HERITAGE AND SOCIAL MEDIA

Heritage and Social Media explores how social media reframes our understanding and experience of heritage. Through the idea of 'participatory culture' the book begins to examine how social media can be brought to bear on the encounter with heritage and on the socially produced meanings and values that individuals and communities ascribe to it.

To highlight the specific changes produced by social media, the book is structured around three major themes:

- *Social Practice.* New ways of understanding and experiencing heritage are emerging as a result of novel social practices of collection, representation, and communication enabled and promoted by social media.
- *Public Formation.* In the presence of widely available social technologies, peer-to-peer activities such as information and media sharing are rapidly gaining momentum, as they increasingly promote and legitimate a participatory culture in which individuals aggregate on the basis of common interests and affinities.
- *Sense of Place.* As computing becomes more pervasive and digital networks extend our surroundings, social media and technologies support new ways to engage with the people, interpretations and values that pertain to a specific territorial setting.

Heritage and Social Media provides readers with a critical framework to understand how the participatory culture fostered by social media changes the way in which we experience and think of heritage. By introducing readers to how social media are theorized and used, particularly outside the institutional domain, the volume reveals through groundbreaking case studies the emerging heritage practices unique to social media. In doing so, the book unveils the new issues that are emerging from these practices and the new space for debate and critical argumentation that is required to illuminate what can be done in this burgeoning sector of heritage work.

Elisa Giaccardi is Associate Professor at the Universidad Carlos III de Madrid (UC3M), where she is affiliated with the Department of Computer Science and the Institute for Culture and Technology. She works at the intersection of interaction design and social media, with an active interest in living heritage practices. Her contributions to this subject comprise research and design work on collective memories, affective geographies and emerging curatorial practices.

HERITAGE AND SOCIAL MEDIA

Understanding heritage in a participatory culture

Edited by Elisa Giaccardi

 Routledge
Taylor & Francis Group

LONDON AND NEW YORK

First published 2012
by Routledge
2 Park Square, Milton Park, Abingdon, Oxon OX14 4RN

Simultaneously published in the USA and Canada
by Routledge
711 Third Avenue, New York, NY 10017

Routledge is an imprint of the Taylor & Francis Group, an informa business

British Library Cataloguing in Publication Data
A catalogue record for this book is available from the British Library

Library of Congress Cataloging in Publication Data
Heritage and social media : understanding heritage in a participatory
culture / edited by Elisa Giaccardi. – 1st ed.
     p. cm.
   Includes bibliographical references and index.
   1. Social media. 2. Technological innovations–Social aspects.
   3. Cultural property. I. Giaccardi, Elisa.
   HM1206.H47 2012
   302.23'1–dc23   2011051624

ISBN: 978-0-415-61662-1 (hbk)
ISBN: 978-0-415-61667-6 (pbk)
ISBN: 978-0-203-11298-4 (ebk)

Typeset in Bembo
by HWA Text and Data Management

CONTENTS

PART II
Public formation 87

PART III
Sense of place 159

FIGURES AND TABLES

Figures

Tables

CONTRIBUTORS

Nicola J. Bidwell, PhD is a principal researcher at CSIR-Meraka and an honorary associate professor at Nelson Mandela University, South Africa. Since 2003 she has focused on human–computer interaction for rural contexts, and Australian Indigenous and African cultural views. She applies situated, ethnographic and participatory research methods by living in geographically remote areas.

Luigina Ciolfi, PhD is a lecturer and senior researcher at the Interaction Design Centre, University of Limerick, Ireland. Her research is concerned with the design and evaluation of interactive technologies augmenting human interaction in place, and is based on an understanding of the lived relationship between people, activities and the physical world.

Martin Conreen is an artist, designer and senior lecturer at Goldsmiths, University of London. Earlier work has included investigations on new and emerging materials and crafts, and the intersections of material culture, contemporary art and manufacturing. His current interest is in rapid prototyping/manufacturing materials and their relationship to digital technologies.

Richard Coyne publishes on digital media, technoromanticism, the digital economy, and design. His latest book *The Tuning of Place: Sociable Spaces and Pervasive Digital Media* (2011, MIT Press) explores smartphones as devices that tune social relationships. He is an architect and was Head of the School of Arts, Culture and Environment at the University of Edinburgh.

Audrey Desjardins is an MA student at the School of Interactive Arts and Technology at Simon Fraser University, Canada. Her research interests combine industrial design and interaction design. Her thesis topic relates to understanding the ways and techniques people use artefacts in ways designers did not intend.

Rachel Charlotte Smith is a PhD fellow in Social Anthropology and Interaction Design at Aarhus University, Denmark, and a member of the Center for Digital Urban Living. She studies how digital technology can provide new ways of engaging audiences in cultural heritage.

Chris Speed, PhD is Reader in Digital Spaces at the Edinburgh School of Architecture and Landscape Architecture. Speed engages in a critical enquiry into how digital technology can engage with the field of architecture and human geography through a combination of art and design based practices and funded research projects.

Dagny Stuedahl, PhD is a senior research scientist at InterMedia, Faculty of Education, University of Oslo. She has a background in ethnology and has participated in several multidisciplinary research projects that transcend disciplinary boundaries between humanities, informatics and educational studies. Her research work investigates the transformative impact of social media on museums and cultural heritage organizations, with a particular focus on how digital media is changing notions and practices of participation and community.

Karen Tanenbaum is a PhD candidate at the School of Interactive Arts and Technology at Simon Fraser University, Canada. Her dissertation work is on adaptivity and ambient intelligence for ubiquitous and tangible computing environments. She has worked on several projects involving the creation of novel wearable, handheld and tabletop computing platforms and applications.

Ron Wakkary, PhD is an associate professor in the School of Interactive Arts and Technology at Simon Fraser University, Canada. His research is in interaction design with a focus on museums and technology, interaction design practices and everyday design.

Heike Winschiers-Theophilus, PhD is Dean of the School of Information Technology at the Polytechnic of Namibia. She has lived in Namibia and lectured in software engineering at the University and Polytechnic since 1994. Her research includes cultural appropriation of design, evaluation concepts and methods, and community-centred design of information systems.

Peter Wright is Professor of Social Computing at Newcastle University (Culture Lab). He has over twenty years of experience as a human-centred design researcher and over 130 publications in the area of human-computer interaction and experience-centred design. In 2004, he co-authored with John McCarthy *Technology as Experience* (MIT Press) which sets out a new theoretical foundation for user experience research. In 2010, again with John McCarthy, he co-authored *Experience-centred design: Designers, users and communities in dialogue* (Morgan Claypool), which describes contemporary methods of experience-centred design.

ACKNOWLEDGMENTS

I would like to thank all the authors of this volume for their thought-provoking contributions and for bearing with my editing. This project would not have been possible without their inspiration and commitment. I also would like to thank Liam Bannon, Gerhard Fischer, Neil Silberman and Roger I. Simon for comments and suggestions on my own writing. A special thanks goes to all the participants in the workshop 'Heritage inquiries: a designerly approach to human values' organized at Aarhus University, Denmark, in August 2010 as part of the conference 'Designing Interactive Systems', for giving me motivation and ground to pursue this project. Another special thanks goes to Routledge for believing in the project of this book from the very start, and to Amy Davis-Poynter for her kind assistance throughout this last year.

OTHERS

A prologue

Graham Fairclough

This foreword first took shape in my head in the Baltic Centre for Contemporary Art in Gateshead (UK) whilst looking at paintings by George Shaw in the 2011 Tate Turner Prize exhibition, held somewhere other than London for only the second time since it began in 1984. Sponsored, or as the publicity put it, 'Connected', by Nokia, the Baltic on the day of my visit was a model of interactivity and participation: Shaw's hyper-realistic paintings landscape ordinary places in an unremarked suburb of Coventry, in a narrow radius of at most a kilometre from his childhood home on the Tile Hill estate, Coventry. The Prize web page said that the area is '[t]ypical of post-war British social housing ... [it] could belong to any city or have originated at any point between the early 1950s and the late 1970s, promoting the timeless, placeless quality of Shaw's work', and it is clearly 'other' in respect of conventional landscape art. It is an example of everyday heritage, another layer of unofficial heritage in which the role of the expert is diminished or different; viewing it encourages an active participation as opposed to a passive consumption, offering a demonstration of heritage being 'taken' not given, created not provided.

Shaw was the 'popular' if unofficial favourite to win the Prize, although the art elite (perhaps not wholly trusting of popular taste?) suggested that this was only because he was more traditional, painterly and conventional than the other three shortlisted artists, and in the event he did not win. But his work is distinctly non-traditional in its relentlessly (the artist himself might say 'bleakly') ordinary, everyday landscapes of suburban house and waste ground, back alleys and garage doors, red phone boxes and demolished roadhouses. It is unconventional in its medium, too, because Shaw paints with the oil-based enamel paints in tiny tins used mainly by, indeed mainly manufactured for, young teenage boys making Airfix kits in the 1950s and 1960s and beyond; today, many of that age group are instead amongst those we call digital natives, primary users of iPhones, Facebook and all the other components of the ever-shifting proprietary landscape of social media.

Inspiration had also come to me a few weeks earlier, whilst participating at a COST workshop in Tallinn on 'culture in sustainability' funded by the European Union in rooms full of (mainly) social scientists but also geographers, political scientists and other 'others'. Their interdisciplinary discussions prefigured many of this book's themes, and they were not unaware in their attempts to define the breadth and scope of culture that culture and thus heritage changes even as we try to describe. Many at the conference saw 'culture' as nothing less than the whole process of being/becoming in the world, of the creation of identities, of social interactions, and of the relationship between people and their cognitive, imaginative, emotional landscapes. The superiority of process (the acts of interaction, dialogue and communication) over product is a key thread through the chapters that follow, and the use of social media is an important part of the process.

Participative social media affects both access to and the character of cultural activity. The majority of contributors to/readers of this book probably come from upper socio-economic layers of the 'West' (in the widest Euro–Anglo–Americanised sense of the term, although one asks when we will finally stop using the word in that way). Technology has allowed that small part of the world's population to 'see into' other cultures almost everywhere, from rain forest to Pacific island, from Sudanese and Mongolian desert to arctic not-as-frozen-as-they-were wastes, and from the poor suburbs of South American megacities to the estates of the so-called under-classes of our own countries. A potentially humbling realisation came to the meeting from a case study by a keynote speaker, that social media is also beginning to allow those other, apparently very different, communities to see into the west's lifeways. This is an unforeseen two-way as opposed to one-way sharing and merging of heritage, culture and landscape on global and cross-cultural scales. A day or two afterwards, a BBC online video showed a protester in Egypt or Syria waving a mobile at a BBC camera with the words 'this is our weapon'.

Reading some of the chapters in this book led me further back into my memory, to David Eagleman's book *Sum*, a series of 40 short tales from possible afterlives, and specifically to the afterlife called *Death Switch* – where human society comes to exist only in disembodied emails, sms txts and similar messages forged by computers refining their initial programming for sending after-death emails to friends and colleagues. A lot of socially mediated heritage, such as genealogical research or the interconnectedness of diaspora communities, is about remembering the dead, and thus in a way bringing them back to life by memories, and we might almost interpret this as the dead learning to communicate with us via social media. An older novel – James Morrow's *This is the Way the World Ends* (1985) – hints at similar cross-generational transfers by inventing the 'ghosts' of the un*born* that haunt those who denied them birth through complicity in nuclear war.

Heritage, whether through social media or other means, can be seen as a conversation between the past and our future. The process of recording and archiving contains the future by anticipating its needs; the future is already here through our desire to pass on our legacy to the generations to come and through the present's appropriation of memories from the past. Heritage itself is a form of memory, and if through Internet or bar-code tagging we give objects their own memories, will they become like the posthumous emails in *Death Switch*? Will they grow from being actants to become actors? Will we have to regard people as actants, *re*acting to things?

We should remember, however, that both heritage and culture are also represented by the concept of landscape, which has its own memories, too, and which in its perceptual, cognitive and representational meanings is a virtual/in-the-mind construct, closely related to the inventions of social media. Each of us carries many landscapes in our heads – that of childhood, that of 'home', that of holidays, that of where our friends live, and so on – which are not all precisely tangible or physical; some no longer exist yet have reality in our heads and hearts. The idea of 'landscape' (not as scenery or historical document, but as how we perceive the world and make sense of it, and as a 'language' through which people can share and contest their views of the world) subsumes a lot of characteristics that in this book are attributed to heritage and is a concept that I now habitually use to frame my heritage thinking.

Social media, and the participation it empowers, offer ways to help us share our mental landscapes, our memories and identities, our heritage and culture. The chapters in this book dispel any remaining notion that social media should be or can be used just as a new method of disseminating and promoting existing heritage 'knowledge' to new or broader audiences. The opportunities created by social media are not mainly about the consumption of heritage offered by others (experts, politicians) but instead, allow (require?) people to create their own, shared heritage, culture and landscapes. This book shows many examples of social media creating new heritage through cultural processes. The process of participation becomes the most important thing, and realising in a museum context that 'engagement becomes the exhibition' simply raises the question of why the process should take place in a museum at all. The walls of a museum are potentially dissolved by social media, just as they dissolve the walls between the special and the everyday, between academic disciplines, between the expert and the lay, between past and future, between 'us' and 'others'. Put another way, if the everyday is to be brought to the museum, why not simply take the 'museum' out to the everyday? Such ideas are embedded in the philosophy of the Florence (Landscape) and Faro (Social Value of Heritage) Conventions, and perhaps represent the continued broadening of heritage to a more democratic and ubiquitous, inclusive level. The heritage that this book considers and that Faro, for example, concerns is not the special (guarded by regulated canons of taste and thoughts, protected by experts), but the ordinary (which turns out not really to be ordinary because people are not ordinary). Social media reunites or merges heritage with the everyday.

Social media starts by offering a way to 'widen the audience', 'reach new constituencies' but it ends by changing heritage and by asking everyone to participate in its construction, encouraging openness not closure of interpretation and valuation, making flux, uncertainty and doubt critical. The permanently-always-connected lifestyle facilitates this, so that heritage becomes a daily culture, not something you buy and consume while on holiday. This can be radical and revolutionary, and of course it is a viewpoint that readily comes under attack from those for whom relativism risks a loss of control, and by those hankering for simpler stories of the national past ('good' taste and high art, knowing what matters, as they say).

Graham Fairclough
St Albans
December 2011

INTRODUCTION

Reframing heritage in a participatory culture

Elisa Giaccardi

Heritage and Social Media explores how social media reframe our understanding and experience of heritage by opening up more participatory ways of interacting with heritage objects and concerns. Through the idea of 'participatory culture' the book begins to explore how social media can be brought to bear on the encounter with heritage and on the socially produced meanings and values that individuals and communities ascribe to it.

Ubiquitous personal memory devices and social media technologies (e.g. multimedia recorders, camera phones, online media sharing and social networking sites) are giving rise to a new age of information and communication technologies characterized by participatory and grassroots activities. The impact on heritage discourse and practice is significant, as new digital technologies alter and transform the complex set of social practices that interweave memories, material traces and performative enactments to give meaning and significance in the present to the lived realities of our past. Yet this is among the first scholarly publications that critically address the profound and transformative impact of social media on our understanding and experience of heritage.

New heritage frontiers

From private memorabilia and scrapbooks to family inheritance and traditions, from the collective storytelling of historical events to the performative reification of a living connection to land – heritage is today about far more than museum artifacts and historic buildings, and how they are to be preserved and communicated. It is about making sense of our memories and developing a sense of identity through shared and repeated interactions with the tangible remains and lived traces of a common past.

Like the farmers of the Norwegian Jæren landscape – which as described by Setten (2005) have measured their own farming against those of other family members as well as present and past farmers in their local community – we live and practice heritage within situations that are 'personal and yet social, private and yet public, of the present and yet of the past and the future' (Setten 2005: 74). In other words, we socially construct heritage in the context of our own lives and imaginations to interact meaningfully with our past and shape our vision of the future (Thomas 2004; Lowenthal 2005). This fundamental understanding emphasizes that heritage meanings and values are not attached to artifacts, buildings or sites. Neither are they frozen in time. They are the results of repeated and ongoing interactions in the lived world of ordinary people (Byrne 2008).

Changes in the definition and management of heritage are prefigured in the Faro Convention on the Value of Cultural Heritage for Society (Council of Europe 2005). Setting the broader understandings of heritage that have been emerging over the last decades into a wider social, political and economic context, the Faro Convention proposes a more comprehensive and holistic view of what should be intended as cultural heritage, and emphasizes the importance of people's participation and engagement – rights as well as responsibilities – in the making of place and local identities. New scales and new frontiers are prefigured for heritage practice, which set no boundaries or limits to what heritage can be and how is to be intended. At the core is a definition of heritage practice that focuses not just on the protection of the material and temporal fabric of heritage but more importantly on 'the management of change' (Fairclough 2009): the use of heritage in a broader cultural, political and social context to express and perform 'constantly evolving values, beliefs, knowledge and traditions' (Council of Europe 2005, from Art. 2). Such a definition voids of meaning distinctions between tangible and intangible heritage, between conventional heritage and 'new heritage' (i.e. digitally born forms of heritage), and between prospective logics of 'future heritage' (i.e. what we may value in the future) as opposed to retrospective logics of preserving what of value we have inherited from the past.

Today mobile and ubiquitous technologies are accelerating these changes by enabling users to participate, spontaneously and continuously, in activities of collection, preservation and interpretation of digitized heritage content and new digitally mediated forms of heritage practice. Heritage institutions and practitioners are urged to use emerging information and communication technologies – in particular social media – to encourage visitors to actively interact with heritage content and connect socially with one another (Simon 2010). Yet little emphasis is given to people's autonomous engagement with cultural heritage in the context of their own lives and in association with the unique character of the places and communities in which heritage comes to matter. In other words, there is little understanding of how emerging technologies are powerfully connecting heritage experience to people's lives and settings. Even though increasing attention is being paid to the construction of personally and socially meaningful experiences, issues of heritage value and its wider social significance have not yet been placed at the core of the design, management and renewal of heritage experience (Giaccardi, 2011).

The rise of the participatory culture

This book examines the impact of ubiquitous personal memory devices and social media technologies on heritage discourse and practice through the idea of participatory culture. But what is a participatory culture? According to Jenkins *et al.* (2006), a participatory culture is one in which 'not every member must contribute, but all must believe they are free to contribute when ready and that what they contribute will be appropriately valued' (Jenkins *et al.* 2006: 7). This culture is characterized by relatively low barriers to public artistic expression and civic engagement, strong support for creating and sharing one's creations with others, and frameworks for formal and informal mentorship to novices. In such a culture, people feel socially connected with one another, all the time (Shirky 2008). Even though acting at different levels of motivation and expertise, they belong to communities that provide, according to Jenkins *et al.*, 'strong incentives for creative expression and active participation' (Jenkins *et al.* 2006: 7). Participatory culture or in the plural, cultures of participation (Fischer 2011) value the creative process and how engaging socially in creative activities changes how we think about the others and ourselves. As emphasized in Jenkins, a participatory culture is one that shifts the focus from individual expression to community involvement, and reframes literacy from matters of interactive technology to issues of cultural attitude. Participatory culture is not just about producing and consuming user-generated content; it is also manifested through diverse forms of affiliation, expression, collaboration, and distribution (Jenkins *et al.* 2006).

Participatory cultures are not new. For example, amateur cultures are an instance of participatory culture. In addition to the numerous historical societies, preservation societies and literary societies that could be mentioned here, the Amateur Press Association of the middle of the nineteenth century is perhaps one of the most widely known historical examples. However, we are witnessing today a broader and more profound phenomenon. This is the result of a combination of several socio-technical factors. Creating, publishing and distributing content requires less time and less money today than in the past. Software that does not require sophisticated programming skills is available and easy to use. With Web 2.0 (O'Reilly 2005) and the spreading of web applications and services that facilitate online information sharing and collaboration, there is not even the need for additional software to be installed on the computer. All can be done online, quite naturally. From encyclopedic collaborative projects (e.g. Wikipedia) to question-and-answer websites (e.g. Quora), from non-profit crowdsourcing projects (e.g. Ushahidi for microblogging) to crowdsourcing projects where people are paid for taking on open tasks (e.g. Amazon Mechanical Turk) or competing in open contests (e.g. Userfarm), from do-it-yourself (DIY) websites where people share knowledge and tips on how to make things (e.g. Instructables) to web services for the sharing and tagging of a large variety of digital content (e.g. Flickr for photos, YouTube for videos, SoundCloud for sounds, Google 3D Warehouse for 3D models, including even Wikileaks for whistle-blowing), from social tagging (e.g.

Delicious or StumbleUpon) to collaborative web mapping (e.g. OpenStreetMap, an editable geographical map that is also a wiki and a crowdsourcing project)… the list of services and websites supporting the production and distribution of digital content has no end. This production and distribution is facilitated by social networking, that is, the way in which social media (which builds on the ideological and technological foundations of Web 2.0) fosters the emergence of online communities around affinities and topics of interest, transforming traditional one-way media communication into an active conversation. From generalist social networking sites (e.g. Facebook) to specialized networks (e.g. LinkedIn), from custom social networks (e.g. Ning) to microblogging services (e.g. Twitter), people aggregate and engage in conversation in many and various ways.

Additionally, with the spread of iPhone, Android and BlackBerry smartphones, which combine the functions of a mobile phone with that of a small personal computer, and with other high-end mobile devices such as Apple iPod Touch and iPad, or Amazon Kindle (just to name the most well known today), social media are increasingly becoming mobile. They are contributing to new mindsets and skill sets, fostering a culture of participation unrestricted by schedules and locations. This mobility promotes a continual activity of interaction in which we are immersed and involved, all the time (Greenfield 2006). Moreover, there is now the possibility of attaching digital data to artifacts in the real world through social media suites for augmented reality, the tagging of uniquely identifiable objects, or the sensing of patterns of activity and specific behaviors around those artifacts (Ashton 2009). Thus the fabric of participation and conversation offered by social media is not simply made of online interactions and virtual experiences; it is also interwoven with physical objects, places and activities that are augmented and enhanced with social data and connectivity. From the cloud of networked web infrastructures, services and data to the real world (and back again), the participatory culture is radically changing the rules of the game.

Implications

The idea of participatory culture is challenging and in some cases recasting the way in which industries do business, citizens engage in civic and political life, teachers and students prepare and learn, and people engage in forms of creative expression and new craftsmanship. The long-term implications of this change are impossible to know, but they raise significant issues. In this more plural and collaborative culture, 'the boundaries between amateur and professional, consumer and producer, grassroots and mainstream are breached, if not erased' (Leadbeater 2010: 46). The impact of social media and emerging cultures of participation on our understanding and experience of heritage is blurring. This leads to a questioning of the boundaries between official and unofficial heritage, reshaping and creating new relations between audiences and institutions, fostering grassroots understandings and manifestations of heritage practice, and in general bringing to the front the living and performative aspects of heritage as part of our present-day existence.

The way in which we capture our living experiences, the nature of our artifacts, and the ways in which we share them are changing (Giaccardi *et al.* 2012). Aspects of our lives are increasingly captured and shared with others who can themselves annotate and augment these digital traces with their own perspectives. Preserving, making sense and exchanging everyday artifacts and practices is increasingly becoming a matter of heritage: it brings the past to matter in the present, helping us to tell stories about who we are. In this sense, heritage artifacts and practices not only constitute a legacy to future generations, but they also play a crucial role in shaping our sense of place and identity: 'Heritage begins with you as an individual and grows all the way to the whole world' (LeBlanc 1993).

What we see emerging is not simply an opportunity to widen the visitor experience from personal to communal interactions; it is an unstable, fluid shift in our understanding of what is at the core of heritage experience and why it is important. If we acknowledge this challenge, then it becomes clear that we cannot widen the margin of how people participate (though diversely) in the social significance of heritage artifacts and places, unless we begin to understand how we experience and construct heritage as a result of the emerging technologies and social practices that are shaping and being shaped by the spreading of participatory cultures and attitudes, in an upward spiral of possibilities and expectations. Social media is giving people a more central position, creating networked meanings and even more importantly contexts that are subject to rapid change and renegotiation (Van Oost 2012). In other words, social media create infrastructures of communication and interaction that act as places of cultural production and lasting values at the service of what could be viewed as a new generation of 'living' heritage practices. This is a critical and fundamental consideration that goes beyond learning how to use social media effectively. It urges heritage professionals and designers to address thoughtfully the new series of issues that come with social media, including the loss of curatorial voice and the challenges of multivocality, the redistribution of curatorial activities and the fluid 'coming together' of heritage narratives, the duty of memory and the limits of the social syntax of mainstream social media, the digital (un)sustainability of embodied practices and knowledges, and the ways in which participation and dialogue are configured – just to name the issues most frequently discussed in this collection.

About the book

The book explores from different perspectives the idea that heritage is defined more by the cultural work of ordinary people than by official heritage lists, as discussed in Susie West's *Understanding Heritage in Practice* and Laurajane Smith's *Uses of Heritage*. This idea is also emphasized by heritage scholars such as Rodney Harrison, David Byrne and Graham Fairclough, who look at heritage as a form of social action. Referring to these ideas and to emerging notions of technology as experience (as advocated by Peter Wright and John McCarthy in *Technology as Experience*), *Heritage and Social Media* expands current ideas of 'digital heritage' and 'new heritage' to investigate the radical impact of social media on our understanding and experience of heritage. In doing so, the book moves beyond traditional museological concerns and presents unconventional heritage ideas and experiences ranging from bottom-up forms of participatory curation in the museum (see Iversen and Smith, this volume) to everyday grassroots practices unique to social media (see Liu, this volume). The book also moves beyond an account of the opportunities and challenges of using emerging technologies in the conventional museological activities of collection, interpretation and exhibition, as it examines the broader landscape of social interaction with material artifacts and environmental settings that is opened up by mobile and ubiquitous social technologies 'in the wild'.

Heritage and Social Media highlights the complexities of heritage discourse and practice in the context of the participatory culture shaped by social media. The book accounts empirically for socio-cultural issues of archiving and representing 'digital stuff', and critically speaks to how experiences, memories and identities are constructed, valued and passed on in a society in which people come together to generate, organize and share content through an ongoing interchange of thoughts and affects, opinions and beliefs, attachments and antipathies.

In filling a significant gap in the available heritage literature, this book represents a significant cross section of ideas and practices associated with the use of social media for heritage-related purposes. The book also offers important material for designers and technologists in the emerging field of cultural informatics, and provides conceptual resources for future research in the field. The contributors to this volume come from a wide array of disciplines, including heritage studies, anthropology, museology, archaeology, history, human geography, sociology, architecture, computer science, interaction design, digital media and human–computer interaction.

Themes and chapters

To highlight the specific changes produced by social media, the book is structured around three major themes: social practice, public formation and sense of place. Each section contains four chapters: the first three chapters address issues of heritage, social media and participatory culture within a broader context; the fourth chapter is more specific to the museum sector and related issues of institutional change.

Social practice

New ways of understanding and experiencing heritage are emerging as a result of novel social practices of collection, representation and communication that are enabled and promoted by social media. A renewed legitimacy of personal accounts and community-based practices are capturing the dialectical and often conflicted relations between people and their environment. Collective memories (see Silberman and Purser, this volume), digital memorials (see Pitsillides, Jefferies and Conreen, this volume), and grassroots curatorial practices (see Liu, this volume) are just a few examples of how social media are giving new meaning to notions such as public heritage and curation. What categories of cultural objects do social media enable us to capture, and what forms of curation do they support? How do these heterogeneous 'social traces' (see Ciolfi, this volume) recast participation in a museum context?

Chapter 1, 'Collective memory as affirmation: people-centered cultural heritage in a digital age' examines the potential of several kinds of social media in support of community-based heritage activities using examples from the United States, South America, Fiji, South Africa, Asia and Europe. The chapter stresses how the value of cultural heritage in a digital age lies in its power to stimulate ever-evolving community-based reflection and conversation on past, present and future identities.

Chapter 2, 'Socially distributed curation of the Bhopal disaster: a case of grassroots heritage in the crisis context' describes self-organizing curatorial activities by members of the public using social media in times of disasters. Based on the findings of a large-scale empirical investigation, the chapter discusses the potential of social media technologies as both tools and sites for grassroots heritage practices of online curation, focusing on the crisis narratives of the 1984 Bhopal gas leak as a case study.

Chapter 3, 'Museum of the self and digital death: an emerging curatorial dilemma for digital heritage' reviews current practices around online data storage in relation to memory and death. The chapter offers a critical discussion of the various strategies concerning how the personal legacy data that people leave behind could be accessed, curated and engaged for historical and heritage purposes, while at the same time being shared and kept 'alive' within communities of loved ones.

Chapter 4, 'Social traces: participation and the creation of shared heritage' reflects on the author's work in interactive exhibition design and her participation strategies. The chapter discusses how the 'social traces' that visitors leave on the exhibit can be used to facilitate broader connections, and create new communities and patterns of social interaction around the heritage. Based on this reflection, the author draws insights on the role that social media can have in redefining curatorial practices in the context of established museums as well as more informal heritage sites.

Public formation

In the presence of widely available social technologies, peer-to-peer activities such as information and media sharing are rapidly gaining momentum, as they increasingly promote and legitimate a participatory culture in which individuals aggregate on the basis of common interests and affinities. New publics are forming and evolving around focusing events that will grow to have historical and cultural significance (see Simon, this volume), around the everyday blogging of crafts and traditions (see Stuedahl and Mörtberg, this volume), around online and offline curation of social media content (see Iversen and Smith, this volume), and also in the context of convergent museum practices (see Russo, this volume). What practices of public formation and aggregation do social media support, and what possibilities for knowledge and dialogue are still unrealized or inherently problematic?

Chapter 5, 'Remembering together: social media and the formation of the historical present' explores how social media redefine the temporal and spatial boundaries of a historical event, and discusses how social media can support the formation of new publics by enabling strangers to share their experiences and renegotiate their relations to specific historical events and to each other. The chapter offers a critical understanding of how social media are currently being used for 'remembering together', and addresses the possibilities left unrealized by such practices.

Chapter 6, 'Heritage knowledge, social media, and the sustainability of the intangible' discusses how digital technologies and social media can be integrated in sustainable ways to support the documentation and sharing of intangible heritage knowledge and practices. Through cases studies concerning intangible heritage knowledge of craftsmanship related to the building of traditional wooden boats, the chapter illustrates how cultural sustainability concerns the ways in which participation is configured, and draws attention to the challenges of bringing continuity to the performed and changing character of intangible cultural heritage when re-manifested in digital forms.

Chapter 7, 'Connecting to everyday practices: experiences from the Digital Natives exhibition' describes how social media can be used, and even mimicked, to mediate between a museum's exhibition space and audiences' social practices. By unpacking the design and outcomes of the Digital Natives interactive exhibition, the chapter discusses how active audience engagement is not an end in itself, but a means to renew the connection between audiences' everyday lives and matters of heritage, and to create unique moments of dialogue and interaction inside the exhibition space.

Chapter 8, 'The rise of the "media museum": creating interactive cultural experiences through social media' provides an overview of how social media and social networking technologies are becoming increasingly important in the development of museum communication, and how audiences are invited to engage with cultural content. The chapter discusses the need for a shift in emphasis from issues of cultural content (whether consumed, crowdsourced or shared) to issues of cultural experience. This shift requires a finer understanding of audience participation and engagement in the context of convergent museum practices.

Sense of place

As computing becomes more pervasive and digital networks extend our surroundings, social media and technologies support new ways of engaging with the people, interpretations and values that pertain to a specific territorial setting. Creating or strengthening a sense of place means creating communication and interaction spaces capable of exploring and sustaining renewed forms of engagement with the physical and social settings of the heritage. Quick Response (QR) tagging (see Speed, this volume), photo sharing and collaborative mapping (see Coyne, this volume), and social gaming (see Wakkary *et al.*, this volume) are just a few ways of re-articulating our sense of place through social media (even in the museum).

How can social media be used to expose and sustain the system of experiences, interpretations and expectations that contribute to continuous heritage interpretation and construction? What are the criticalities to account for when working with different knowledge systems, in different parts of the world? (See Bidwell and Winschiers-Theophilus, this volume.)

Chapter 9, 'Mosaics and multiples: online digital photography and the framing of heritage' offers a critique of amateur digital photography and examines the role and impact of emerging online practices (from online photo sharing to collaborative mapping) concerning how people come to understand space, place and heritage. The chapter discusses how the exponential growth of digital photographic archives has both the potential to expose differences that might otherwise go unacknowledged by comparison (the mosaic), and to defamiliarize and occlude by profusion aspects of heritage and place (the multiple).

Chapter 10, 'Mobile Ouija boards' reflects on three software projects and art interventions that were designed by the author with the intent to explore the opportunities offered by mobile social media and introduce elements of temporal reflection in our interactions with material artifacts and physical sites. Through a criticism of the rhetoric of contemporary technology, the chapter offers an alternative approach to how social networks can be placed at the core of digital heritage, in both its tangible and intangible manifestations.

Chapter 11, 'Extending connections between land and people digitally: designing with rural Herero communities in Namibia' describes the endeavors of the authors to enable rural people of the Herero tribe, in southern Africa, to extend their local knowledge practices digitally. The chapter offers an empirically grounded critique of how technologies (even social media) privilege particular ways of encountering, organizing and making sense of the world, and how these can conflict with the heritage that is lived in the connections between land and human dwellers in different parts of the world.

Chapter 12, 'Situating the sociability of interactive museum guides' analyzes emerging research approaches for interactive museum guides to describe the move from information delivery to sociability. Using several examples, the chapter discusses the need to refine what is meant by sociability with respect to technologies in museums, and what impact the trajectory toward museum guides as social technology tools has on the notion of the interactive museum guide.

Summary of aim and contribution

Heritage and Social Media provides readers with a framework to understand how the participatory culture fostered by social media changes the way in which we experience and think of heritage. Introducing readers to how social media are theorized and used, particularly outside the institutional domain, the volume reveals through groundbreaking case studies the emerging heritage practices unique to social media. In doing so, the book unveils the new issues that are emerging from these practices and the new space for debate and critical argumentation that is required to illuminate what can be done in this burgeoning sector of heritage work.

References

Ashton, K. (2009) 'That "Internet of Things" thing', *RFID Journal*, 22 June. http://www.rfidjournal.com/article/view/4986 (accessed 7 December 2011).

Byrne, D. (2008) 'Heritage as social action', in G. Fairclough, R. Harrison, J. Schonfield and J. H. Jameson (eds) *The Heritage Reader*, London: Routledge.

Council of Europe (2005) Faro Convention on the Value of Cultural Heritage for Society. http://www.coe.int/t/dg4/cultureheritage/heritage/identities/default_EN.asp (accessed 6 December 2011).

Fairclough, G. (2009) 'New heritage frontiers', in D. Therond and A. Trigona (eds) *Heritage and Beyond*, Brussels: Council of Europe Publishing.

Fischer, G. (2011) 'Understanding, fostering, and supporting cultures of participation', *Interactions*, 18(3): 42–53.

Giaccardi, E. (2011) 'Things we value', *Interactions*, 18(1): 17–21.

Giaccardi, E., Churchill, E. and Liu, S.B. (2012) 'Heritage matters: Designing for current and future values through digital and social technologies', *Proceedings of CHI 2012*, New York: ACM Press.

Greenfield, A. (2006) *Everyware: The Dawning Age of Ubiquitous Computing*, Berkeley, CA: New Riders.

Jenkins, H., Puroshotma, R., Clinton, K., Weigel, M. and Robison, A.J. (2006) *Confronting the Challenges of Participatory Culture: Media Education for the 21st Century*. Chicago, IL: The MacArthur Foundation. http://www.newmedialiteracies.org/files/working/NMLWhitePaper.pdf (accessed 3 November 2011).

Leadbeater, C. (2010) *Cloud Culture: The Future of Global Cultural Relations*, London: Counterpoint.

LeBlanc, F. (1993) 'Is everything heritage?' *ICOMOS Canada Bulletin*, 2(2): 2–3.

Lowenthal, D. (2005) 'Stewarding the future', *CRM: The Journal of Heritage Stewardship*, 2(2): 6–25.

McCarthy, J. and Wright, P. (2004) *Technology as Experience*, Cambridge, MA: The MIT Press.

O'Reilly, T. (2005) *What is Web 2.0: Design Patterns and Business Models for the Next Generation of Software*. http://oreilly.com/web2/archive/what-is-web-20.html (posted 30 September 2005; accessed 6 December 2011).

Setten, G. (2005) 'Farming the heritage: On the production and construction of a personal and practised landscape heritage, *International Journal of Heritage Studies*, 11(1): 67–79.

Shirky, C. (2008) *Here Comes Everybody: The Power of Organizing Without Organizations*, New York: Penguin Press.

Simon, N. (2010) *The Participatory Museum*, Santa Cruz, CA: Museum 2.0.

Smith, L. (2006) *Uses of Heritage*, London: Routledge.

Thomas, J. (2004) *Archeology and Modernity*, London: Routledge.

Van Oost, O. (2012) 'Rethinking the museum: Cultural heritage and the Internet of Things', in C. van den Akker (ed.) *Museum Transfigurations. Curation and Co-creation of Collections in the Digital Age*, Oxford and New York: Berghahn Books.

West, S. (2010) (ed.) *Understanding Heritage in Practice*, Milton Keynes: The Open University.

PART I
Social practice

1

COLLECTIVE MEMORY AS AFFIRMATION

People-centered cultural heritage in a digital age

Neil Silberman and Margaret Purser

Introduction

Over the last 15 years, the character of the public administration of cultural heritage – long based on rigid standards of authenticity and monumentality – has undergone a far-reaching change (Araoz 2011). As most powerfully expressed by the 2003 United Nations Educational, Scientific and Cultural Organization (UNESCO) Convention for Safeguarding the Intangible Cultural Heritage, intangible cultural heritage and, by extension, all of cultural heritage, is 'constantly recreated by communities and groups in response to their environment, their interaction with nature and their history, and provides them with a sense of identity and continuity' (UNESCO 2003). This wholehearted acceptance of re-creation and adaptation as essential aspects of heritage significance places a new emphasis on process rather than product, thus opening up exciting new potential for digital technologies as facilitators of people-centered cultural heritage.

This chapter will examine the potential of social media as a framework for such community-based heritage activities. These applications provide varying combinations of visual, spatial and auditory representations that can be contributed to (or commented upon) by individuals, yet which also simultaneously comprise a constantly changing and expanding mosaic of collective memory. Case studies of digital applications and innovative uses of online social networks will be presented, demonstrating the richness of a dynamic, ever-evolving, participatory heritage praxis quite distinct from the older, static conceptions of heritage as unambiguous, expert-defined and needing *protection* from the forces of change.

This kind of interactive heritage – like traditional collective memory – is continuously transformed as a kind of meta-history itself. The role of heritage curators and conservators in the coming years must therefore become increasingly that of facilitators rather than authoritative scripters and arbiters of authenticity and significance. Although professional expertise in historiographical method, heritage policy and site management will certainly always be useful, in a digital world of multivocality of memory, these skills will not be the only ones. The task of heritage professionals will be rather to enable contemporary communities to digitally (re)produce historical environments, collective narratives and geographical visualizations that cluster individual perspectives into shared forms and processes of remembering. These interactions are reminiscent of the conversations that once occurred much more frequently at corner bars, in town squares and by evening campfires (cf. Putnam 2001) as a vital part of the exercise of cultural diversity that is now seen as a central component of world heritage (UNESCO 2005).

Un-inventing heritage: the transformatory power of participation

The acceptance of carefully designed and authoritatively presented narratives as the normative structure for public heritage communication is a tradition that extends back for centuries (Silberman 1995). From Herodotus, through medieval pilgrim guides, through the national monuments and heritage sites of the present, the main trajectory of communication has been from an author or an expert to a reader or hearer, relating a sequence of carefully chosen details, often with a subtext of contemporary political significance. As modern Western nations adopted official versions of their national story – to be taught in public schools and transmitted through national park systems – collective memory became a Janus-faced phenomenon. Official public commemoration projected forward into future generations of national- and international-scale human societies, while private collective memories looked backward through more localized and intimately performed narratives of a smaller, more circumscribed, but nonetheless shared past. And although the audience for state-sponsored heritage was never completely passive (neither accepting the authorized narrative at face value or refraining from expressing one's own reaction) that interactivity remained largely unacknowledged by public institutions and was rarely used to enrich the public interpretation of the heritage itself. In important ways, that popular or individual reaction to official interpretation has carried the character of rumor, ridicule or gossip – frowned upon by the institutions of the state and its educational system, but enormously important in constructing unofficial communities of sympathy (Fine 2007).

This sort of unofficial, community-based reaction to official heritage narratives has, throughout history, thrived on all kinds of alternative conspiracy theories and explanations that have contested the official version. Groups and sometimes especially creative and persuasive individuals have used these counter-narratives to give voice to feelings of historical exclusion or disempowerment. Whether it was the popular explanations of the Ten Lost Tribes, the Moundbuilders, the Von Däniken thesis, Velikovskyism, JFK conspiracy theories, or even the wild rumors of responsibility for the 9/11 attacks on the Twin Towers, disenfranchised sectors of the public have been able to contribute to the interpretation of public events and icons only by contesting the power of the authorities as being intentionally deceptive and or factually incorrect. At times, these contests can and do spill over into an equally unambiguous and exclusionary nostalgia. It is expressed in the kind of scorched-earth xenophobic nationalism that currently fuels anti-immigrant sentiment and propels religious fundamentalism into the center of political discourse all across the world (Roy 2010). It is manifested in pitched battles at national and local levels over the relative purity and authenticity of history textbook narratives (Castenell and Pinar 1993). In both these forms – the official and the reactionary – lies an assertion that there is only one truth to be had, accessible only through narratives that are inherently authoritarian and didactic.

None of the competing claims for a totalizing, absolute truth reflect the socially inclusive and fluid modality of genuinely collective memory. Indeed the alternatives in the realm of collective memory have always flown beneath the radar in a series of face-to-face or family encounters, almost always transmitted orally, that describe a different warp and weave of time. Instead of interpreting and tracing the history of the *big* heritage subjects like technological progress, the succession of aesthetic styles through history, and the rise and fall of nations, it has produced a thick anecdotal description of how the world works based on membership in a social collectivity (Zerubavel 1996). That membership can be read simultaneously on many levels: in the place names of a particular territory, in the recipes prepared on special occasions, in a yearly round of holidays linked to religious or cultural traditions, and, of course, in the telling of family stories at gatherings of kin. In whatever its form, it remains (with the exception of the examples systematically collected by modern folklorists, from the Grimm brothers onward) largely unrecorded and borne through time by the active exercise of identity. In other words, it is what Paul Connerton (1989) identifies as 'performative memory' that absolutely *requires* the personal, physical participation of its adherents, not merely an assent to or passive acceptance of an official historical narrative.

Even as collective memory on the local and family level has been progressively shattered in industrialized nations by globalizing mobility, urbanization, suburbanization and the disintegration of extended families in individual-centered service economies (Connerton 2009), some pockets of viable community and family 'performative' identity still exists. As we will suggest in the following pages, the active awareness and performance of shared habits, places, celebrations and recollections is a vital channel of human communication (and not only intergenerational inheritance) in healthy and dynamic societies (cf. Misztal 2003). No wonder then, that as a vibrant, collective consciousness of the past has progressively receded in large segments of the industrialized world, a hunger for *personal* connection with ancient places, traditions and customs has arisen alongside 'official' heritage narratives.

The interactive element in public heritage interpretation was never completely absent in the historical sites and initiatives that steadily increased in the Industrial Age. The birth of house museums (West 1999); the proliferation of community-inspired historical pageants (Glassberg 1990); the establishment of open air museums (Rentzhog 2007); and the evolution of historical re-enactments (McCalman and

Pickering 2009) merged the hunger for older and apparently more stable ways of life with routinized visits to what might today be called an 'immersive environment' (Lowenthal 2002). Yet even in these mass-produced venues for performative memory, there remains a sharp distinction between those that remained faithful to officially dictated narrative and academically authenticated facticity (at places like Plimoth Plantation and Colonial Williamsburg in the US, Bokrijk in Belgium, and Skansen in Sweden among others), and the eclectic and creatively anachronistic Renaissance Fairs, Wild West towns, and other quasi-historical reenactments that encourage participation in communal re-creations of a consciously imagined and idealized past (Gunnels 2005). The limitation of all these interactive environments, however, is their carefully bounded extent in both space and time. Whether in visits to open air museums or historically themed events, participation is explicitly defined by the way they are set apart from everyday life. They require special acts of pilgrimage and expenditure; participants travel to and from them as consumers of momentary experience with a beginning and an end.

'Performative memory' as a component of collective experience and identity is something quite different. It is an ongoing process that is also at least potentially transformative. Each performance of inherited, shared traditions is not necessarily a discrete occasion, but often a fleeting moment in which, by tweaking the performance itself, the meaning or relevance of the memory itself can be changed. As suggested in the UNESCO definition of intangible cultural heritage mentioned above, it is additive, and conversational, and has no clear beginning or end. Such performances (and the conversations about them) can extend over months or decades; old threads dropped in the past can be picked up again when the need arises, or interest returns. These moments can be both serendipitous and purposeful. But in either case, the narratives constructed are not totalizing, absolute or singular. They do not resolve in a single answer. Rather, they are contemplative, experimental, evocative and essentially mundane. They occur in the almost unnoticed moments of changing the recipe inherited from mothers-in-law or first cousins; in retelling alternate versions of remembered events with a childhood friend; or walking home along a well-worn path for the first time with a new neighbor or a grandchild. There is no sense of separation from everyday life; in fact, it is just the opposite. These performances are the way that people weave rational connections between past and present, taking apart elements of the remembered past and reassembling them to make sense of an ongoing, dynamic present, and to negotiate the currents of power and authority that shape daily life (Scott 1990; Glassie 1995; Zerubavel 2004).

Yet in a world in which communities of memory are far-flung, hybrid and diasporic, and where face-to-face interaction between siblings, old schoolmates, former colleagues and childhood friends is increasingly replaced by the digital communication of email, websites and social networks, new kinds of 'virtual' communities are being built. It is our contention that digital technologies offer a new medium not only for conversation and contact, but also for the construction of viable, continuous 'memory communities' that creatively reassemble fragments from a shared past into a dynamic, reflective expression of contemporary identity.

The potential of these digital communities to restore a sense of collective memory is enormous, as we will suggest in the following sections. But the technologies that animate them must be used with caution, lest they merely enhance the dominance of the authorized, official narratives that have degraded and in many cases replaced the creative power of both individual and collective memory.

Realer than real: the seductive misuse of digital technologies

The amazingly lifelike images of new generation computer reconstructions of ancient sites, immersive environments and personalized content are powerful new elements in the presentation of official heritage. Through the first two decades of the twenty-first century, the development of digital applications has blossomed with funding from such major sources as the European Commission (Digicult, Minerva and EPOCH being among the most well-funded EU projects); the US National Park Service through its National Center for Preservation Technology and Training; heritage non-profits such as CyArk, Archives & Museum Informatics and the Virtual Heritage Network, and with increasing investment from a large number of private firms in the computer and museum design industry (cf. VAST, VSMM and Eurographics conferences). Digital applications have become standard features of archaeological and architectural research, public heritage presentation and even site management, with a new body of theory emerging for the most effective use of digital heritage for both research and educational uses (Parry 2005; Cameron and Kenderdine 2010). Even though concerns have been voiced about the durability of digital media (Addison 2007), it is taken as a given that digital heritage is essential for the preservation of the world's heritage. Yet what is its effect on performative collective memory?

Visualization is perhaps the most conspicuous of the new digital heritage applications, though it is hardly an innovation or novelty in the field of heritage (Molyneaux 1997). Ever since the birth of what might be called antiquarian interest in the Renaissance with their meticulous architectural reconstructions of Greek and Roman architecture through the melodramatic tableaux of the pageants and panoramas of the nineteenth century, to the Hollywood costume epics of the twentieth century, graphic imaginings of the past have always been a standard medium of popular historiography. As stirring or romantic artists' impressions, these pencil-drawn, oil-painted or cinemascoped Technicolor images have created indelible popular images of the past. Those images have been constantly changing over time, as artistic styles and contemporary tastes transformed the conventions and styles with which and by which antiquity was represented in graphic form, and cultural modalities of visual accuracy and authenticity evolved.

The rise of 3D computer modeling of ancient structures, sites and landscapes (Barceló et al. 2000) can be seen as a continuation of that long tradition. But it also marks a considerable rise, at least in some circles, in expectations for both passive consumption and its historiographical authority. The increasing sophistication of laser scanning and excavation database-driven reconstructions has tied the visualization of the heritage site or heritage object ever more closely to digital processes, seemingly based on empirical evidence alone. The increasingly sophisticated rendering has given rise to a style of pseudo-photographic representation that has unparalleled authority in a world of computer images and video games. In its increasing use as a standard feature of visitor centers, augmented reality kiosks, immersive environments and other interpretive installations for public presentation, the character of 3D modeling as realer than real has been 'enhanced' by a range of new applications that populate the reconstructed scenes with wholly artificial 'people' (Tecchia *et al*. 2002) and even fill the unexcavated or undocumented spaces with sophisticated applications (Willmott *et al*. 2001) to camouflage with pixels the inevitably fragmentary information we have about the past. As a result, the formerly tangible, experiential distinction between excavated site or surviving ruin and 'artist's reconstruction' blurs, or disappears altogether: the observer cannot tell the representations of empirical or phenomenological 'fact' from pixilated speculation.

The danger to public participation (of more than a purely passive kind) in the kinds of collective memory mentioned above is not only the increasing authority of 'expert' presentation; it is the isolating and highly individualizing way in which the past is perceived via these media. Although there is unquestionably a useful role in 3D documentation of endangered or destroyed cultural resources, the quest for ever greater visual realism and the increasing introduction of navigational rules, simulation protocols and participation in heritage activities in virtual worlds such as Second Life (Bogdanovych *et al*. 2011) substitute the stimulating experience of being in a life-like but virtual environment for possible reflection on the relationship between past and present, and the relationship with a meaningful memory community.

The past indeed becomes a 'foreign country' for most visitors to heritage sites – a place of wonder and escape from the present that is static in its representational perfection, with none of the consequences, uncertainties or imperfections that both the past and our knowledge of it share (Lowenthal 1999). 'Digital heritage' or 'virtual heritage' holds the danger of becoming all visualization and factoids, delivered to individual viewers or receivers not only through the computer-generated images on fixed video screens and smartphones but also through the delivery of global positioning systems (GPS) heritage through handheld devices or standard mobile phones (Benini, *et al*. 2002; Ancona *et al*. 2007). That is not to say that digital visualization has no place in the gathering and analysis of data; our emphasis is, rather, on its danger as the increasingly common face of public heritage. For a public increasingly accustomed to the passive consumption of historical content, there is a dangerous illusionary aspect of which digital archaeologists, humanists and heritage professionals need to be aware. The examples cited above are highly individualized and isolating. In particular, there is nothing collective here, other than the sum of individual experiences. In most instances, individuals interact with software, not each other. The scripts for exploration and application are pre-set by scholars, museum curators or curriculum designers; there is little or no real option for the kind of conversational transformation that is so essential to the constant recreation 'by communities and groups in response to their environment, their interaction with nature and their history, and provides them with a sense of identity and continuity' (UNESCO 2003, Art. 2.1).

Yet the digital technologies do, in fact, have a great potential to make interaction really potent: the continuous contribution of data from end-users (as well as scholars, curators and educators) not only makes the process of learning about and reflecting upon the past dynamic and unique to the place and community. It is a digital version of Raphael Samuel's 'theatres of memory' – places, events and opportunities where the community as a whole and the individuals within it can reflect on the past and create an evolving image of themselves (Samuel 1996). That evolution only occurs when people interact with each other. It is the ability to hear someone else's version of the story, or see a 'map' of someone else's memory of a place, that creates the open cognitive space in which you can change your own. This theater does not have to be simultaneous or synchronous; experiences can be layered over time as well, as when successive generations inherit and use places and spaces, rituals and habits. But the sense of collective engagement has to be present somehow, before digital versions of interaction can escape the old one-directional frame of the museum panel or the textbook chapter.

In the following sections we explore the potential for digital technologies (from early participatory geographic information systems (GIS) to social networking) to serve as tools for the reconstruction and constant reformulation of performative collective memories in the dimensions of space, community and individual identity.

Re-enchanting places: the collective memory of GIS

Place is a powerful theater for memory, both individual and collective. In recent years, participatory GIS projects have evolved from a field researcher's labor-saving strategy for data-gathering into genuine attempts to employ the technology as a place-based medium for both collective remembering and transformation. The Levuka Cultural Landscape Project is one such effort (Purser 2012). Levuka, Fiji, is a small island port community of about a thousand people with a rich and diverse history. It is currently being nominated to the World Heritage List by the Fijian government for its role as the British colonial capital of Fiji in the 1870s (Harrison 2004).

The Levuka Cultural Landscape Project grew out of the need to find some mechanism for enabling the local community to participate in the heritage nomination process. The goal was to design an accessible medium, or platform, for first documenting what community members wanted to have acknowledged as elements of the town's heritage, and then conveying that information to authorities from their own government as well as an array of international consultants, functionaries and decision makers. In this sense, the project was grounded in and driven by an existing, physical community. The digital technology became a very locally focused medium, or platform, first for discussing memories and meanings amongst themselves, and then for generating what became a truly alternative 'map' of what local Levuka community members defined as 'heritage', and its 'significance', in contrast to definitions being driven increasingly by outsiders.

Over the course of five field seasons in seven years, successive layers of information were imbedded in the GIS. Each season was designed around a series of open community workshops and meetings. Participants in these meetings worked on three things: reviewing the new images produced by previous season's work; developing the new information for that season, and deciding what kinds of information should be recorded next. Each successive season's maps were generated based on what the previous work revealed.

Over the years, it became very clear that while the end-product of the GIS, with all its detailed map data and comparative power, was very useful, it was the process of creating it that had the greatest impact for people in Levuka who took part in the workshops. More important than making the maps was deciding what should go on the maps, and why. More important than creating the document was the power to see what had been invisible made visible. Conversations sparked and crackled around how to draw boundaries, label neighborhoods with local names, chart the routes and pathways that carried daily foot-traffic, and tell the remembered (but often conflicting) stories about past uses for a house, a lot or a district. Prior to starting the project, all official attention on Levuka's 'heritage' had been focused on important public structures related to Fijian national history, and a picturesque and accessible commercial strip where a localized heritage tourism was already well developed. The GIS process expanded the physical scale of what might count as heritage into the residential neighborhoods and more remote enclaves well away from the civic and commercial sector. But it also created an inherently intangible and constantly evolving, yet instantly and immediately visual means of asserting that others also held an authority to define what counted.

In the process of remembering, things were also discovered. New ideas about the relationships between past and present emerged, and literally took shape on the map. Areas of town that had been perceived as occupied only by 'newcomers' were found to be vibrant enclaves of families and individuals with local roots going back four generations. Places socially perceived as 'outside' town were found to be within the official town boundary. And perhaps most importantly, people who thought their histories had been forgotten or ignored by the town's current residents not only got to perform their own memories, but discovered that others remembered as well (see Simon, this volume). Stories began to overlap like the digital layers of the GIS, palimpsests of place-based memories held by individuals, families, neighborhoods, all the town's church groups, alumni societies for the different schools, occupational clusters of storekeepers, government workers, schoolteachers and so on. Out of the rich interaction of these distinct but connected and overlapping 'memory communities' came an increasingly clear demand on the part of town residents to be given a greater voice in the next phases of the heritage nomination process.

In essence the ultimate product of the Levuka project may have been awareness and mobilization – not that there was none there before, but the generative process of the GIS development definitely supplemented and supported earlier efforts, giving them new impetus. Several years before the Levuka Cultural Landscape Project was begun, a consortium of local schoolteachers and community leaders had painstakingly collected a wide range of town family histories, carefully including as many as possible of the ethnically diverse groups represented in the town's population. They published these in a slim volume that constituted the townspeople's first response to the externally driven and monument-focused heritage nomination process.

Entitled *Levuka: A Living Heritage*, and authored by 'The People of Levuka' (2001), the book argued instead for a focus on the people themselves, and their generations-long collective and collaborative stewardship of this special place. The participatory GIS project did more than simply map that community engagement onto built space and form. It took the representational, but sequential, linear and ultimately finite performance of family histories and individual identity that had been captured in the book, and translated them into a dynamic and continuing conversation about how and why those diverse but shared histories connected local people to both the place and each other. And Levuka's residents, in turn, have used that conversation as the basis for asserting their role in defining the town's future.

Reconstructing community: the digital diaspora as home

There is perhaps no clearer case of the stubborn maintenance of the cultural heritage tradition and collective memory of a diasporic community than that of District Six in Cape Town, South Africa (Jeppie and Soudien 1990). The exiles from the racially mixed (and bulldozed) neighborhood – scattered to different places with the actual location torn down – retained precious intangible memories of a time and a place that survived only in that community's mind. After the fall of apartheid, and a greater freedom to talk not only about resistance, but deep cultural resistance to the racially segregated order, the District Six Museum was founded. The memories were organized and collected in a former church now serving as a local memory institution. Through the contributed user content of evocative artifacts (like the street signs collected and kept by one of the bulldozer operators) and through the medium of a large map of the streets and squares of the former district painted on the church's floor, former residents, their children and grandchildren taped their notes and memories of their lost homeland to create a collective imagining of life in District Six that expanded the more straightforwardly documented history (Julius 2007).

It is interesting how this larger vision of collective history envelops and gives meaning to a recent attempt to represent shared memories of District Six through 3D modeling (de Kadt *et al.* 2009). Here, like a similar case in the very different context of the destroyed and abandoned town of Rosewood, Florida (González-Tennant 2010), visualization becomes an aid to collective memory along with other mnemonic techniques (see http://www.virtualrosewood.com/, accessed 4 April 2011). What process of collaborative digital memory-making can supplement the painted lines and yellow Post-its on the floor of the District Six Museum or the stories told about Rosewood? In the absence of the physical landscape that gave rise to the memories, a virtual landscape constructed digitally from both empirical evidence and collected reminiscences can map the community of memory itself.

That community of memory can be displaced geographically from its place of origin as well as distanced across time. In recent studies of the 'Newfoundland diaspora' and people's cultural yearning to remain connected with the traditions and sites of Newfoundland through the creation of digital communities, we can see immigrant heritage not as a place or a product but an ongoing process in which digital technologies play an essential role (Hiller and Franz 2004). At first instrumental in helping the relocating migrants find jobs and accommodations in their new homelands, in this case in far western Canada, the Internet ultimately becomes a bearer of culture in later stages of diasporic existence, when the 'homeland diaspora' system has replaced the original idea of territory. Facilitated by the participation of the staff and membership of a cultural organization, the Internet is transformed from a source of practical information that facilitates the move to a source of cultural capital when the immigrants' identity begins to erode. Digital social networks maintain a sense of connection during the migration period, dealing mostly with contemporary family events and one-to-one communication. But as the bonds of the 'immigrant village' begin to fray and the natural process of assimilation occurs, the digital media become a source of deeper heritage information, as people attempt to maintain, and ultimately to construct entirely anew, the basis of a composite identity.

The key distinction made by Hiller and Franz is between new ties, old ties and the search for lost ties – and it is in this search that heritage as performative memory can be facilitated digitally. Case studies have shown that diasporic peoples as different as Trinidadians and South Asian Indians go through the same processes of community maintenance, cultural identity expression and information sharing that were simply not possible before social media. Where before the mechanisms that defined shared cultural heritage were territorially bounded or required physical presence, those connections can now be maintained digitally. As Hiller and Franz observe (2004: 747) 'instead of being an alien outsider in a strange land, the online community allows the migrant to belong and to be a member of a shared community'. And that feeling of being a member of a collective is what the appreciation of heritage, whether completely ancient or more modern, is presumably all about: the sense of a living, dynamic and useful cultural heritage that is, as we have repeatedly mentioned, 'constantly recreated by communities and groups in response to their environment, their interaction with nature and their history, and provides them with a sense of identity and continuity'.

Another intriguing case study is the diasporic use of digital heritage among overseas Chinese for sharing and interpreting traditional Chinese poetry (Chang 2006). In this application, the online activity is shifted 'from path finding and selection to the user's ability to create content and meaning' (Chang 2006: 174). The most common digital heritage applications, guided by (external) expert opinion, prevent the user from doing just that. Yet in the context of diasporic communities, such meaning-making is a public act that expands or subtly transforms the collective memory of the wider community. This is a far cry from the use of digital technologies merely to reproduce and disseminate catalogues of expert information, which divert the power of the communicative medium from its potential to serve as a platform for performative collective memory.

Silvia Mejía Estévez notes a similarly instructive example of the use of Internet communications by new Ecuadorian immigrant communities in Spain (Estévez 2009), who are assisted by non-profit initiatives like the Programa Migración, Comunicación y Desarrollo to obtain digital access to their home communities. Estévez suggests that constant access to a virtual community encompassing both homeland and diaspora in a web of communication, content and shared culture – through websites, chatrooms, Skype links and emails – leaves neither time nor space for isolation or nostalgic longing. The digital tools (however simple and straightforward) help strengthen a sense of community belonging, by providing both the moments and the media for potentially transformative conversations about the character of membership in the community. These performative and self-reflective aspects of constantly evolving collective memory are at the heart of community-based heritage.

As in the case of Fiji above, a collective consciousness linking past and present is maintained, but here it does so in places where the distances between members of the community are great. This collective process is something that standard heritage presentation of monuments and sites cannot offer, for in their static official nature they discourage rather than enhance cultural creativity. And what of the case when the process of even greater alienation has occurred and the search by individuals for their 'lost ties' must be conducted not only through space but also through time?

Genealogy as a social network: digital memory communities

The quest to restore 'lost ties' noted in the scattered Newfoundland digital communities, and the attempt to maintain cultural continuity through the use of the Internet by the Ecuadorian diaspora can be seen in yet another form in the new rituals of 'Highland Homecomings' described in detail by Paul Basu (2007). This is performative heritage in all its dimensions, creating processes of remembering (or experiencing a perceived sense of remembrance) that weave together national and ethnic narrative with place and personal experience. This produces what Basu calls 'an answering image' to an assimilated diasporic existence through the use of representations of the past and the social ties drawn from it. Here is diasporic heritage ritualized back in the 'homeland' wherever and however that homeland is perceived to be. In combining historical research with specific points on the Scottish landscape, the homecoming walks and visits create a community of memory with very concrete social implications, quite apart from the documentation of the tangible and intangible traditions. These connections and recollections are now both maintained on websites created by the Scottish National Trust and by innumerable contemporary 'clans'. The easiest part of the digital performance is in planning and recording this nostalgic, identity-rich connection. But there is something else of great interest in the possibilities of digital technologies facilitating a physical return.

It is the idea of a diaspora being overcome by a new kind of digital genealogy that crosses the boundaries of both time and space. These are pilgrimages of intentional memory creation: the act of returning to physically stand on the street where a storied great-grandfather once walked is the literal embodiment of a generational connection between past and present. So by definition, these journeys create repeated moments of opportunity for exploring personal meanings of and for a shared diasporic past. Moreover, these moments are themselves often shared, creating in effect new memory communities with others in the tour group not even necessarily of one's own family, but on the collective pilgrimage themselves. The fundamental difference between the shared exploration of memory in place, and the shared purchase of an authoritatively guided tour at a conventional heritage site, is this active, collaborative conversion of experience into heritage.

Another use of digital technology to facilitate and document the collective memory of scattered or fragmented communities is in the realm of genealogy. As Tamara Hareven long ago noted, identity and consciousness are dependent on the depth of generational memory, and the quest to extend the reach of family connections has become an 'exercise of "tribal rites" in an advanced technological society' (Hareven 1978: 145). The kinds of fact-based public history (digital or analogue) in which individuals are informed of events and cultures far beyond living memory do not result in a meaningful connection between personal circumstances and collective history. It is therefore significant that genealogical activity has become for many, particularly in the United States and the United Kingdom, an increasingly popular activity that is for the most part quite unconnected with 'official' heritage. In the transformation of genealogy from a passively acquired record of a pedigree to reinforce elite social status or inheritance claims has been upended. It has been transformed from product (title, status, inherited property) to a process of individuals from many walks of life hoping to find out 'who they are' (cf. Mason 2008). In a sense, like the other cases we have mentioned, digital heritage can serve not merely as a purveyor of archaeological information or historical visualizations, but as a facilitator of reconnection – in this case, to history.

And here is the digital connection: the concerted effort by government bureaucracies, particularly in the industrialized world, to digitize their records has created an unparalleled abundance of raw material for personal genealogical connections – in the form of birth records, death certificates, census forms and tax rolls, increasingly accessible on the Internet. Private firms, the most well-known and largest being Ancestry.com (Saito-Chung 2011), have offered subscription-based access to their growing network of genealogical resources. Following the pattern set by the earlier BBC version of *Who Do You Think You Are?*, the search for roots by select celebrities that is sponsored by such firms during the US TV primetime (National Broadcasting Company 2011) shows all the advantages and drawbacks of other entertaining forms of digital heritage: passive consumption of packaged narratives, in vivid visualized form. This is vicarious heritage with its generalized lessons for the public: how a starlet, sports hero or singer traced the unexpected twists and turns of his or her family's history.

The opportunity to participate in one's own quest to link his or her forebears to the sweep of official history certainly offers more of a process, but is it yet another isolating activity that works against the kinds of collective memory that are coming to be recognized as the dynamic and meaningful face of public heritage? An important step towards answering this question has been made by Labrador and Chilton (2009) in their examination of the restructuring of digital heritage databases – a suggestion with profound implications for all the other applications based on community engagement that we have surveyed in this paper. Recognizing that the basic structure of digital collections of data reproduces that of the traditional archive – constructed and selected by experts for passive consumption by other scholars or the general public, they ask pointedly, 'What if non-"expert" heritage archive users were acknowledged as imaginative information seekers willing, able, and wanting to create their own meanings? And what if this meaning-making process was more formally accepted as part of a new archival process, the creation of a self-consciously created new memory palace?' (Labrador and Chilton 2009: 4).

In understanding that a shift to a truly user-oriented database approach would entail a fundamental shift in construction, they go on to propose a transformation from the collection and handling of huge amounts of data for research purposes to a construction that would make individual searches for specific items of information more accessible. Indeed the growth in the individual versus research uses of institutions like the US National Archives is indicative not only of a growing hunger to bridge the gap between individual identity and collective memory, it is an important factor in how the archives – and by extension digital databases that underlie the collections of museums, archives and archaeological data banks – will be reshaped in the decades to come. And that brings us back to the theme of digital genealogy where in a digital, interconnected world, the process of searching through the data is not necessarily a solitary one.

Digital technologies can create heritage networks that resemble real-time social networks like Facebook, except with the added dimension of historical time. Points of contact between separate searches lead to communication between seekers and new connections in both present and past. As Labrador and Chilton put it, 'Here the meaning-making process is socially mediated – the inherent contradictions between personal histories are not presented as public multiple narratives, but are encountered as moments of contact during contiguous heritage quests with multiple intersections of shared nodes' (2009:6). This is quite different from most currently conceived user-generated content that is used to create museum exhibitions or digital repositories of multiple memories. It is light years distant from the digitization of expert-driven collections of objective (arti)facts. It represents a new means of creating social contact through heritage search and reflection – in other words, the facilitation or creation of digital memory communities.

Such social networking sites – along with other more spontaneous uses of social media create a virtual kitchen table, backyard fence, corner bar conversation that, because of the textual and visual format, are instantly accessible yet at the same time archived, preserving the structures of collective memory, even while the memories themselves evolve and change. This allows for contemplation, for coming back the next week with a new comment, or when a new set of photos goes up on someone's wall or when a new connection is found. And the community participating in the conversation can be expanded, but it is a community of active seekers, producers and preservers of cultural heritage information, not an essentialized and anonymous 'audience' for predigested heritage.

Conclusion

These examples from the United States, South America, Fiji, South Africa, Asia and Europe show that the creative value of digital heritage lies not only in information processing through instantaneous communication networks or databases of precise scientific documentation, but in its power to stimulate unique, community-based reflection on past, present and future identities. We have presented these examples of the potential of digital technologies as media of memory in a fragmented, amnesiac and diasporic world. It is clear that digital technologies and social media do indeed represent a new way for us to reflect upon the past. But they must not be allowed merely to intensify the power of old top-down structures.

The key is indeed to favor process over product in the cultural production of our relationship to the past. And it is through the communicative and connecting nature of social technology that new 'realms of belonging', in the words of Anne-Marie Fortier (1999) can be established, maintained and transformed in our fragmented and diasporic world. Digital technologies can help individuals, communities and communities-in-the-making escape the conventions of standard visualization and top-down heritage presentation, but they cannot do it alone. The 'software' for such a radical reversal in the process of heritage lies in the very fact that collective memory – now largely missing or highly regimented in our world of individualism and media conventions – is a prerequisite for productive social action and cohesive, dynamic communities.

Heritage has the potential to restrict or empower; its significance lies not in the objects and places of the past or their digitized documentation. As we have seen, digital technologies have the capacity to make the artificial and contemporary seem ancient; they have the power to make carefully scripted interactive games and simulation seem like the passage of historical time. But contingency, agency, surprise, contemplation, serendipity and, above all, creativity are the secret ingredients of the human-made past. It is in enhancing the scripting and performance of this rich cognitive software that the true value of social media lies. And that software is the ever-changing collective conversation about past and present – about space, identity and emerging selfhood – that constitutes the dynamic core of meaningful human memory.

References

Addison, A.C. (2007) 'The Vanishing Virtual: Safeguarding Heritage's Endangered Digital Record', in Y. Kalay, T. Kvan and J. Affleck (eds) *New Heritage: New Media and Cultural Heritage*, London: Routledge.

Ancona, M., Conte, D., Quercini, G. and Casamassima, M. (2007) 'Attention-Aware Cultural Heritage Applications on Mobile Phones', in *Proceedings of the Twelfth International Symposium on a World of Wireless, Mobile and Multimedia Networks (WoWMoM 2007)*, 1–8. Los Alamitos, CA: IEEE Computer Society.

Araoz, G. (2011) 'Preserving Heritage Places under a New Paradigm', *Journal of Cultural Heritage Management and Sustainable Development*, 1 (1): 55–60.

Barceló, J.A., Forte, M. and Sanders, D.H. (2000) *Virtual Reality in Archaeology*, Oxford: Archaeopress.

Basu, P. (2007) *Highland Homecomings: Genealogy and Heritage Tourism in the Scottish Diaspora*, London: Routledge.

Benini, L., Bonfigli, M.E., Calori, L., Farella, E. and Riccò, B. (2002) 'Palmtop Computers for Managing Interaction with Immersive Virtual Heritage', in *Proceedings of EUROMEDIA 2002*, 183–189. Erlangen: SCS Publishing House.

Bogdanovych, A., Rodríguez, J., Simoff, S., Cohen, A. and Sierra, C. (2011) 'Developing Virtual Heritage Applications as Normative Multiagent Systems', *Agent-Oriented Software Engineering*, 10: 140–154.

Cameron, F. and Kenderdine, S. (2010) *Theorizing Digital Cultural Heritage: A Critical Discourse*, Cambridge, MA: MIT Press.

Castenell, L.A. and Pinar, W. (1993) *Understanding Curriculum as Racial Text: Representations of Identity and Difference in Education*, Albany, NY: SUNY Press.

Chang, P.-L. (2006) 'Exploring Interactivity: User Ability and the Chinese Diaspora', *Digital Creativity*, 17 (3): 174.

Connerton, P. (1989) *How Societies Remember*, 1st edn, Cambridge: Cambridge University Press.

Connerton, P. (2009) *How Modernity Forgets*, 1st edn, Cambridge: Cambridge University Press.

de Kadt, C., Gain, J. and Marais, P. (2009) 'Revisiting District Six: A Case Study of Digital Heritage Reconstruction from Archival Photographs', in *Proceedings of the 6th International Conference on Computer Graphics, Virtual Reality, Visualisation and Interaction in Africa (AFRIGRAPH '09)*, 13–21. New York: ACM Press.

Estévez, S.M. (2009) 'Is Nostalgia Becoming Digital? Ecuadorian Diaspora in the Age of Global Capitalism', *Social Identities*, 15 (3): 393–410.

Fine, G.A. (2007) 'Rumor, Trust and Civil Society: Collective Memory and Cultures of Judgment', *Diogenes*, 54 (1): 5–18.

Fortier, A.-M. (1999) 'Re-Membering Places and the Performance of Belonging(s)', *Theory, Culture & Society*, 16 (2): 41–64.

Glassberg, D. (1990) *American Historical Pageantry: The Uses of Tradition in the Early Twentieth Century*, Chapel Hill, NC: The University of North Carolina Press.

Glassie, H.H. (1995) *Passing the Time in Ballymenone: Culture and History of an Ulster Community*, Bloomington, IN: Indiana University Press.

González-Tennant, E. (2010) 'Virtual Archaeology and Digital Storytelling: A Report from Rosewood, Florida', *The African Diaspora Archaeology Network Newsletter* (September 2010). http://www.diaspora.uiuc.edu/news0910/news0910-1.pdf (accessed 4 November 2011).

Gunnels, J. (2005) 'Let the Car Burn, We're Going to the Faire: History, Performance, Community and Identity within the Renaissance Festival', PhD dissertation, University of Texas at Austin. http://repositories.lib.utexas.edu/handle/2152/7626 (accessed 4 November 2011).

Hareven, T.K. (1978) 'The Search for Generational Memory: Tribal Rites in Industrial Society', *Daedalus*, 107 (4): 137–149.

Harrison, D. (2004) 'Levuka, Fiji: Contested Heritage?', *Current Issues in Tourism*, 7 (4/5): 346–369.

Hiller, H.H. and Franz, T.M. (2004) 'New Ties, Old Ties and Lost Ties: The Use of the Internet in Diaspora', *New Media & Society*, 6 (6): 731–752.

Jeppie, S. and Soudien, C. (1990) *The Struggle for District Six: Past and Present*, Cape Town: Buchu Books.

Julius, C. (2007) *Oral History in the Exhibitionary Strategy of the District Six Museum, Cape Town*, Cape Town: University of the Western Cape.

Labrador, A.M. and Chilton, E.S. (2009) 'Re-locating Meaning in Heritage Archives: A Call for Participatory Heritage Databases', in *Proceedings of Computer Applications to Archaeology 2009 (CAA 2009)*. Williamsburg, VA: CAA Press. http://www.caa2009.org/articles/Labrador_Contribution386_c (1).pdf (accessed 4 November 2011).

Lowenthal. D. (1999) *The Past is a Foreign Country*, Cambridge: Cambridge University Press.

Lowenthal, D. (2002) 'The Past as a Theme Park', in T. Young and R. Riley (eds) *Theme Park Landscapes*, Washington, DC: Dumbarton Oaks Publications.

Mason, J. (2008) 'Tangible Affinities and the Real Life Fascination of Kinship', *Sociology*, 42 (1): 29–45.

McCalman, I. and Pickering, P.A. (2009) *Historical Reenactment: From Realism to the Affective Turn*, Basingstoke: Palgrave Macmillan.

Misztal, B. (2003) *Theories of Social Remembering*, Maidenhead: Open University Press.

Molyneaux, B. (1997) *The Cultural Life of Images: Visual Representation in Archaeology*, London: Psychology Press.

National Broadcasting Company (2011) 'Who Do You Think You Are?' http://www.nbc.com/who-do-you-think-you-are/ (accessed 4 November 2011).

Parry, R. (2005) 'Digital Heritage and the Rise of Theory in Museum Computing', *Museum Management and Curatorship*, 20 (4): 333–348.

Purser, M. (2012) 'Emptying the Magician's Hat: Participatory GIS-based Research in Fiji' in J. Carman, C. McDavid and R. Skeates (eds) *The Oxford Handbook of Public Archaeology*, New York: Oxford University Press.

Putnam, R.D. (2001) *Bowling Alone: The Collapse and Revival of American Community*, New York: Simon and Schuster.

Rentzhog, S. (2007) *Open Air Museums: The History and Future of a Visionary Idea*, Jamtle: Carlssons.

Roy, O. (2010) *Holy Ignorance: When Religion and Culture Part Ways*, New York: Columbia University Press.

Saito-Chung, D. (2011) 'Ancestry.com Forms a Tie with Facebook', *Investors.com – Investor's Business Daily*. http://www.investors.com/NewsAndAnalysis/Article/567857/201104011910/Ancestrycom-Touts-Genealogy-Database.htm (accessed 4 November 2011).

Samuel, R. (1996) *Theatres of Memory: Past and Present in Contemporary Culture*, London: Verso.

Scott, J.C. (1990) *Domination and the Arts of Resistance: Hidden Transcripts*, New Haven, CT: Yale University Press.

Silberman, N.A. (1995) 'Promised Lands and Chosen Peoples: The Politics and Poetics of Archaeological Narrative', in P.L. Kohl and C. Fawcett (eds) *Nationalism, Politics, and the Practice of Archaeology*, Cambridge: Cambridge University Press.

Tecchia, F., Loscos, C. and Chrysanthou, Y. (2002) 'Visualizing Crowds in Real Time', *Computer Graphics Forum*, 21 (4): 753–765.

The People of Levuka (2001) *Levuka: A Living Heritage*. Suva: University of the South Pacific.

UNESCO (2003) Convention for the Safeguarding of Intangible Cultural Heritage. http://www.unesco.org/culture/ich/index.php?lg=en&pg=00006 (accessed 4 November 2011).

UNESCO (2005) Convention on the Protection and Promotion of the Diversity of Cultural Expressions. http://www.unesco.org/new/en/unesco/themes/2005-convention/the-convention/ (accessed 4 November 2011).

West, P. (1999) *Domesticating History: The Political Origins of America's House Museums*, Washington, DC: Smithsonian Books.

Willmott, J., Wright, L.I., Arnold, D.B. and Day, A.M. (2001) 'Rendering of Large and Complex Urban Environments for Real Time Heritage Reconstructions', in *Proceedings of the 2001 Conference on Virtual Reality, Archeology, and Cultural Heritage (VAST '01)*: 111–120. New York: ACM Press.

Zerubavel, E. (1996) 'Social Memories: Steps to a Sociology of the Past', *Qualitative Sociology*, 19 (3): 283–299.

Zerubavel, E. (2004) *Time Maps: Collective Memory and the Social Shape of the Past*, Chicago, IL: University of Chicago Press.

2

SOCIALLY DISTRIBUTED CURATION OF THE BHOPAL DISASTER

A case of grassroots heritage in the crisis context

Sophia B. Liu

Introduction

This chapter offers an interpretation of how a sense of heritage is shaped through socially distributed curatorial practices emerging from social media use in the crisis domain. Major crises and disasters – natural, technological and human-induced hazards – are shared phenomena that have a societal impact, and tend to be viewed as historic events worth remembering. Although crises typically conjure up thoughts of danger and difficulty, they also provide opportunities to learn how to cope with, recover from and adapt to adverse and unexpected situations that can strengthen community resilience to future disasters. In the digital age, members of the public increasingly document, share and make sense of memories and stories about crises through social media. Methods for curating and communicating the heritage that are emerging from contemporary social practices of collective remembering need to be re-evaluated in light of the new 'technologies of memory' (Van House and Churchill 2008) that we are using in today's society. This chapter brings heritage and crisis events together with the new phenomenon of social media to investigate the emergent socio-technical practices that lie at the convergence of these three domains – a largely uncharted territory.

Historic crises and the emerging role of curation

Historic crises and related commemoration activities engender practices of remembrance that bring together members of the wider public to share and make sense of tragic events in the present day. Social media have increasingly become the new vehicle for commemorating crises and sharing memories and stories that are perceived to be historically valuable as well as personally meaningful. In this context, the idea of heritage is taking on new meanings, and attention is shifting towards the living heritage practices that occur in everyday life outside traditional museum institutions. In this chapter, I refer to these practices as 'grassroots heritage' (Liu 2011).

At the convergence of heritage, crises and social media is the element of 'curation'. Curation is an active and intentional process of making choices about what is most meaningful to preserve and pass on to future generations. This task is typically associated with the role of professional curators within cultural heritage institutions. However, curation has also become a socio-technical practice involving a large number of ordinary people using emerging information and communication technologies (ICTs) to preserve, manage and share digitally their memories and stories. Emerging ICTs like social media are transforming 'digital memories' into artifacts that can be copied, remixed, (re)presented and ultimately curated online in a distributed fashion. Social tagging, commenting and ad hoc group formation within social media services are some examples of curatorial practices that occur in socially distributed ways, what I call 'socially-distributed curation' (Liu 2011). This concept relates to the 'distributed cognition' framework proposed by Hutchins (1995) and Hollan *et al.* (2000) as a way to understand the interactions between people and technologies. Hollan *et al.* (2000) explain this theoretical model by distinguishing the following three types of 'cognitive processes': (1) a process that is distributed across members of a social group, (2) a process that involves coordination between internal and external structures, and (3) a process that is distributed through time to allow the products of earlier events transform the nature of later events (p. 176).

Based on the findings of a large-scale empirical study conducted between 2006 and 2011, the following sections examine how social media facilitate socially distributed forms of online curation of crisis-related 'artifacts'. They describe how the activities promoted by the distinct design features of social media services support different yet convergent tasks associated with curation (e.g. collecting, organizing, storytelling, etc.). These findings shed light on the unique opportunity and responsibility that designers of social media and ICTs in general have today to influence *how* memories are kept alive – or rather curated.

Investigating curation in the crisis domain

This chapter presents some of the findings from a three-part, multi-method investigation to determine what crisis narratives appear in social media, and how social media are being used to sustain these narratives through curatorial activities (Liu 2011). Part 1 consisted of surveying the social media presence of 111 crisis events that occurred between 1960 and 2010 to examine if and how past historically significant crisis events were being commemorated in the present day through social media. Then, ethnographic and computational collection and analysis methods were used to identify narratives appearing in the social media landscape for the following four crises that exhibited a high social media presence in the survey: (1) the 1984 Bhopal gas leak, (2) the 2001 September 11 attacks, (3) the 2005 Hurricane Katrina, and (4) the climate change crisis. A critical finding that emerged from the first part of this investigation was that in the digital world people sustain the heritage of historic crises by perpetually revising related narratives.

Part 2 consisted of critiquing both the concept of 'curator' (as a profession) and the concept of 'curation' (as a practice) to develop a broader understanding of curation in the context of the social web. Part 3 involved the application and evaluation of this initial conceptual model of curation through the analysis of the curatorial activities that produced the crisis narratives found in the first study. This evaluation led to the articulation of a theoretical model of 'socially distributed curation' meant to inform the design of future technology intended to support long-term preservation of social media activity. The following sections present findings from Part 2 and Part 3 of this research study.

Methods of investigating curation

Critiquing the concept of curation involved a collation and distillation of uses of the term curation within the online context of multiple social media services. Approximately 250 'web artifacts' pertaining to curation in the social web context were collected and analyzed using a technique called 'web sphere analysis' (Schneider and Foot 2005). These artifacts included blog posts, online news articles, videos and the comments within each of these posts. Fifteen people were also interviewed that exhibited expert knowledge on the role of curators within cultural heritage institutions, conducted work in the area of digital history and digital heritage relevant to curation, consistently wrote about curation in their web posts, and/or developed technology to facilitate digital curation. These interviews were conducted face to face, over the phone, via email, through Skype and/or instant messaging. Additionally, five pieces of literature discussing the traditional role of curators in the past and their evolving role in the presence of new media (Thompson 1992; Marincola 2000; Chambers 2006; Thea and Micchelli 2009; Graham and Cook 2010) were critically analyzed to complement the examination of the collected web artifacts.

An initial conceptual model of online curation

The different duties and skills that emerged from synthesizing the meaning of curators and curation in the social web context led to the development of an initial conceptual model of curation containing seven archetypes and several activities associated with each archetype (see Figure 2.1). They are as follows: (1) Like an *archivist*, the curator *obtains*, *collects* and *stores* a representative set of artifacts. (2) Like a *librarian*, the curator *organizes*, *categorizes* and *generates* metadata to add value to the artifacts. (3) Like a *preservationist*, the curator *preserves* and *safeguards* the artifacts for long periods of time. (4) Like an *editor*, the curator *filters* for high-quality, relevant and reputable artifacts and *verifies* their authenticity. (5) Like a *story maker*, the curator *crafts a story* by weaving together the selected artifacts and by producing interpretative material to *communicate a message* to the audience. (6) Like an *exhibitor*, the curator

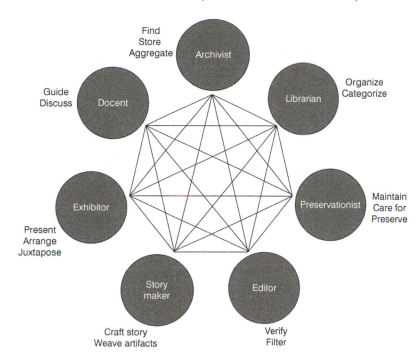

FIGURE 2.1   Online curation: an initial conceptual model

displays, arranges and *juxtaposes* a chosen set of artifacts to create a compelling experience and evoke a response. (7) Finally, like a *docent*, the curator *guides visitors* and *facilitates discussions*.

This diverse set of curatorial activities illustrates how a curator has many functions and how curation is a multifaceted construct. Traditional curators tend to play a mediating role by adapting their curatorial skills to the needs of other stakeholders. Unlike this traditional form of curation, where the curator takes on many roles and functions, curation in the social web context is occurring in a more distributed fashion through a socio-technical process involving many people using a wide array of social media services and technical tools. Instead of just one person categorizing online data about a historic event by means of keywords and tags, it is a multitude of people using social bookmarking services like Delicious to categorize online data while also engaging in other curatorial activities that best fit their own expertise (Figure 2.1). But how does this process unfold in practice?

Assessing online curation in practice

To refine an initial understanding of online curation by ascertaining how crisis narratives are actually curated, data were collected that pertain to how crisis memories and stories are created, shared, and ultimately curated in the social media landscape. By using the initial conceptual model of Figure 2.1 as a guide for analyzing the curatorial activities of a particular crisis narrative, I examined how social media users engaged in memorializing a specific crisis narrative about the 1984 Bhopal gas leak, called the 'second disaster', on the occasion of the twenty-fifth anniversary of the disaster.

The evaluation consisted of creating a spreadsheet to calculate the degree to which the seven curatorial activities described in the initial conceptual model occurred across different social media services regarding this particular narrative. Three or four keywords were used to represent the primary actions associated with each of the seven curatorial activities: (1) *archivist*: identify, find, gather, collect; (2) *librarian*: categorize, tag, label, organize; (3) *preservationist*: store, maintain, copy, republish; (4) *editor*: filter, select, assess, verify; (5) *story maker*: synthesize, provide context; (6) *exhibitor*: display, distribute, juxtapose; and (7) *docent*: guide, discuss, mediate, reflect.

For this study, five popular social media services were examined to ensure a broad coverage of different media types as well as to compare and contrast curatorial activities across different social networking platforms. Facebook is currently the most visited social media service with an Alexa ranking of 2; this study examined Facebook groups, pages and causes pertaining to the Bhopal gas leak. YouTube is the second most visited social media service with an Alexa ranking of 3; this study examined YouTube videos, channels and playlists relevant to the Bhopal crisis. Wikipedia is also a commonly visited social media service that tends to be the first result in a Google search and has an Alexa ranking of 7; this study examined Bhopal-related Wikipedia articles with their associated discussion pages as well as relevant Wikipedia category pages. Twitter is another popular social media service with an Alexa ranking of 11; this study examined tweets about the Bhopal disaster collected between September and December of 2009 during the twenty-fifth anniversary. Finally, Flickr is the most visited photo-sharing service with an Alexa ranking of 34; this study examined Bhopal-specific Flickr photos, groups, sets and photostreams.

These particular data points within each social media service were selected because they were at an appropriate level of analysis for examining the seven curatorial activities. They had to be large enough data points to encompass curatorial activities at a socially distributed level. For example, Facebook groups were chosen because the social features and practices within these groups facilitate large-scale curatorial efforts in a distributed manner, whereas wall posts that appear in a Facebook group are usually too small a data point to examine the socially distributed aspects of curation online.

Case study: the 1984 Bhopal gas leak

On 3 December 1984, over 40 tons of toxic gas called methylisocyanate (MIC) leaked from the Union Carbide pesticide plant in Bhopal, the capital of Madhya Pradesh, India. The number of deaths remains debated. Official estimates by the government of Madhya Pradesh in India tabulated around 3,787 immediate deaths and 11,000 casualties (Browning 1993), but others estimate as many as 8,000 to

10,000 immediate deaths while leaving as many as 200,000 permanently injured with long-term health effects (Eckerman 2005; Perrow 2007). The current death toll is now estimated to be around 25,000. As such, many consider the Bhopal gas leak to be 'the world's worst industrial disaster' because it is the deadliest chemical leak in history. Although Simon's chapter on 'remembering together' (this volume) also examines the social media activity pertaining to the Bhopal disaster, his chapter more broadly addresses sociality issues around collective memory practices through networked technology, whereas this chapter focuses more specifically on the socially distributed curatorial activities emerging from the use of social media.

One of the narratives that particularly emerged in the social media landscape pertaining to the Bhopal gas leak was what many call the 'second disaster'. The 'second disaster' refers to the contamination of the underground water supply in Bhopal, India, due to the leaking chemicals left at the Union Carbide pesticide plant. Nearly 25,000 Bhopali residents are currently using this groundwater for drinking, bathing and other daily needs. Many of them now report serious long-term health effects, including skin disorders, missing palates and a wide range of birth defects. Some argue that this environmental hazard began when Union Carbide opened its Bhopal plant in 1968 and began dumping toxic waste in nearby solar ponds. The attention around the 1984 gas leak as being the 'worst industrial disaster', particularly on the twentieth and twenty-fifth anniversaries, has helped shed light on the hidden and forgotten aspects of the Bhopal disaster that continue to affect Bhopalis on a daily basis. According to Stringer and Johnston's (2002) report, the toxins are not only poisoning the soil, groundwater and vegetables but also mothers' breast milk. This is why many argue that it was not just gas contamination but also water contamination that have affected the second and third generations. According to Aquene Freechild who works with the International Campaign for Justice in Bhopal, the Bhopal disaster is an 'unfinished story' that continues with the youngest Bhopali survivors being born today.

Curating the 'second disaster' narrative

After examining Facebook, Flickr, YouTube, Twitter and Wikipedia, 136 data points were found that pertained to the Bhopal 'second disaster' across these five social media services. A rating scale was used to evaluate the amount of curatorial activity for each data point across the seven curatorial activities. For example, the data points that exhibited a high amount of activity were marked with a '2'. The data points that exhibited low activity were marked with a '1'. The data points that exhibited no activity were marked with a '0'. After examining each data point, the average was taken across the total data set for each of the seven curatorial activities as well as for each of the five social media services. Table 2.1 shows the numerical ratings for each of the 136 data points as well as the average ratings for each social media service.

The initial conceptual model of curation (see Figure 2.1) used for this evaluation provided a helpful way to isolate different curatorial activities based on conventional

TABLE 2.1 Results of the evaluation of social media activity for the second Bhopal disaster, based on the proposed curation model

- Case study: Ongoing Bhopal narratives pertaining to the 'second disaster, water contamination, and cleanup'.
- Curatorial roles: Archivist – identify, find, gather, collect; Librarian – categorize, tag, label, organize; Preservationist – store, maintain, copy, republish; Editor – filter, select, assess, verify; Story Maker – synthesize, provide context; Exhibitor – display, distribute, juxtapose; Docent – guide, discuss, mediate, reflect
- Amount of activity for each curatorial role: 2 = high activity; 1 = low activity; 0 = no activity

Social Media Platform	Data Point	Name of Data Point	Archivist	Librarian	Preservationist	Editor	Story Maker	Exhibitor	Docent	Description of Curatorial Activity
Facebook	Groups	Bhopal Gas Tragedy [25,000+ dead and counting] Facebook group volunteer organization	2	2	2	2	1	2	2	Admin posted most wall posts all of which are just links, he also 'liked' the posts other people posted, no discussions or comments between members, some photos preserved, mainly copy/pasted web content, credentials based on weblink, long description but it was copied from an article online
		no more bhopals Facebook group common interest activities	0	2	0	0	0	0	0	Only 4 members, no posts, no content, only category and description of group
		Bhopal Gas Tragedy...a travesty of justice.. Facebook group common interest beliefs and causes	1	2	1	1	2	1	2	Sharing of links, one spam post, some discussions between members
		Bring justice to Bhopal gas tragedy victims. Facebook group	2	2	0	1	2	1	2	One admin posted most materials, copy/pasted news articles as discussion posts, 32 admins but only the creator posted items
		Justice for Bhopal gas tragedy Victims Facebook group	1	1	1	1	2	2	2	Over 3,000 members mainly discussing, not many links, some spam, more wall posts from a variety of members
		Justice for Bhopal Facebook group – common interest beliefs and causes	2	2	1	1	2	1	1	Only 37 members but does provide a helpful synthesis in description
		Protest Against Bhopal Judicial Disaster Facebook group common interest current event	2	1	2	2	2	2	2	Over 1,600 members, different members make wall post, some with comments, more posts about reflections
		The Truth about Live Earth and Dow Chemical Facebook group organizations	1	2	2	2	2	2	2	Over 470 members, some very long wall posts, more commenting on people's wall posts, some images
		BHOPAL XXV Facebook group organizations	2	2	2	2	1	2	1	About 370 members, based on images that are shared in the photos section as a copy, some comments, more labeling of links shared
		Bhopal Gas Tragedy ....a shame on Indian Government,a travesty of justice.. Facebook group common interest beliefs & causes	2	2	1	1	1	1	1	Just over 120 members, some wall posts from other members, more discussions

Facebook		Name								Description
Groups		The Unfinished Story of Bhopal 1984 Facebook page	2	2	2	1	1	1	0	Creator of page finds relevant up-to-date links and post them on the wall, Likes to other related Facebook groups/pages, people liking some wall posts but not a lot of engagement
		Bhopal Gas Tragedy – World's Worst Industrial Disaster awaits Justice Facebook non-profit org page	1	2	2	1	1	1	0	Only one post not from creator that mentions the water contamination, links with explanatory text
		SUPPORT TODAYS VICTIMS OF 1984 BHOPAL CHEMICAL DISASTER and BOYCOTT DOW !!! Facebook group advocacy organization	2	2	1	1	2	2	2	In depth description or story, more commenting and engagement between members, some spam
		Students For Bhopal Facebook group advocacy organization	2	2	2	2	2	2	2	Over 1,900 members with 9 admins, a lot of engagement from members, more descriptions added to shared links
		Indra Sinha begins hunger strike over Bhopal Facebook group common interests politics	1	2	1	1	1	2	2	Around 490 members with 2 admins, some spam, engagement from members, some descriptions with shared links
Pages		Bhopal Gas Tragedy 1984 Facebook community page	1	2	2	1	2	1	1	Creator of page tends to share links and resources, more photos with juxtapositions
		Justice for Bhopal Gas Tragedy Victims Facebook community page	1	2	2	1	1	1	2	More comments and rhetorical questions among members/fans
Causes		Campaign for Justice in Bhopal	2	2	2	2	2	2	2	Over 2,200 members, donated over $4,200, indepth description with latest bulletins
		Justice for Bhopal	2	2	2	1	2	2	2	Over 4,000 members, donated over $380, indepth description with latest bulletins, some spam
		One Night in Bhopal – The World's Most Horrific Gas Accident	1	2	1	1	2	1	0	Only 21 members, donated $25, indepth description, creator of cause shows the most activity
		International Action for Bhopal	2	2	2	2	2	2	2	Over 4,300 members, different posts from different members
		Justice for Bhopal Gas Disaster victims	0	1	1	0	0	0	0	Only 2 members, explicitly states water contamination issues in about section
		JUSTICE FOR THE BHOPAL VICTIMS.	0	2	0	0	2	0	0	Only 1 member, long description in about section
		JUSTICE FOR THE BHOPAL VICTIMS.	1	2	1	1	1	2	2	Over 7,500 members, same description as above cause but more members and recruiting through members
		Bhopal Tragedy – Injustice to the Innocents	1	2	1	1	1	0	0	Only 2 members, post from administrator
		Justice for Bhopal Gas Tragedy Victims	0	1	0	0	1	0	0	Only 8 members, post from administrator
		Fight for justice for the Bhopal gas victims.....	0	2	0	0	1	1	0	Over 170 members, indepth description in about section, few posts from others

Social Media Platform	Data Point	Name of Data Point	Archivist	Librarian	Preservationist	Editor	Story Maker	Exhibitor	Docent	Description of Curatorial Activity
Flickr	Groups	Lest we forget – Bhopal gas tragedy Flickr group	2	2	2	2	2	2	1	Only 64 items many of which were included based on admins request, some description for group and in some photos, not many comments or discussions
	Photostream	ICJB photostream	1	1	1	2	2	1	0	Some photos have a description, no comments, some had no titles
	Photostream	an equilibrium always exists photostream	1	2	1	1	1	2	0	Artwork, paintings and sketches with a long caption that included summaries and links to websites on broad issues related to the artwork, comments not allowed
	Sets	Open Wounds: Bhopal 1984-2009	1	2	2	2	2	2	0	Professional photos of the Bhopal survivors and their environment, personal stories and descriptions for each photo, quite a few views but no comments
	Sets	B'Eau Pal Water	1	1	1	2	2	2	0	The description for each photo is the same and it juxtaposes the image and provides a historical background on Bhopal water, no comments or engagement
	Sets	Bhopal 25	1	1	1	2	2	2	1	Same description for each photo, juxtaposes with image, authoritative information based on user type, not much engagement from others, many viewed it
	Sets	Bhopal Portraits	1	2	1	2	2	1	1	Same description for each photo, juxtaposes with image, authoritative information based on user type, not much engagement from others, many viewed it
	Sets	Bhopal 25 years later	1	2	1	1	1	1	0	Photos are from photojournalists credited in caption, caption contains story, a few tags, no comments
	Sets	Bhopal Today	1	0	1	1	1	1	0	Short titles and caption, no tags, some juxtaposing titles with photos, no views
	Sets	Art for Bhopal – Water Pots	1	2	1	2	1	2	1	Photos of art some with in-depth descriptions of the reason for water pots, some have many tags, not many comments, not many views
	Photos	bhopal gas disaster: 25 years too late	1	2	2	2	2	2	2	Each photo has its own unique story, also appears in other groups, more comments and engagement by others, many tags and titles
	Photos	bhopal gas disaster 25 years and counting	2	2	2	2	2	2	2	Contains a story in the description with mention of source, many views and quite a few comments, photo appears in other groups
	Photos	Clean up Bhopal Now	2	2	2	2	1	2	1	The caption is personalized, many views and some favorites, most comments request the photo appear in other groups

	Title								Description
Flickr / Photos	Born from Hell: Innocent Victims of a Chemical Legacy_hapu	1	2	2	1	2	1	0	Caption contains a story of the photo with tags, no comments, not in other groups, many views
	नवि वाघ	2	0	2	2	2	2	1	Artwork with a lengthy caption, no tags, a couple of comments, many views, juxtaposition in the art itself
	Bhopal gas Tragedy 20000 dead and counting	2	1	2	2	2	1	1	Story in caption, not many tags, comment from user, quite a few views, appears in one set
	Bhopal Medical Appeal Vigil 2	1	2	1	2	2	1	0	Caption contains history, many tags, some views, no comments, appears in one set
	BHOPAL	2	2	2	2	2	2	2	Caption is in Italian, many comments and views, appears in groups and sets, image appears in other places online, many tags, geotagged
	Union Carbide Gas Tragedy memorial, Bhopal	1	1	2	2	2	1	0	Long caption with text from Wikipedia, some tags, many views, no comments
	'Freedom is the art of human release.'	2	1	2	1	1	2	0	Artwork, paintings and sketches with a long caption that included summaries and links to websites on broad issues related to the artwork, comments not allowed
	gallery-2-2	2	0	2	2	2	1	0	Photo and caption taken from Greenpeace, no tags, no comments
	IMG_3974.JPG	1	0	1	1	1	1	0	Photos for a TV program, not many tags, generic title, same caption for all Bhopal photos, no comments allowed, not many views
	IMG_3981.JPG	1	0	1	1	1	1	0	Photos for a TV program, not many tags, generic title, same caption for all Bhopal photos, no comments allowed, not many views
	IMG_3987.JPG	1	0	1	1	1	1	0	Photos for a TV program, not many tags, generic title, same caption for all Bhopal photos, no comments allowed, not many views
	DSC02192	1	0	1	1	1	1	0	Photos for a TV program, not many tags, generic title, same caption for all Bhopal photos, no comments allowed, not many views
	DSC02198	1	0	1	1	1	1	0	Photos for a TV program, not many tags, generic title, same caption for all Bhopal photos, no comments allowed, not many views
	Open Wounds: Bhopal 1984-2009	1	2	2	2	2	2	0	Photo has a story specific to the image, many tags, no comments
	Polly Morgan – 'Chemical Plant'	1	2	1	2	2	2	0	Photo of artwork that juxtaposes the story in caption, a lot of tags, no many views, a few favorites, no comments
	Bhopal Disaster 1984	2	0	2	1	1	2	0	Photos are from other sources but no credit of photo, no tags, no comments, short caption
	Futile, Red	1	0	1	1	1	0	0	Photo with short caption, no tags, no views
	Children are reflected in groundwater, believed to be contaminated, near the site of the deserted Union Carbide factory in Bhopal, India, by Daniel Berehulak 2009	2	0	1	2	1	1	0	Long title that includes source, no tags, not many views, no comments

Social Media Platform	Data Point	Name of Data Point	Archivist	Librarian	Preservationist	Editor	Story Maker	Exhibitor	Docent	Description of Curatorial Activity
Flickr	Photos	8-yr-old Annan suffers from cerebral palsy – 25 years after the biggest industrial disaster in history, toxic material continues to affect the people of Bhopal, by Daniel Berehulak 2009	2	0	1	2	1	1	0	Long title that includes source, no tags, not many views, no comments
		Dow Chemical Co. took over Union Carbide in 2001 and claims it is not responsible for cleaning up the site of the 1984 Bhopal gas leak disaster, by Manish Swarup 2009	2	0	1	2	1	1	0	Long title that includes source, no tags, not many views, no comments
YouTube	Channels	bhopalbhopal	2	2	2	2	2	2	1	Many videos with caption if not in English, short description, accurate title, some tags, categorized, no comments, not many subscribers
		The Bhopal Medical Appeal	2	2	2	2	2	2	1	Many videos specific to second disaster in English, descriptions for each video, many tags, has friends and subscribers, not many comments
		WaterWideWeb.org	1	1	2	2	2	2	2	Two videos related to Bhopal appear on this Channel, this provides a broader understanding of water crises around the world, many subscribers a few comments
		toogoodius	2	1	2	2	2	1	0	This channel contains longer videos that help promote Bhopal Medical Appeal, long descriptions, many tags, no comments, no subscribers
		JusticeforBhopal	1	2	2	2	2	2	1	Two videos, 14 subscribers, 1 comment, favorites other videos
		ICJBinNYC	1	2	2	2	2	2	1	Only 4 videos and 5 subscribers but a lot of comments on some of the videos, a long caption with the story of Bhopal, some tags with informative titles
	Playlists	chernobyl and other disasters	2	2	2	2	2	1	0	A mashup of multiple industrial disasters, 46 videos, 227 views
		Chemicals	2	2	2	2	1	1	0	A mashup of videos related to chemical crises, 109 videos, 68 views
		07. Dow chemical Company	2	2	2	2	2	2	0	A mashup of videos related to Dow Chemical, 57 videos, 3,161 views
		It Happened In....	2	1	2	2	0	0	0	A mashup of videos related to disasters around the world, 29 videos, 9 views
		Environment	2	1	2	2	0	2	0	A mashup of videos related to environmental hazards, 151 videos, 453 views
		Crimes Against Humanity	2	1	2	2	1	1	0	A mashup of videos related to crimes against humanity, 200 videos, 231 views

	Videos								Description
YouTube	Remembering Bhopal gas Disaster 1984	2	2	2	1	2	2	2	Mashup of news clips, title and tags, caption in video mentions ongoing contamination, over 8,700 views, 15 comments
	Toxic Water–Bhopal's SECOND Disaster 3	1	2	2	2	0	0	0	The caption provides details on this second disaster, quite a few tags and includes a category, no speaking just ambient sounds and captions of the toxins in video, no comments and not many views, just one video mashup
	Bhopal 25 Years On	2	1	2	2	1	1	1	BBC news clip not uploaded by BBC, title and tags are not detailed, no caption, 200 views, 2 comments
	25 years on: Bhopal still contaminated	2	2	2	2	2	2	0	NDTV news clip, title and caption add info about contamination but the clip is about the disparity in compensation, comments disabled, over 1000 views
	Indians of Bhopal Protest Over U.S Union Carbide Industrial Toxic Poisoning	2	1	2	2	1	2	0	RT news clip uploaded by RT, contains long title, some tags, no comments, 25 views
	short documentary on bhopal gas tragedy-4/5	2	1	2	2	1	2	1	This is a short documentary that appears in other places, no description, some tags, a few comments, over 8,200 views
	Killer gas: Toxic legacy of World's worst industrial disaster in India	1	1	2	2	1	2	2	RT news clip uploaded by RT, contains long title, some tags, 19 comments, over 2000 views
	It happened in Bhopal – 27 Aug 07 – Part 2	1	2	2	2	2	2	2	AlJazeeraEnglish news clip, contains title and tags, over 50 comments and over 18,000 views
	Bhopal the endless tragedy	1	2	2	2	2	2	2	Documentary created by user, short caption, some tags, includes interviews with key stakeholders, 11 comments, over 13,000 views
	Bhopal Disaster – BBC – The Yes Men	2	2	2	2	2	2	2	One version of the BBC clip of the Yes Men, title and tags and over 180,000 views, this video appears in multiple playlists
	the yes men	2	2	2	2	2	2	2	Another version of the BBC clip of the Yes Men, title and tags are short, over 270 comments and over 439,000 views, this video appears in multiple playlists
	Union Carbide Kills 8,000 In One Day in Bhopal	1	1	2	2	1	2	1	BBC news clip not uploaded by BBC, contains title and caption, tags not broad enough, interviews with high official, 1800 views, 3 comments
	Interview – The Bhopal Disaster: 25 Years Later	2	2	2	2	2	2	1	Radio interview with stakeholders, contains caption and title but not specific, many tags, 5 comments, over 1,700 views
	BBC Interview with the Yes Men, Five Years On – Part I	2	2	2	2	2	2	1	BBC interview with Yes Men, contains caption and title, some tags, 6 comments, over 2,500 views
	The Bhopal Chemical Disaster: Twenty Years Without Justice	2	1	2	2	2	2	2	Documentary created by user with interviews with key stakeholders, 54 comments and over 37,000 views, brief caption, some tags
	The Curse of Bhopal – Tropic Of Cancer – Episode 4 Preview – BBC Two	1	2	2	2	2	2	1	BBC video clip links to photos shared on Flickr, contains caption and title, 10 comments and over 2,300 views
	no more bhopals.avi	2	1	2	2	2	2	0	Artistic video with a long caption at the end with story, contains long caption, few tags, 1 comment, over 400 views

Social Media Platform	Data Point	Named Data Point	Archivist	Librarian	Preservationist	Editor	Story Maker	Exhibitor	Docent	Description of Curatorial Activity
YouTube	Videos	'B'EAU-PAL' WATER SCARES DOW EXECS INTO HIDING	2	2	2	2	2	1	1	Video about the process of making the B'eau-Pal spoof water, explaining the juxtaposition, long caption, some tags, 1 comment, 230 views
		Bhopal: Locals oppose disposal of Carbide waste	2	2	2	2	2	1	0	NDTV news clip, title and caption provides info, some tags, comments disabled, 155 views
		We drink toxic water.mov	2	2	2	2	2	1	1	Juxtaposition between images and caption, title and tags, 2 comments 99 views
		Hush Baby - Bhopal Continues to Suffer	2	2	2	2	2	2	0	Mashup of images, like a lullaby with a poem like narration, caption, many tags, over 2,200 views, 1 comment
		Bhopal Torch Rally Dec. 2nd 2009	2	2	2	2	1	1	0	Video contains 'water contamination' as tag and in caption, video focuses on rally, 100 views, no comments
		Exclusive: A generation grapples with Bhopal gas tragedy	2	2	2	2	2	2	1	Video contains 'water contamination' as tag and in caption, over 570 views, one comment with others marked as spam
		Collecting Water in Oria Bustee	2	2	2	2	2	1	0	Video contains 'water contamination' as tag and in caption, video juxtaposes with caption which has long story, over 140 views, no comments
		Art For Bhopal - Skullduggerous.mov	1	2	2	2	2	2	0	Video advertising gallery with long caption explaining history, many tags, over 300 views, no comments
		Riding rickshaws at election time in Bhopal.... going nowhere, fast!	1	2	2	2	1	1	0	Video contains 'water contamination' as tag and in caption, video shows people in streets, 70 views, no comments
		The chemical waste fields Bhopal	2	2	2	2	2	2	0	Video shows evidence of water contamination, explained in caption, no comments, over 1,300 views
		Sathyu Sarangi comments on official CES India contamination report 1/12/09	2	2	2	2	2	1	0	Explains a scientific report to prove contamination, link to report, short caption, few tags, only 46 views, no comments
		The Yes Men Fix The World, P2P Edition FULL MOVIE (2009) (HQ)	2	2	2	2	2	2	2	Part of a longer documentary by the Yes Men, title and caption and tags do not mention bhopal, 49 comments, over 11,400 views
		Dominique La Pierre on Dow Chemicals 1/12/ 09.	2	2	2	2	1	1	0	Video contains 'water contamination' as tag, over 160 views, no comment
		Bhopal- India.... The cost of Corporate neglect	2	2	2	2	2	1	0	Video from Bhopal Medical Appeal, copied and shared, no comments, 92 views, contains the same long description appears with story of contamination

Platform	Category	Item								Description
YouTube	Videos	BMA Event Video – 'Bhopal's Second Disaster'	2	2	2	2	2	1	0	Video backdrop with a mashup of images and captions that mention water contamination, no comments, 26 views, relevant title, some tags
		Bhopal 26 Years Later – Search for Justice Continues	2	2	2	2	2	2	1	Video was shared widely on 26th anniversary, contains a short caption and few tags, over 4,200 views, 7 comments
		India-Bhopal Anniversary	2	2	2	2	2	2	1	VOA news clip, title and caption, 555 views, 1 comment
Twitter	September Tweets	Clean up India's ground zero, Dow Chemical! RT @BhopalMedAppeal: Water still a killer at #Bhopal... http://bit.ly/cmAPGC - @GMWatch	2	1	2	2	1	2	2	User RT @BhopalMedAppeal who identified a relevant link, and added more info, included multiple hashtags, provided a brief comment, coming from a known user, 10 RTs, authoritative source
		Bhopal water still toxic, 25 years on... http://fb.me/AxehroBz #Obama #Dow #Bhopal #BP - @BhopalMedAppeal	2	1	2	2	1	1	0	User identified a relevant link, added some info for context, add hashtags, 1 RT, authoritative source
		Dow Liable for Bhopal Disaster... http://thomassroche.wordpress.com/2008/06/02/dow-liable-for-bhopal-disaster/ - @BhopalMedAppeal	2	0	1	2	2	1	0	User identified a relevant link, brief title, no hashtags, 3 RTs, authoritative source
		15. Bhopal Water Still Toxic Twenty-five Years After Deadly Gas Leak http://dlvr.it/6MRjD - @infokubo	2	0	1	2	2	1	0	Sharing a weblink, no hashtags, part of a larger list of articles
	October Tweets	After 25 Years, Bhopal Water Poison http://bit.ly/aWnU9y #water #eco #green #ecomonday #waterwednesday - @SuperWaterMan	2	2	1	2	2	1	0	Sharing a weblink, 5 hashtags, connecting it to water issues
		On polluted open wells near Bhopal Bihar. Need to clean 'em up http://bit.ly/aEn6GP make 'em sanitary wells #groundwater #water @ahambhumika - @zenrainman	2	2	1	2	2	1	0	Sharing a weblink, 2 hashtags focused on water, related issue
		Indian Govt confusion over Bhopal court cases? Water and gas disasters are SEPARATE ISSUES http://fb.me/MSaGHz5E - @BhopalMedAppeal	2	1	1	2	2	2	2	Sharing a weblink, clarifying that there are two separate disasters, authoritative source, asks a question
		I hate those Dow 'human element' commercials because it's a giant lie, if they cared about people they'd clean up Bhopal, India. - @rynthelyn	0	0	0	0	2	2	2	A comment about Dow, conversation and opinion oriented
		The Bhopal clean-up MUST be done properly http://fb.me/srjj10Ar #Obama #Dow #Bhopal - @BhopalMedAppeal	2	2	1	2	2	1	0	Sharing a weblink, a request, 3 hashtags; authoritative source

Social Media Platform	Data Point	Name of Data Point	Archivist	Librarian	Preservationist	Editor	Story Maker	Exhibitor	Docent	Description of Curatorial Activity
Twitter	November Tweets	Bhopal Water Contamination - Available on the Corbis website at http://tinyurl.com/32fov6k - @AlexMasiPhoto	2	0	1	2	2	1	0	User promotes his own pictures at a website, no hashtags. 1 RT
		@BDUTT CBI has failed in 2 decades after bhopal. Should it be disbanded to cleanse it up. Please start a dscsn. I wish to be a part.` - @Shashi_99	0	0	0	0	2	0	2	Request to start a discussion
		The children of Bhopal risk their lives by playing cricket on fields contaminated by a horrifying past	http://es.pn/aEqojh - @espncricinfo	2	0	1	0	2	2	0	Sharing a weblink to a video. 6 RTs
		Watch B'eauPal 'Advert' on Vimeo! http://vimeo.com/7990750 #Obama #Dow #Bhopal - @BhopalMedAppeal	2	2	1	2	1	1	0	Promoting a video that is a spoof, 3 hashtags, authoritative source
		Will India now participate in US law suit regarding Bhopal water contamination? - Bhopal - @BhopalMedAppeal	0	0	0	0	2	1	2	Poses a question, authoritative source
	December Tweets	15. Bhopal Water Still Toxic 25 Years After Gas Leak 16. Universal Jurisdiction On Crimes Against Humanity Dies In Spain... - @Outellect	1	0	0	1	1	0	0	Mentions one of the articles related to Bhopal but does not provide weblink, the inclusion of the 16 article provides context
		#15. Bhopal Water Still Toxic Twenty-five Years After Deadly Gas Leak: http://wp.me/p13L0q-da - @PhxProdOnline	2	0	1	2	2	1	0	This one includes the weblink to this article 15, title shows ongoing nature
		@primary_red @alpeshtwiiting @centerofright @gkhamba @greatbong @anandmahindra Dow chemical must clean up the Bhopal site.Plz RT Mak it trnd - @rushie82	0	0	0	0	1	0	2	Encourages a discussion by mentioning 6 people in tweet, request to RT and make it a trending topic in Twitter
		@BDUTT @bomanirani @BollywoodGandu @bhogleharsha @earth2angel @flyyoufools @GabbbarSingh Dow chemical must clean up the bhopal site. Plz RT. - @rushie82	0	0	0	0	1	0	2	Encourages a discussion by mentioning 7 people in tweet, request to RT and make it a trending topic in Twitter
		25th anniversary of the Bhopal disaster http://bit.ly/93m8Hq	2	0	1	2	1	2	0	A weblink to the Boston Big Picture photos of Bhopal, this weblink was appeared around 25 times
		Today is the 26th Anniversary of the Bhopal Disaster. Twenty-six years later, we are still storing tons of hazardous chemicals on-site in US - @nanopatents	0	0	1	1	2	2	0	A tweet that tries to relate the crisis to the US and chemical contamination issues, no sources, not specific

Wikipedia

		Archivist	Librarian	Preservationist	Editor	Story Maker	Exhibitor	Docent	
Article and Discussion	Bhopal disaster	2	2	2	2	2	2	2	Main Wikipedia page aggegates multiple sources of information and reorganizes in a way to tell the larger story, it does not preserve the references
	Dow Chemical Company	2	1	1	1	1	2	2	The article does not explicitly mention the water contamination and Dow's responsibility to take care of this, it only contains a very short section on Bhopal
	Union Carbide India Limited	1	1	1	1	1	1	1	This is a very short article but half of it talks about Bhopal and a brief mention of cleanup of the plant
	International Campaign for Justice in Bhopal	1	1	1	1	1	1	0	This article is somewhat short in an outline format, it does mention their mission to demand Dow to cleanup the site, no discussions
	International Medical Commission on Bhopal	2	2	2	2	2	1	0	This article is lengthy and compiles a lot of the work about this organization and mentions briefly the water contamination issue
	Sambhavna Trust	1	1	1	1	1	1	0	Briefly mentions the chemical pollution, provides more info about resources and related literature
	The Yes Men	2	2	2	1	2	2	2	There is a section on Dow Chemical and the need for cleanup, aggregates many sources about this hoax, provides a lengthy enough story on this
Category	Category: Bhopal disaster	2	2	1	1	2	1	2	Includes the crisis, perpetrators, victims, advocacy organizations, authors; categorized by editors
	Category: Man-made disasters	1	2	1	1	2	1	2	Provides an overview of man-made disasters but only includes a select few

Analysis of curatorial activities	Archivist	Librarian	Preservationist	Editor	Story Maker	Exhibitor	Docent	Summary of analysis
TOTAL	200	190	198	210	217	189	99	Maximum of 272 if all are '2' and maximum of 136 if all are '1'
AVERAGE	1.47	1.40	1.46	1.54	1.60	1.39	0.73	Most curatorial activities have average presence, storymaking activities are the highest, docenting activities are the lowest
Analysis of each social media platform — Facebook	1.26	1.85	1.26	1.07	1.48	1.26	1.19	Most curatorial activities have an average presence, librarian activities are highest, editorial activities are the lowest
Flickr	1.36	1.03	1.39	1.64	1.52	1.42	0.39	Most curatorial activities have an average presence, editorial and storynmaking activities are highest, docenting activities are the lowest
YouTube	1.76	1.74	2.00	1.96	1.74	1.57	0.72	Most of the curatorial activities have a higher than average presence with preservation and editorial activities as the highest, docenting activites are lowest
Twitter	1.35	0.60	0.70	1.30	1.75	1.10	0.70	Half of the curatorial activities have an average presence; but librarian, preservation, and docenting activities are the lowest
Wikipedia	1.44	1.56	1.33	1.22	1.33	1.56	0.78	Most of the curatorial activities have an average presence, librarian and exhibition activities are the highest, docenting activities are the lowest

cultural heritage professions. However, assessing the validity of the model in the context of the Bhopal 'second disaster' narrative led to the final model of socially distributed curation. This model, while retaining the basic structure of the initial model, describes how socially distributed curation happens in practice.

Socially distributed curation model

The socially distributed curation model (see Figure 2.2) depicts what is happening in practice but also alludes to what could be better supported with technical tools. In this model, each curatorial activity plays an important role in making curation successful, even though some activities may exist all the time while others may not be supported very well yet. Different types of arrows are used to indicate the relationships between each of the curatorial activities and communicate the complexity of how socially distributed curation happens in practice (see Liu 2011 for details).

Seven curatorial activities

The initial conceptual model of curation was based on seven activities that distilled the primary duties traditionally associated with professional curators. The final model shifts the focus away from traditional curatorial roles towards the following seven curatorial activities intended as actions rather than roles: (1) Preserve and maintain, (2) Collect and archive, (3) Categorize and organize, (4) Edit and verify,

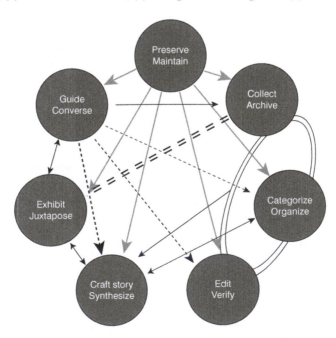

FIGURE 2.2 Socially distributed curation model

(5) Craft a story and synthesize, (6) Exhibit and juxtapose, and finally (7) Guide and converse. The following subsections describe each of these seven activities in detail. These descriptions include findings from the assessment of curatorial activities for the Bhopal 'second disaster' narrative (see Table 2.1).

Preserve and maintain

One of the overarching purposes of curation is to preserve and care for an artifact so as to maintain its longevity for the benefit of future generations. A critical aspect of preservation is identifying what is worth remembering and maintaining over time. The challenge in the social media landscape is how to preserve social media artifacts (e.g. blog posts, online news articles, online videos and the comments associated with each of them). Is it necessary to preserve the entire social media service? Is there additional value in doing so? Or is a screenshot of a Facebook wall post or the text of a tweet from Twitter sufficient?

Based on the assessment of the curatorial activities for the Bhopal 'second disaster' narrative, YouTube scored the highest in preserving artifacts concerning this narrative because the majority of videos about Bhopal and the descriptions for each of these videos do mention the ongoing water contamination issue. Twitter scored the lowest because the tweets examined during the investigation did not directly mention issues of water contamination; they only contained a link and not the 'actual' web artifact (e.g. blog post or media content) discussing water contamination. However, measuring the degree to which a social media service preserves the artifacts concerning a particular narrative can be quite difficult. Even if a Facebook group, Wikipedia article, YouTube video, or tweet contained information about the 'second disaster' narrative, the impact of this social media artifact may be difficult to determine depending on who viewed it, shared it or recorded it.

What may presumably be forgotten if the medium itself is not preserved are the social norms and practices that have emerged from the use of a specific social media service. There may be value in maintaining the technical design and social principles that facilitated a certain phenomenon in order to have the ability, for example, to view the artifacts in their original socio-technical environment.

Collect and archive

Another important aspect of socially distributed curation is deciding where and how to build a collection of digital memories and artifacts using archiving techniques. One might consider Flickr or YouTube as an amorphous collection of multimedia content from the wider public. Any type of search conducted within these social media services automatically generates a topic-specific collection. Facebook groups and blogs may also be considered sites that aggregate artifacts into a collection. Ultimately, it is the metadata generated by the users (i.e. folksonomies) that allows keyword-specific collections to be created on demand.

Based on the assessment of the collecting and archiving curatorial activities for the Bhopal 'second disaster' narrative, YouTube scored the highest since the primary function of this site is to maintain a public video collection. Also, many of the YouTube channels, playlists and videos archived mainstream news reports and clips from professional documentary films, which tend to be ephemeral artifacts not easily accessible. Facebook scored the lowest in part because many of the Facebook groups, pages and causes did not exhibit any social activity between Facebook members and instead only provided relevant information in the description section.

Archiving involves maintaining the collection by keeping it current and up-to-date. Some social media services use algorithms to automatically collate the 'most recent' content uploaded to their site. This ability to automatically display the content shows that a social media service is constantly being updated with new content. Yet, administrators of social media groups manually post and share new content on a regular basis as a way to show that these groups are consistently updated. With socio-technical activities such as building and maintaining online collections, there is likely to be a mix of human and algorithmic filtering and aggregation happening at multiple levels. One may use Google Search to look for relevant news articles, but non-algorithmic decisions are still made regarding what to share in a Facebook group.

Categorize and organize

Categorizing and organizing items in a collection are also important maintenance activities associated with socially distributed curation. This typically involves users in creating keywords and tags for each artifact in the collection to make it easier to search and find content.

Based on the assessment of the curatorial activities for the Bhopal 'second disaster' narrative, Facebook scored the highest in categorizing and organizing because many of the Facebook groups, pages and causes contained extensive details about the water contamination issue in their titles and descriptions. This allows multiple groups, pages and causes to appear in the Facebook search results even though there may not be a lot of activity within each of these Facebook artifacts. Twitter scored the lowest in organizing and categorizing, since hashtags[1] were not frequently used in tweets related to the Bhopal disaster. Also, there were no hashtags specifically associated with the water contamination issue, thus making this 'second disaster' narrative less visible than Bhopal's most well-known narrative about the gas leak that happened in 1984.

Organizing activities by subject matter experts are likely to produce historically more relevant tags and categories. Still, tagging and categorizing can be a tedious activity, and potentially unnecessary when web services and search engines automatically index web artifacts and harvest the metadata associated with them using natural language processing techniques.

Edit and verify

The adoption of the term 'curation' in the social media landscape put particular emphasis on editorial activities and on being able to verify what artifacts are included in the collection. Typically, this involves filtering for relevant and reliable information and assigning editorial weight on the basis of one's subject matter expertise – an aspect of the curatorial process that can be quite critical when the amount of information is large. To some extent, this reflects the relationship between journalism and history in terms of how news articles contribute to the shaping of contemporary history, and how the editorial practice of journalists relates to curating history.

Based on the assessment of the curatorial activities for the Bhopal 'second disaster' narrative, YouTube scored the highest in editing and verifying because there was a high 'signal to noise' ratio and the channels, playlists and videos typically contained credible information largely from mainstream news reports, professional documentary films and other reputable sources. Trusted sources may also include content from traditional media outlets as well as scientific reports. Raw and unfiltered content from ordinary citizens was not frequently shared unless they were eyewitness reports, and even then an aggregation of eyewitness reports appeared more frequently and were more credible than just a single report. However, during more recent crises, mainstream media outlets increasingly rely on eyewitness reports to provide critical information at a time when information dearth occurs during the emergency period.

Craft a story and synthesize

Another aspect of socially distributed curation has to do with synthesizing the information from each artifact to craft a story. Crafting a story involves weaving together web artifacts and packaging them in a meaningful narrative that can be passed on to future generations. Stories are an important way in which collective memories are kept alive. They have the ability to safeguard memories and connect people to a distant past that has relevance to the present by making history timeless. Memorable stories with lessons from the past are passed on for these lessons to be learned in the present. Creating memorable stories is also critical for making sense of traumatic situations that arise from historic crises. In this case, the key to crafting and then telling a good story is that it must be evocative enough to awaken people to the actions needed to strengthen community resilience.

Based on the assessment of the curatorial activities for the Bhopal 'second disaster' narrative, Twitter scored the highest because the restriction of 140 characters for messages sent through this microblogging service was an enabler to making Twitter users synthesize multiple pieces of information in the size of a 'tweet'. Wikipedia scored low in synthesizing and crafting a story partly because Wikipedia articles related to Bhopal that were included in the assessment did not mention the second disaster, and thus were not places where this memory was kept alive.

The Unfinished Story of Bhopal 1984
http://www.tehelka.com/story_main38.asp?filename=Ne050408air
_water.asp

Tehelka - India's Independent Weekly News Magazine
www.tehelka.com

The factory that killed 15,000 in 1984 is still poisoning new victims. As survivors march to Delhi, RAGHU KARNAD tells the chilling story of Bhopal's ongoing disaster

August 31, 2010 at 2:02am · Like · Comment · Share

FIGURE 2.3   Automated summary generated from sharing a link as a wall post in 'The Unfinished Story of Bhopal 1984' Facebook group (created on 31 August 2010)

Social media services are also beginning to automate some aspects of the story making process. For example, many of the wall posts in a Facebook group are links to news articles. Instead of just showing the URL address with a hyperlink to the news article, Facebook automatically produces a short snippet of the article, typically showing the first few lines of the text (see Figure 2.3). However, when linking to a news article, some Facebook users do make an effort to manually add further information or provide his or her own reflections and interpretations. These 'user-generated' syntheses provide the readers of a wall post with different interpretations about what is relevant and worth remembering about these historic crises.

Exhibit and juxtapose

Another aspect of socially distributed curation involves exhibiting the story in a compelling way by juxtaposing the artifacts within the story. Social media services and the features within it are increasingly becoming exhibition spaces for crafting and presenting these stories. A critical aspect of making the story compelling is through juxtapositions. The act of displaying, arranging and re-presenting a set of artifacts in an effective and understandable way helps to draw attention to the proposed narrative and make it more memorable.

Based on the assessment of the curatorial activities for the Bhopal 'second disaster' narrative, YouTube and Wikipedia scored the highest in facilitating exhibiting and juxtaposing activities. Many of the YouTube videos were spoofs related to the Yes Men's B'eau-Pal[2] drinking water and BBC hoax,[3] both of which used creative and artistic skills to create compelling juxtapositions regarding the water contamination issue in Bhopal. Twitter scored the lowest in part because the restriction of 140 characters does not provide a significant amount of space to exhibit and juxtapose compelling content.

One example of a juxtaposition that appeared in the Bhopal disaster narratives was the multimedia spoofs of Dow Chemical Company's Human Element campaign that began in 2006. YouTube contains six videos[4] that are spoofs of Dow Chemical's Human Element TV advertisement. Some of the videos use the audio narration

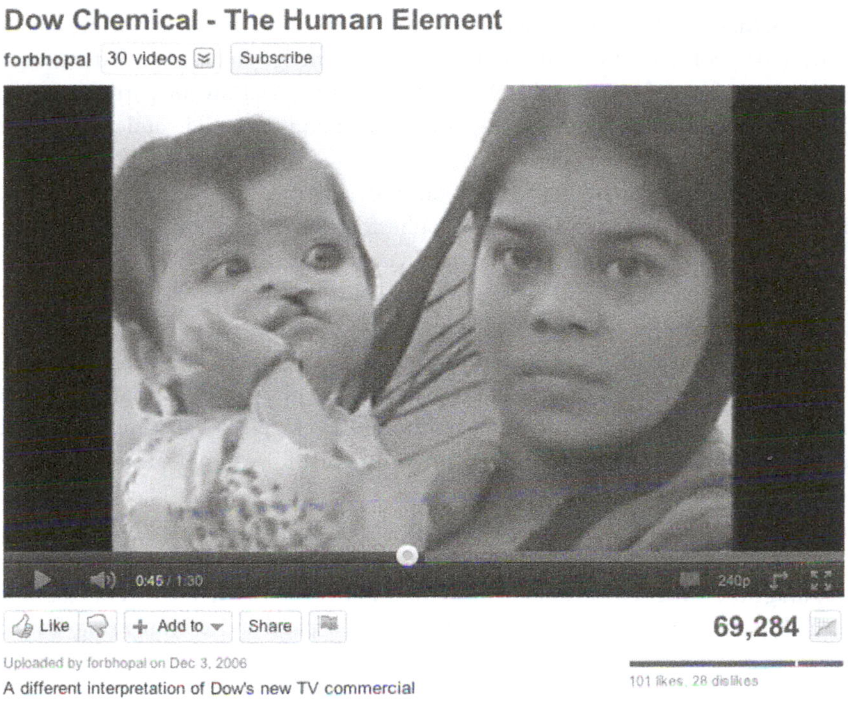

Dow Chemical - The Human Element

forbhopal   30 videos ⚥   Subscribe

👍 Like 👎   ＋ Add to ▼   Share 🖼   69,284 ✎

Uploaded by forbhopal on Dec 3, 2006
A different interpretation of Dow's new TV commercial

101 likes 28 dislikes

FIGURE 2.4   Screenshot of 'Dow Chemical – The Human Element' YouTube video (uploaded by forbhopal on 3 December 2006)

from the Dow Chemical commercial and then juxtapose the audio with images of the Bhopal disaster victims (see Figure 2.4) as a way of drawing attention to the irony between Dow's human-centered branding message and its environmental track record.

The curatorial activities of exhibiting and juxtaposing involve decisions regarding what type of medium should be used to exhibit the story and how this medium should be used. Social media are both exhibiting platforms for viewing stories and distribution channels for sharing stories. Ultimately, what makes such stories memorable is if they are exhibited in a way that creates a compelling experience worthy enough to share and discuss with others in the community.

Guide and converse

One final aspect of socially distributed curation involves guiding and conversing, which are activities often associated with docents. Typically, docents are knowledgeable guides, community leaders, mentors and enthusiasts who volunteer their time to interface with the public and share knowledge about a particular topic. Since social media services fundamentally facilitate conversations and engagement with the public, one might argue that many social media users engage in docenting activities. Many of the social media users I interviewed and observed were personally motivated to volunteer their time to share their knowledge and engage in discussions with others about the crisis. There is no financial motivation for participating in these curatorial activities; instead, it is about educating the public and engaging in conversations with them.

Based on the assessment of the curatorial activities for the Bhopal 'second disaster' narrative, Facebook scored the highest in conversing and guiding because Facebook groups and pages tend to facilitate conversations through wall posts, comments to wall posts and the discussion pages. Facebook has become ubiquitous at a nearly global level, making it the central hub for engaging in daily conversations independently of when people are connecting and of where they are connected from. Flickr scored the lowest because many of the photos related to the Bhopal disaster did not receive any comments. Although Flickr photos that relate to more controversial topics generate hundreds of comments (for example, issues of racism in the aftermath of Hurricane Katrina), most of the comments in Flickr tend to be oriented towards aesthetic and photographic concerns.

Conversing and discussing represent features of social media services that encourage the wider public to participate in other curatorial activities. For example, the Talk page in Wikipedia articles, the discussion page and commenting feature in Facebook groups and pages, the discussion section and commenting feature in Flickr, the commenting feature in blogs, and the reply/mention feature in Twitter are all examples of socio-technical features that allow some users to engage in conversations and guide others to seek, collect and organize additional information relevant to the subject of interest.

Conversing is the constant human element of the socially distributed curatorial process and it would be potentially unconscionable to try and automate this process. However, new features and tools could be designed to enable users to make it easier to engage in discussions, provide feedback and listen to others. People are already beginning to engage daily in these activities in a more streamlined way thanks to the nearly ubiquitous access to popular social media services offered by portable and mobile ICTs.

Socially distributed curation: now and beyond

Socially distributed curation is a socio-technical practice involving people, cultural artifacts and information and communication technology. It is a process where it can be difficult to determine the beginning and the end of a curatorial activity – particularly when the very products of curation become new artifacts to curate. This type of curation occurs in a collaborative and distributed way, thus creating shared ownership over the stewardship of the living memory that is being preserved. It is a participatory, bottom-up approach that makes each curatorial activity transparent to allow other interested parties partake in the curatorial process. Making reference to the 'distributed cognition' processes described by Hollan *et al.* (2000), we can say that socially distributed curation takes place when: (1) each curatorial activity is carried out in a decentralized fashion that allows multiple people to participate in different parts of the curatorial process; (2) memories and artifacts are externalized and made shareable to allow others to curate them into meaningful and visible narratives; and (3) the curatorial process is distributed through time to allow past curated narratives affect and transform future narratives.

As observed in the Bhopal 'second disaster' narrative, two primary types of experts are helping to sustain this curatorial process: subject matter experts and curation experts. Subject matter experts are knowledgeable about the subject being curated (in this case, they have 'expertise' pertaining to historic crises, and the Bhopal disaster specifically). They might include people directly affected by the crisis, researchers who have studied that crisis or others who can share expertise related to the crisis. For example, the top contributors for the 'Bhopal disaster' Wikipedia article included a medical doctor, a chemical engineer, a chemist, people interested in the Bhopal disaster, an Indian native and an enthusiasts interested in editing current event articles related to disasters.

Curation experts are those who have expertise in conducting any of the seven curatorial activities discussed in this chapter. These types of experts tend to have social media literacy and know how to use web-based tools to curate digital content. More specifically, a curation expert may have expertise in identifying reputable sources, knowing how to verify a source, filtering out irrelevant content or removing spam. Generally, these types of experts are enthusiasts who are passionate and resourceful about the topic. However, curation enthusiasts are also on the rise and highly motivated to participate as a form of brand marketing to increase their online influence and social capital (see Rosenbaum 2011).

Conclusion

Although the 1984 Bhopal gas leak continues to be the worst industrial accident in history, many people today still do not know the story of Bhopal. In a book titled *Bhopal: Its Setting, Responsibility and Challenge* written just a year after the gas leak, Sufrin (1985) foresees the forgotten narrative of Bhopal but urges the importance of sharing its lessons in the following excerpt:

> The Bhopal accident soon will become a social memory with a line or two in history books and a page in law books. Soon the afflicted people will become a sad fixture in a small geographical segment of India, largely forgotten. The more than 100 score of dead will become memories, ever [sic] growing dimmer in the thoughts of their families. But Bhopal as a lesson and as an example of the indifference and thoughtlessness of modern industry will not, and indeed cannot and should not, become a mere historical incident. Bhopal and what happened at the Union Carbide plant shortly after midnight on December 3, 1984, is a dramatic signal that responsibility is a real and pervasive necessity and not only the subject of academic and empty discussion.
>
> (Sufrin, 1985: 23)

The memory practices emerging in the social media landscape pertaining to the Bhopal disaster appear to be preventing Bhopal from just being a line or two in a history book. The memory of the Bhopal disaster is alive through the creation of a full length 'Bhopal disaster' Wikipedia article, the sharing of Flickr photos and YouTube videos, the writing of blog posts and tweets, and the creation of Facebook groups. These spontaneous curatorial activities are not only preserving the memories of the 1984 Bhopal gas leak but also transforming the ongoing narrative of the contamination in Bhopal, India, today. The Bhopal legacy will continue to change and be passed on as long as there are 'lessons' to be discovered and learned by those in the present and future generations.

Notes

1 Hashtags are a community-driven convention that appears in http://twitter.com to provide additional metadata or context to the tweet. They tend to be words or phrases prefixed with the hash (#) symbol.
2 http://theyesmen.org/blog/dow-runs-scared-from-water (accessed 29 November 2010).
3 http://theyesmen.org/hijinks/bbcbhopal (accessed 29 November 2010).
4 http://www.youtube.com/view_play_list?p=493CD2130EA3D55B (accessed 3 October 2010).

References

Browning, J. (1993) 'Union Carbide: Disaster at Bhopal', in J.A. Gottschalk (ed.) *Crisis Response: Inside Stories on Managing Image Under Siege*, Detroit, MI: Gale Research.
Chambers, E.A. (2006) 'Defining the Role of the Curator', in S.L. Williams and C.A. Hawks (eds) *Museum Studies: Perspectives and Innovations*, Washington, DC: Society for the Preservation of Natural History Collections.
Eckerman, I. (2005) *The Bhopal Saga: Causes and Consequences of the World's Largest Industrial Disaster*, Hyderabad: Universities Press.
Graham, B. and Cook, S. (2010) *Rethinking Curating: Art after New Media*, Cambridge, MA: MIT Press.
Hollan, J., Hutchins, E. and Kirsh, D. (2000) 'Distributed Cognition: Toward a New Foundation for Human-Computer Interaction Research', *ACM Transactions on Computer-Human Interaction (TOCHI)*, 7(2): 174–196.
Hutchins, E. (1995) *Cognition in the Wild*, Cambridge, MA: MIT Press.
Liu, S.B. (2011) 'Grassroots Heritage: A Multi-Method Investigation of How Social Media Sustain the Living Heritage of Historic Crises', PhD Dissertation, Boulder, CO: University of Colorado.
Marincola, P. (ed.) (2000) *Curating Now: Imaginative Practice/Public Responsibility*, Philadelphia, PA: Philadelphia Exhibitions Initiative.
Perrow, C. (2007) *The Next Catastrophe: Reducing our Vulnerabilities to Natural, Industrial, and Terrorist Disasters*, Princeton NJ: Princeton University Press.
Rosenbaum, S. (2011) *Curation Nation: How to Win in a World Where Consumers are Creators*, New York: McGraw-Hill.

Schneider, S.M. and Foot, K.A. (2005) 'Web Sphere Analysis: An Approach to Studying Online Action', in C. Hine (ed.) *Virtual Methods: Issues in Social Research on the Internet*, Oxford: Berg.

Stringer, R. and Johnston P. (2002) *Technical Guidelines for Cleanup at the Union Carbide India Ltd (UCIL) Site in Bhopal Madhya Pradesh, India*, Greenpeace Research Laboratories, Department of Biological Sciences, University of Exeter, UK. http://www.greenpeace. org/international/PageFiles/24481/bhopal_cleanup_guidelines.pdf (accessed 29 March 2010).

Sufrin, S. C. (1985) *Bhopal: Its Setting, Responsibility and Challenge*, Delhi: Ajanta Publications.

Thea, C. and Micchelli, T. (2009) *On Curating: Interviews with Ten International Curators*, New York: Distributed Art Publishers, Inc.

Thompson, J.M.A. (ed.) (1992) *Manual of Curatorship: A Guide to Museum Practice*, Oxford: Butterworth-Heinemann Ltd.

Van House, N. and Churchill, E.F. (2008) 'Technologies of Memory: Key Issues and Critical Perspectives', *Memory Studies*, 1(3): 295–310.

3

MUSEUM OF THE SELF AND DIGITAL DEATH

An emerging curatorial dilemma for digital heritage

*Stacey Pitsillides, Janis Jefferies and
Martin Conreen*

Introduction

This chapter is primarily concerned with exploring the connection between digital legacy of data that people currently leave behind and how this data can begin to form a part of our collective 'digital heritage'. By reviewing current practices around online data storage in relation to memory and death, the chapter considers the value of 'digital memory objects' for the growing field of digital heritage. It also discusses the significance and implications of designing new contexts and systems for the future management of personal legacy data. By using the transformative properties of the 'digital memory object' itself, the chapter presents various strategies concerning how this data could be both (re)used and (re)evaluated, making it a useful asset in our contemporary collective; for both history and heritage.

What does death have to do with heritage?

We are all currently 'living'. We generally go about our lives, have experiences and feelings, observe and make mental annotations about the world around us. Often the day-to-day 'living' of our lives goes unrecorded and is often un-recordable. However, we do leave the mark of our 'living' in the physical world. The traces of us, embedded in the objects of our everyday, carry within their form the memory of living. Do you remember a time when someone taught you how to do something that seemed impossible at the time – to stand at a graveside, to survive a deep grief, to celebrate a life? Do you also remember watching your own hands, perhaps awkwardly at first, but then with a smoother motion, holding a baby, kneading the dough, mixing the currants into a cake, sewing a bouquet made of beads for a wedding, make a wreath of roses, tending the garden or making a gift of wood or cloth?

Objects, things we carry with us, are markers of complex personal histories and it is in this sense that they take on the cultural markers of memory and of time. Objects tell stories of our relationship to the world and to others, and they offer a material base not just in terms of production – hand, industrial or even digital media – but in relation to how we consume them, long for them and even obsessively collect them. These 'memory objects' can be owned by the self in many surprising ways (Jefferies 2005). A historical example might be the knife that a person in prehistoric times carried around and used for many years to kill animals, cut food, protecting his family. Through its use, the knife will have gained a specific 'hand shaped' ware, carrying information about who used it and how it was used. So because of the knife's materiality, history and the fact that as a hard object it is relatively stable, it 'can preserve information about "how to cut" for tens of thousands of years' (Flusser 1990).

This 'possession' is, according to Susan Stewart (1993), a guarantee of the presence of the absent other. The magic or power bestowed on such objects is precisely dependent on the fact that they are a possession, an extension of the self, which also reminds us of the threat of loss. Objects regarded as personal memorabilia can be addressed in relation to memory, grief and remembrance and are supplemented by a narrative discourse through the language of longing (Stewart 1993). This supplement further contributes to a surplus of significance with its reference to the past, rites of passage and ceremony, in so far as it permits objects to conjure a kind of magic aura and phantasms of fictional histories beyond any objective reality.

Material is of prime importance here. Like in the example of the stone cutter given above, the very matter of the object has to represent and even exceed other kinds of economic value in order to perform an alchemical role in soldering the reality of things to their spiritual equivalent and preserving the memory of its use in life. Objects remain significant; their very material 'thingness' is tangible but any security, which is offered in one moment, is undone by a traumatic shift that directs us to mortality.

What happens then after death? Our physical engagement with objects may no longer exist but as outlined above some of the objects most precious to us may become 'memory objects' that carry within them complex information considered valuable to some of the living. This kind of 'information' would immediately be of interest to friends and family, but if this 'memory object' is kept for long enough and passed down through generations (as heirlooms) then it transcends the barrier of personal memory. Perhaps the person receiving the object will have never met its owner? Nonetheless it begins to become reminiscent of a shared family memory or even cultural memory. As time progresses the 'memory object' becomes more reminiscent of a time period and its culture, and becomes a 'heritage object'.

However, not every object we own or have ever owned or left our trace on is a 'memory object'. There are many objects that we own throughout our lives that are transient and hold relatively uninteresting information. Objects that are worn out, obsolete or void of emotional connections, many of us simply throw them away.

Most of these objects – over time – we won't even remember owning. This is an integral part of growing up and moving on with life. It would be imprudent and uncomfortable to co-exist with every object we have ever owned, from birth to death. If these collections were passed from generation to generation, it would take a lifetime simply to look at, sort through or catalogue this mass. It is obvious that there would be no value in owning these many material possessions because one would never be able to use or appreciate them! Currently, if a person does engage in this practice of keeping everything, in the physical world, it is seen as pathological and society names them 'eccentrics, hoarders, and hermits' (Weiss 2010).

So what would happen to our society and culture if every tiny aspect of our living was automatically transformed into a 'memory object', hooked into our identity and visible to everybody, everywhere, all the time and potentially throughout history?

What is digital death and how does it influence heritage?

Digital death can be broadly seen 'as either the death of a living being and the way it effects the digital world, or the death of a digital object and the way it effects a living being' (Pitsillides *et al.* 2009: 131). When thinking about digital death in relation to cultural identity and cultural memory, we must first consider the relevance of shared data and its impact on our historical and sociological futures. This consideration must also include the potential deletion or unreadability of data in the future. If the information we are inputting into these systems on a daily basis has the potential to provide a detailed account of our present digital society and culture (hence a digital archive of heritage from popular perspective) then it is important we begin to consider what is valuable and how these large amounts of records will be stored and catalogued.

However, it will not be easy to store or catalogue our digital lives, as we are not simply talking about archiving individual bits of data but networks of data and data networked to people which are in turn networked to communities embedded within complex social systems. The concept of 'intangible artifacts' which was proposed by UNESCO in 1952 may provide another way of approaching this. The idea of 'intangible artifacts' and indeed 'intangible cultural heritage' has since grown as a concept and continues to be a central issue for UNESCO as stated within their 'Convention for the Safeguarding of the Intangible Cultural Heritage' report (UNESCO, 2003: 2). The term intangible heritage refers to 'all forms of traditional and popular or folk culture, i.e. collective works originating in the given community and based on tradition' (Kirshenblatt-Gimblett, 2004: 54). In other words, it refers to the active preservation of mastery and traditions, and applies to the preservation of living social networks (which would also include living systems of online culture such as digital social networks).

This perspective enables us to consider living systems online as part of our collective 'intangible heritage', and gives digital historians the opportunity to view individual artifacts within their original network and to sustain and upkeep the 'whole system as a living entity' (Kirshenblatt–Gimblett 2004: 53) rather than individual artifacts in dispersed archives. When it first became possible to create tangible artifacts that could code spoken language (as text) into stable objects, storing vast amounts of reproducible information, a cultural memory was established. This included the formation of various institutions, such as the libraries, that could take responsibility for collecting and sorting this 'huge' store of acquired information (Flusser, 1990: 398). The digitization of text removes this 'stable object' and thus forces the destabilization of our conventional understanding of the role and practice of museums, libraries and archives. Within the digital world the 'static' record of the traditional library has been socially augmented and has become much harder to trace, document and store. Concerning digital death, it becomes obvious that there will continue to be a proportional rise in the amount of 'memory objects' being passed on, collected or simply hoarded online.

As seen in recent work on bereavement (Odom *et al.* 2010: 1835), the passing on of objects is a complicated area and in many cases people convey 'uncomfortable feelings about [physical] objects they had been bequeathed, but nonetheless felt obligated to hold onto. These instances represented strange paradoxes in which participants could neither come to terms with objects nor get rid of them' (Odom *et al.* 2010: 5) When it comes to digital objects, things are even more complicated. This situation exasperates and reveals the lack of provision around people's digital lives, and the need for radical change in the way we deal with, store and pass on the mass of digital content we produce (Winer 2007). For example, we must consider the particular value of the digital object itself when they are not bequeathed to one person in particular. They simply continue to exist online, in the public realm where the original object itself may be shared (e.g. by taking care of a person's 'memorialized social network' after death). It must also be taken into account how this sharing of responsibility alters the value of the object for the person's family and friends. Does a sense of custodianship and the fact that this object was given to 'me' make it special? If so, how does sharing change this relationship? Can the sharing in some cases add value to the object by removing some of the burden of its ownership, through a sort of communal stewardship, thus increasing in value throughout its existence within a community of 'loved ones'?

According to Stiegler (1998), there is and has always been a co-development of society (i.e. the 'way' we exist within the world as human beings) and the 'way' we make our world (i.e. our technics). Teasing out Stiegler's argument, one thing we must consider when thinking about digital heritage is the 'way' we are developing our technologies. This is intrinsically connected to the 'way' we are developing within those systems as human beings and the institutions that are built to support them. In the context of our contemporary human condition, however, there is no way of separating what is intrinsically natural (i.e. to collect and to pass on objects) from the technologies we have created (i.e. systems of storage, archives, museums). Taking this concept further, we question how can we begin to construct any basis from which to critique or to evaluate the human significance of objects (digitally born or otherwise), especially when we are so intrinsically built into these systems (cf. Turkle 1995; Hayles 1999). These systems are also not only having an effect on our day-to-day lives but are affecting how our brains work, how we conduct research, evaluate and more generally deal with information about the world. However, we cannot simply continue living digitally without some kind of systemic analysis and planning for the 'effect' of these developments.

When we engage with the concept of digital death and question the ethical significance of the technological mediation of our condition, within the context of grief and bereavement, we must look at these systems in a fundamentally different way. Through grief we are compelled to (re)consider the ways in which we act within contemporary technological systems, and further investigate how these systems are affecting us in our most vulnerable condition. By questioning whether technology does have any profound effect on the nature of grief or whether it simply allows people to develop and use new tools that amplify or suppress that which is already inherently 'natural' is a paradox in itself. However, in this fast-paced modern world the slowness of grief is still apparent; as stated by Halamish and Hermoni, 'grief ... [is] really a dinosaur in modern life. You can get a meal in three minutes from a fast food place, in a minute you can get any information you want from the internet, but pregnancy and grief still take a long time' (Halamish and Hermoni 2007: 72). So the creation of better technological solutions is not *always* the best answer. What we must reflect on instead is whether there is some way other than acting directly through new technology to readdress these issues; how bereavement, grief and identity are being digitally 'augmented' and are changing; and how we as human beings (symbiotically technical beings) can breathe and move culturally 'within our technology(s)'.

> In a passage of *Prometheus Bound* ... [the Titan states] 'I stopped mortals from foreseeing death,' [by giving them hope] ... housed among humans [hope] constitutes through her very blindness the anecdote to foresight. She is not a cure for death, which has none ... [but] finding her place within the very seat of mortal life, Elpis can balance out the consciousness of death with lack of knowledge of the moment when and the matter in which death will come and take this life.
>
> (Stiegler 1998: 197)

If the foreknowledge of death precludes life, how then do we as human beings begin to plan for what happens to our 'digital memory objects' after death, especially in a system as fluid and clogged with data as the Internet? We may at first consider the use of standardized systems like the 'last will and testament', which are already being used by some to plan their digital afterlives (Walker 2011). However, we believe that this system would need a radical overhaul if people, en masse, were to start to include their digital possessions, which so often need to be altered and updated. Perhaps in this scenario one would be almost constantly planning their death, as a day-to-day activity; not a pleasing thought for most. The problem is bigger than simply what to do with our data after death.

What does it mean to keep 'everything, forever'?

Immortality has always been the fascination of human beings resulting in myriad myths, legends and stories centering on this theme (Hayles 2002). However, often, within these myths and stories, the protagonists are left divided between those who are actual immortal beings and those who have immortality thrust upon them (Adams 1982). These stories where characters find, receive or are attacked with immortality are often shrouded in warning with protagonists left feeling overwhelmed, regretful or even cursed (Ferrucci *et al.* 2006).

As discussed earlier, the physical world creates very clear, finite boundaries. Therefore there is a pressure to constantly re-evaluate the objects around us and to make the sometimes difficult (and emotional) choice of throwing things away. However, in the digital world space is relatively cheap (often free) and fairly easy to acquire – the choice flipping from 'Do I need it? Can I keep it?' to 'Do I delete it?' It becomes clear that new protocols and cultures need to be developed if we wish to avoid becoming a kind of digital hoarder. A recent estimate from the International Data Corporation (IDC) suggested that 'the amount of digital information created and replicated in a year will increase to 35 zettabytes, or 35 trillion gigabytes' (Herring 2010). This is particularly relevant if (after death) you are the one to receive this hoard of digital possessions from all your loved ones (Odom *et al.* 2010).

Can we conceive of 'forever'? What does it actually mean, and if we are unable to conceive it, then why does it continue to be something we both crave and promise? Theoretically, if things are to 'exist forever' then whose responsibility is it to pay for them forever? These were some of the questions to arise during the first 'Digital Death Day',[1] 26 May 2010. These questions were flagged up through the comments of representatives from two major digital asset companies, Entrustet[2] and Legacy Locker.[3] Digital assets companies are a fairly new but growing collective of companies online which offer services related to bequeathing your online data to loved ones after death. They have a vested interest in opening dialogues centered around the question of 'what should happen to our digital data after death?' and there are a variety of opinions around how this *could* be done, why this *should* be done and how the data is kept. Within this particular conversation, it was flagged up that companies, across the board, often receive emails from people wanting to know if they can store '*all their digital assets forever*'.

This question leads us to speculate on what these and other companies working in the area of digital death (and preparation for digital afterlife) are really offering or being pushed to offer. We begin by looking at a cross section of statements from digital asset companies' websites, considering the type of language they are using to describe what they offer. To list a couple of examples, Death Switch[4] is a website offering digital legacy preparation with the tagline 'Bridging Mortality'; 1000 Memories[5] is a data storage facility stating that they aim to provide new ways 'to remember the people we care about' and offer a place 'where their memory will be maintained forever'.[6] On the reverse side, the Web2.0 Suicide Machine[7] is a site offering people a button that will delete all data on their chosen social networks and scramble all passwords so they can never log in again. This service offers the strap line 'Faster, safer, shorter, better. Sign out forever!' There is something dramatic and unsettling about the use of 'forever' as a sales pitch in all these sites, even when it is used ironically, as in the above example.

The greater problem is that this kind of languaging is only encouraging users of digital assets companies to feel like they can and should be able to store *all* their digital possessions forever. Despite the existence of websites like Suicide 2.0, an increasing number of people (and technology communities) are looking for more concrete and better ways to store and save data. As reflected by James Gleick: 'we complain about our oversupply of information. We treasure it nonetheless. We aren't shutting down our e-mail addresses. On the contrary, we're buying pocket computers and cellular modems and mobile phones with tiny message screens to make sure we can log from the beaches and the mountaintops' (Gleick 1999: 90–91).

Perhaps there is a better solution than either deleting everything entirely, as suggested by Suicide 2.0, or keeping everything forever. This process of evaluation should involve more consideration than simply trying to predict or empathetically plan for what future generations may want or find value in. First we must consider the key question of 'why' we want to save any piece of data.

We must then reflect on how we can begin to form our own personal criteria of relevance in a digital world. This particular thread of critique is contemplated in a recent article by Sellen and Whittaker (2010) where there is an extensive critical discussion articulating recent developments and goals of the 'lifelogging'[8] community. The article questions what are the criteria of relevance for the technologies that the lifelogging community is producing and what advantage there is (if any) of 'capturing everything'. The article is primarily concerned with provoking the technology industry to reconsider the lack of use of human-centric design principles and the concurrent devaluing of the 'human memory system'. Sellen and Whittaker call for a new conceptual framework focusing on how technology could better serve humans through having a greater understanding of human beings' inner workings and psychological needs. We agree with this critique of the technology industry but will expand on their argumentation and its relation to the critical effect of technology. By stressing that there must also be a consideration of 'why' we choose to develop a particular media or technology in the first place, it is important to move from questions concerning human memory simulation and augmentation (Sellen and Whittaker 2010) to the consideration of how technologies are affecting societal and cultural development when they are adopted on a larger scale. In other words, it is critical to consider the effect of 'digital memories' on society when they, as opposed to biological memory, are left 'behind' in technologically mediated social networks after a person dies.

In particular, Joanna Garde-Hansen focuses on the way in which human memory is affected by 'social archives' in her chapter 'My Memories? Personal Digital Archive Fever and Facebook' (Garde-Hansen 2009). By looking at widely adopted social archives such as Facebook, she critiques their use of computer database logic and questions their position and prevalence in society today as opposed to older media, which include various forms of narrative logic (Garde-Hansen 2009: 141). By considering social networks as human archives, Garde-Hansen is inherently questioning how these archives are adapting human beings to fit in to the principles of technology (i.e. computer databases). When various archiving technologies become an adopted system of practice, such as Facebook, being used almost globally, the technological mediation of memory begins to become the accepted norm rather than the augmentation (Turkle 2011). This forms an ever-changing time-based cycle of effect, containing within it the paired functions of technology and memory and the way they are being used and viewed within contemporary society.

Museum of the self: how to provide a context for digital heritage within the social web

In addition to understanding how digital memory objects, and the narratives we produce through them, add new layers of meaning into the construction of heritage both at the personal and broader cultural level, we must also consider what it means to narrate the self online, (re)mediating ones thoughts, emotions and ideas in online platforms. Is this the practice of an indulgent writing about oneself, the building of 'fictional' identities, or the (perhaps unconscious) act of getting to know or taking care of oneself (Foucault 1988)? As stated by Barthes (1982), one of the effects of direct recording is that people may lend themselves to the social game – we may pose and know that we are posing and this posing results in a paradoxical reciprocal recording system of self and other. However, although Facebook and other social memory archives allude to self preservation (i.e. the ability to save a part of yourself online), memory mediation encourages the personal 'urge' to fully capture and share the stories that we tell about ourselves with others. This demands new forms of critical analysis as our 'fictional' identities become ever more complex.

In the case of a social networking site like Facebook, your personal ability to 'edit' and narrate the self to your liking is questionable. This is partially due to the multiple authorship function engendered by Facebook's system of comments and tagging, which dictates that despite you having control over your own personal input, there is always a collaborative identity and history being built. Through systems like Facebook we are experiencing the 'panoptic' force, control and conformism (Foucault 1977) of not knowing if we are being constantly 'monitored' (watched) by our group of 'friends'. This must be taken into account if any online record is to later be considered as an entirely accurate recount of personal history and/or memories.

To expand this slightly, let's consider a possible Facebook status update such as: 'Just arrived home, after one canceled flight and a day of delays but, hey, I fly again on Friday, so fingers crossed! 21 December 2010 at 1:14am.' This information is possibly considered by the writer to be both momentary and informative to their close network of friends, as it holds valuable information (1) that the person was out of the country, (2) that they are now back in the country, and (3) that they will soon leave again – a very useful succinct bit of information for anyone that is interested in contacting that person or making arrangements. However, the usefulness of the information within that status for aiding the writer's memory of that period or developing the record of their personal history is dubious. The status will possibly have expired in its usefulness for the person very shortly after it was posted, and most people may consider a lot of their status updates to hold the same transient quality. So if these statuses we consider to be transitory were to become a part of our personal history, then on reflection would we be able to recognize ourselves (and our society) within the networks of micro-transactions that occur on a day-to-day basis within a person's status or tweet?

How can either society (in relation to the discussed notion of 'museum of the self') or loved ones (in the case of deciding what data to keep after death) know or predict what are the important aspects of a person's digital life, if this is not indicated by the person themselves? It is evident that throughout the ages both narratives and artifacts have played a key role in keeping the memory of ancestors and important people alive (Walter 1996). However, as we inevitably live more of our lives digitally and have digital access to a 'perfect' memory of both our own and other people's histories (Mayer-Schonberger 2009), there will undoubtedly be an accumulation of digital paraphernalia. In today's society, if people do not begin to set up structures for the future of their data after death, we could be in danger of losing any understandable personal narrative in favor of the vast collection.

If one was to consider this solely from a heritage perspective, and personal profiles were to become a part of our collective history, to return to our example of a status detailing plane trouble in 2010 in Europe, then we must reframe our answer. We would consider that if this status was to be archived, aggregated and properly mined, then perhaps it would document one of the worst winters for travel in Europe, and become historically relevant. From these two very different analyses of one status it becomes clear that there is a danger in trying to build a universal case for what must be done with data left online after death. There must be a distinction drawn here between what the criteria of relevance are for historical records as opposed to what an individual may consider to be personal criteria of relevance. Should this data therefore be placed in a digital museum, at the funeral, be stored in a historical archive, a library – or all of the above?

The British Library stated in a recent report from their 'Digital Lives' project that that they consider the role of personal archives, including social networks and other personal data online, to be of great social interest and importance. They also argued that the researching of personal archives is of increasing value and benefit both to society and to individuals (John et al. 2010). Better research resources are also directly relevant to individuals who wish to manage their own person digital collections for family history, biographical and other purposes. The value is that people have better control over their collections and a sense of satisfaction and well-being. This valuing of digital data sources has also been reflected by the Library of Congress in the United States, which has been collecting online data since 2000 and now holds more than 167 terabytes of digital data including the revelational donation of twitter's entire archive in 2006 (Raymond 2010). This kind of forward planning or planning for data's value and use historically (i.e. for the future) is not only seen at a national or govermental level, it is also seen in various independent websites, including the Internet Archive,[9] The Long Now Foundation[10] and research projects like the Museum of the Person,[11] which is an online museum aimed at collecting, gathering, preserving and sharing the narrated lives of individuals across the globe.

For researchers and historians generally (given the right tools), the more data there is available, the better picture of the past they are able to build. But where friends and family are concerned with looking for memories of a person after death, there must be both meaning and narrative behind the data, for memories to be experienced and treasured meaningfully. How do we begin to design systems that work as 'living networks' but also allow data to be accessed, curated and engaged within a multitude of contexts and on different levels? If we, as individuals, do begin to engage in the preservation and passing on of our personal online traces after death, then perhaps we have begun the process of building up a new kind of 'institution', a decentralized museum of the self. When contemplating the emergence of this museum of the self, we must consider the mass of data typically being produced every day via social networks and other online platforms. This data includes photos, popular music, films, messages, links, statuses, websites, blogs etc. and grows exponentially. If this information is to be kept, for heritage, family or personal memory, then we must begin to consider what the context for relating to this information about one's digital life should be, especially after death. Current online practices of remembrance are becoming less about the process of recalling a once loved object or person, and more about the topological skills and ability to locate and identify fragments of memory multiplied and scattered through several media. Information and communication technology supports the inherent inclination of memory (via its objects) to store and revise, to download and upload, to recollect, project and invent (van Dijck 2007). However, two significant questions remain, concerning the organizing of what happens to our data after death. That is *who* is to be responsible for the overall management of this sensitive data, and *how* are they to go about collecting, archiving, updating and potentially curating it (Churchill and Ubois 2008)?

Future systems of data organization and management must reflect the attributes of interconnectivity and fluidity of social media (and its ability to introduce substantial 'information noise'). As mentioned in the introduction of this chapter, we must consider systems for 'living' intangible heritage that do not remove or copy the various digital objects from within their contexts, as you would do if working with something stationary like a last will, a singular website or even a standalone interface. We must instead work alongside the current model of the decentralized web, and begin to think through a system for personal data and legacy management with enough flexibility to allow the same data in the same network to be used and engaged in a variety of ways. In terms of personal legacy management there is the potential for personal data tagging to be used in order to mark a person's intent. This practice could be modeled on the Creative Commons idea of a modular system of licenses (in this case a modular system of 'intent' after death), which would allow the information producer to independently tag data, personal websites, comments, images etc. with a symbol stating their intent – for example:'I do not wish this data to live beyond me' or 'I wish this data to be passed on as legacy.'

These last considerations address primarily the technological infrastructure (and thinking) need to readdress some of the issues produced by the fact that we are currently keeping more information than any single person can process (Shenk 1997). However, as articulated throughout this chapter, the authors recognize that this is a complex social and cultural problem as well. When attempting to organize our own digital presence (within any system) the first question we should be asking ourselves is: is everything worthy of archiving (Derrida 1996)? This is a topic of much contention within history, and even more in today's society of the instant record. As more and more things are being converted to and being produced primarily (or solely) in digital format, we find ourselves at an important time of increasingly changing forms of cultural memory. Our altering perspective on cultural and social memory has a profound effect on society: on the social and technological institutions we have created to hold memory; the way we recall and mark personal memory; the way we take care of the memory of a loved one we lost; and even on the remembered experiences carried within our being.

Conclusion

This chapter seeks to provide an overview of the emerging curatorial dilemma of how digital data and the networks, which currently 'house' this data, will have an increasingly important role in our growing digital heritage. As a society we must begin to consider what implications this mass of data has on us, both sentimentally and sociologically, especially when this data is currently not being edited or deleted and simply being passed down over the generations. Throughout this chapter, the authors sought to highlight the complex socio-technical relationship we have with 'memory objects' when they are in the form of online data, and to emphasize the effect that developing technological systems around this data have on the ways we can and the ways we wish to remember and narrate the dead. By analyzing how people currently choose, store, seek and value data, this chapter tried to unpack various new approaches to the way we both view and engage with data and legacy management in the digital world. It is obvious that developing increased data storage technology is a double-edged sword: it can give us a richer resource of the past than ever before, but it can also overwhelm us and make us too much reliant on technology and our ever growing museum of the self.

Notes

1 The first Digital Death Day was initiated by the Identity Commons community after experiencing the death of one of their members. The event took place at the Computer History Museum in Mountain View, California. Notes from this and more recent events can be accessed online at http://digitaldeathday.com/.
2 Entrustet, https://www.entrustet.com/.
3 Legacy Locker, http://legacylocker.com/

4 Death Switch, http://www.deathswitch.com/.
5 1,000 Memories, http://1000memories.com/.
6 An appendix was later added to this site stating what they mean by 'saved here forever': http://1000memories.com/what-is-forever (accessed 11 November 2011).
7 Web2.0 Suicide Machine, http://suicidemachine.org.
8 Lifelogging (also known as lifeblogging or lifeglogging) is the continuous technological capture of a person's life. The aim is to build up a complete memory recourse of everything, which the person can refer to at any time. See Bell and Gemmell 2009.
9 Internet Archive, http://archive.org.
10 The Long Now Foundation, http://longnow.org/.
11 Museu de Pessoa, http://www.museudapessoa.net/ingles/.

References

Adams, D. (1982) *Life The Universe and Everything*, London: Pan Books.

Barthes, R. (1982) *Camera Lucida: Reflections on Photography*. Translated by Richard Howard. London: Jonathan Cape.

Bell, G. and Gemmell, J. (2009) *Total Recall: How the E-Memory Revolution Will Change Everything*, New York: Dutton Adult.

Churchill, E. and Ubois, J. (2008) 'Designing for digital archives: the mess we've gotten ourselves into.' *Interactions*. 15(2): 10–13.

Derrida, J. (1996) *Archive Fever*, Chicago, IL: University of Chicago Press.

Ferrucci, L., Mahallati, A. and Simonsick, E. (2006) 'Frailty and the foolishness of Eos', *Journal of Gerontology: Medical Sciences* 61(3): 260–261

Flusser, V. (1990) 'On memory (electronic or otherwise)', *Leonardo* 23(4): 397–399.

Foucault, M. (1977) *Discipline and Punish: the Birth of the Prison*, London: Penguin Books.

Foucault, M. (1988) *Technologies of the Self*, Amherst, MA: University of Massachusetts Press.

Garde-Hansen (2009) 'My Memories? Personal Digital Archive Fever and Facebook', in J. Garde-Hansen, A. Hoskins and A. Reading (eds) *Save As… Digital Memories*, Farnham: Palgrave Macmillan.

Gleick, J. (1999) *Faster: The Acceleration of Just About Everything*, New York: Pantheon.

Halamish, L. and Hermoni, D. (2007) *The Weeping Willow (Encounters with Grief)*, Oxford: Oxford University Press.

Hayles, K. (1999) *How We Became Posthuman: Virtual Bodies in Cybernetics, Literature, and Informatics*, Chicago, IL: University of Chicago Press.

Hayles, K. (2002) *Writing Machines*, Cambridge, MA: MIT Press.

Herring, M. (2010) 'A sea of sensors: Everything will become a sensor – and humans may be the best of all', *The Economist*, 4 November. www.economist.com/node/17388356 (accessed 11 November 2011).

Jefferies, J. (2005) *Ceremony*, London: Pump House Gallery.

John, J.L., Rowlands, I., Williams, P. and Dean, K. (2010) *Digital Lives: Personal Digital Archives for the 21st Century: An Initial Synthesis*, British Library, Digital Lives Research Paper, 03 March 2010, Beta Version 2.0. www.britishlibrary.typepad.co.uk/files/digital-lives-synthesis01a.pdf (accessed 11 November 2011).

Kirshenblatt-Gimblett, B. (2004) 'Intangible heritage as a metacultural production', *Museum International* 56 (1–2): 52–65.

Mayer-Schonberger, V. (2009) *Delete: The Virtue of Forgetting in the Digital Age*, Princeton, NJ: Princeton University Press.

Odom, W., Harper, R., Sellen, A., Kirk, D. and Banks, R. (2010) 'Passing on and putting to rest: Understanding, bereavement in the context of interactive technologies', in *Proceedings of CHI 2010*, 1831–1840. New York: ACM Press.

Pitsillides, S., Conreen, M. and Katsikides, S. (2009) 'Digital Death', in A. Poulymenakou and A. Papargyris (eds) *Images of Virtuality: Conceptualizations and Applications in Everyday Life. An IFIP WG9.5 'Virtuality and Society' International Workshop*, 131–143. Athens University of Economics and Business, 23–24 April 2009, Greece.

Raymond, M. (2010) 'Twitter Donates Entire Tweet Archive to Library of Congress'. *News from the Library of Congress*, 15 April. www.loc.gov/today/pr/2010/10-081.html (accessed 11 November 2011).

Sellen, A. and Whittaker, S. (2010) 'Beyond total capture: A constructive critique of lifelogging', *Communications of the ACM*, 53 (5): 70–77.

Shenk, D. (1997) *Data Smog: Surviving the Information Glut*, New York: HarperEdge.

Stewart, S. (1993) *On Longing: Narratives on the Miniature, the Gigantic, the Souvenir, the Collection*, Durham, NC and London: Duke University Press.

Stiegler, B. (1998) *Technics and Time. 1: The Fault of Epimetheus*. Translated by G. Collins and R. Beardsworth, Stanford, CA: Stanford University Press.

Turkle, S. (1995) *Life on the Screen: Identity in the Age of the Internet*, New York: Simon & Schuster.

Turkle, S. (2011) *Alone Together: Why we Expect More from Technology and Less from Each Other*, Cambridge, MA: MIT Press.

UNESCO (1952) Universal Copyright Convention. http://portal.unesco.org/culture/en/ev.php-URL_ID=35233&URL_DO=DO_TOPIC&URL_SECTION=201.html (accessed 23 February 2012).

UNESCO (2003) Convention for the Safeguarding of Intangible Cultural Heritage. http://www.unesco.org/culture/ich/index.php?lg=en&pg=00006 (accessed 11 November 2011).

van Dijck, J. (2007) *Mediated Memories in the Digital Age*, Stanford, CA: Stanford University Press.

Walker, R. (2011) 'Cyberspace when you're dead', *New York Times*, 5 January.

Walter, T. (1996) 'A new model of grief: Bereavement and biography', *Mortality*, 1: 7–25.

Weiss, K. (2010) 'Hoarding, hermitage, and the law: Why we love the Collyer Brother', *The Journal of the American Academy of Psychiatry and the Law*, 38(2): 251–257.

Winer, D. (2007) 'Future-Safe Archives'. http://scripting.com/stories/2007/12/10/futuresafeArchives.html (accessed 11 November 2011).

4

SOCIAL TRACES

Participation and the creation of shared heritage

Luigina Ciolfi

Introduction

In this chapter I reflect on experiences of working with cultural heritage from the perspective of an interaction designer committed to a participative approach to the design of interactive systems and to engendering novel social interactions around them. This research in interactive exhibition design has been focused on supporting engagement, reflection and appreciation of an exhibit by enabling people's active participation in contributing to the exhibition, both in the context of established art museums and of more informal heritage spaces.

This resonates with recent developments in interaction design for museums and exhibitions that have experimented with ways of facilitating visitors' participation and direct involvement in shaping, and even creating, the content and message of exhibits, rather than just allowing for comments or more limited forms of participant interaction.

I take a more inclusive approach towards the active involvement of visitors as well as all the communities of stakeholders involved in heritage sites, which I study and represent as complex social ecologies surrounding the preservation, creation and sharing of heritage.

Interaction design is a socially oriented and socially sensitive, human-centred perspective, grounded in ideas of participation and dialogue (Bannon 2005, 2011). From this perspective, I consider design for cultural heritage as an activity that does not only lead to the engineering of computer technology in heritage settings, but as a process for supporting the generation, representation and sharing of *social traces*. What I mean by social traces are those immaterial attributes that become inscribed into heritage artefacts and sites and that derive from the ecology of the roles, the contributions, the values and opinions of the communities surrounding, preserving, exploring and communicating heritage.

If we then augment these activities surrounding heritage by means of social technology, we have examples of how the perceivable social traces of the interactions with technology that people have also play a role in redefining curatorial practices and the notion of heritage itself. The more active role that social media and social technology grants to people leads to a new concept of 'shared heritage', whereby institutional content and visitor contributions together make heritage – what Russo elsewhere in this volume calls a 'media museum'.

Making examples from a series of design case studies, I look further at the social traces that became inscribed into heritage when creating interactive installations that are open to contributions and create new communities and new patterns of social interaction around the heritage.

Based on the characteristics of open-ended exhibition designs for museums and public spaces that were realized by the Interaction Design Centre (IDC) at the University of Limerick, Ireland, in the past few years, I offer some insights for future work, particularly focusing on the increasing role that social media can have in communicating to and engaging with participants.

The interaction design approach to participation

Interaction design as a discipline has a strong focus on the *social dimension* of interaction. First of all, by including important insights from the tradition of Computer-Supported Cooperative Work, it is conscious about the importance of collaboration, coordination and sharing around the design and evaluation of interactive systems (Kyng 1991). Interaction design is also concerned with 'appropriation' – that is, the emergent patterns of use of a system that derive from people's own reconfigurations and customization of technology rather than simply its prescribed use (Balka and Wagner 2006; Dix 2007) – and with approaches to design that are open to emergent patterns of use (Giaccardi 2005). Because all these practices of technology reconfiguration usually occur in a socially rich way, such concerns about appropriation are also connected to the social dimension of experiencing technology as it links to new forms of sharing and collaborative use.

Interaction design is also (and importantly) *participative*. The strong tradition of participatory design (Greenbaum and Kyng 1992) has been very influential for many years, advocating a social and inclusive process of design whereby end-users, designers and other stakeholders come together to discuss and propose design solutions.

Within this frame, I adopt activity-centred and place-centred approaches (Bannon 2005; Ciolfi and Bannon 2007) that are crucial in engaging visitors to actively participate in interactive exhibitions, as their contributions resonate with the broader connections and personal ties they develop to environments, communities and practices.

Creating the conditions for participation and sharing means understanding a broad range of concerns – bringing together different actors under an interaction design perspective (i.e. not excluding curators, educators, volunteers, etc. from design). Therefore approaches to interaction design that are inclusive of a wide range of activities within museums and cultural heritage sites and of relationships with the sites themselves are sensitive to this need for inclusion (Walker 2008). Particularly, it is important to explore what technology can do to facilitate social involvement and to enable new possibilities for interaction that can be of benefit to several stakeholder groups. This approach to the design of technology for museums and heritage sites resonates with current developments in thinking about museums as open and participative institutions – something that has emerged relatively recently and has brought significant changes to the concept of heritage.

Participation in heritage sites

The *mission* of museums and heritage sites is to offer visitors information and knowledge, whether they display works of art or antiquities, present scientific and technological themes to the public (e.g. science centres, natural history museums, etc.), or recreate environments and artefacts from another time or space. This presents interesting social implications as museums and heritage sites are increasingly oriented to communities (Simon 2010), and heritage is increasingly intended as what a community values and speaks out to others about their identity (Giaccardi 2011).

Heritage displays are usually created and maintained by skilled professionals in curatorship and conservation, managers, educators and other stakeholders; what is displayed represents these people's knowledge and intents. For many years it has been difficult for visitors to question a museum's content and layout and to make of the museum a place for debate, not to mention the possibility to leave 'traces' of their own meanings and interpretations. Interpretations of heritage were fixed and produced by a curatorial team of experts. Curatorial decisions were kept 'invisible' by offering exhibits as given and authoritative, rather than as the product of a professional practice and of a set of values, intentions and meanings naturally subject to change. Examples of this attitude to curatorship do exist still, although it is now beginning to become the exception rather than the rule.

Hooper–Greenhill notes:

> At the birth of the public museum, a division was drawn between the private space where the curator, as expert, produced knowledge (exhibitions, catalogues, lectures) and the public space where the visitor consumed those appropriately presented products. A deep cleft was formed that separated out the practices of the museum workers from those of the visitor. The experience of the museum, its collections, and its specialist processes, was different on either side of this divide. The lack of knowledge of the work of the curator constituted the visitor as ignorant and the curator as expert in respect of the collections. Conversely, the lack of knowledge of the visitor's reactions and responses constituted the curator as ignorant in respect of the audience for whom the museum's intellectual products were intended. Now, the closed and private space of the early public museums has begun to open, and the division between private and public has begun to close.
>
> (Hooper–Greenhill 1992: 200)

This closed attitude to display and communicate only professional curators' interpretations affected visitors as well as other stakeholder groups (e.g. museum volunteers), who might have been deeply involved with a heritage site, but were not allowed to have an input on either layout or communication, and were not able to see their opinions and thoughts somehow represented.

Over the past two decades, there has been also a growing political commitment at museum management level to enhancing access to museums and galleries by encouraging public participation. This has provoked changes in the way exhibitions are thought and developed by curators:

> The process of introducing community groups to museums is not about high levels of educational achievement. Rather it is concerned with negotiating, confidence-building and provoking opportunities. ... A fundamental change is taking place in the relationship between the public and museums; a change towards a collaboration of joint interest, joint views, feelings and sensitivities.
>
> (Dodd 1994: 132–133)

Elements of participation have been therefore gradually introduced within museums and heritage sites to pervade more and more of the visitor experience. Educational activities and informal learning were possibly the first aspect of the visit to be targeted: from early attempts for participation in educational activities in dedicated spaces (such as lecture theatres and workshop spaces), to fully participative hands-on activities taking place in actual galleries (such as themed treasure hunts, handling sessions, replica making workshops and so on).

The visit itself is now often seen as open, with alternative themes to be chosen, a strong encouragement to use social media to comment on the exhibits, and the role of guides becoming less that of a provider of content and more that of a facilitator of dialogue and debate. The nature of museum visits as inherently social has been discussed in literature on visitor conduct (cf. vom Lehn et al. 2001). As the social element has extended beyond interaction with companions and has begun to pervade the relationship with the institution, the visit is increasingly a 'social experience'.

Many heritage sites also strategically engage in community outreach: they open their doors to other activities to take place on their premises (such as performances, lectures and meet-ups) or they bring themselves (in the form of staff, displays, knowledge or specific artefacts) outside the walls of the institution and into a city or local community.

Increasingly intertwined with several communities, heritage as a notion is now thought of as a participative one. Particularly in interaction design, attempts have recently been made to facilitate the co-creation of heritage: people are encouraged to express opinions, views, engage in activities and sometimes even contribute to the main displays (cf. Bannon et al. 2005; Giaccardi and Palen 2008; Ciolfi et al. 2008; Salgado 2009; Simon 2010).

Social media is proving very effective in facilitating this, with major museums around the world (such as the Metropolitan Museum of Art, the Smithsonian Institution, the Victoria & Albert Museum, to mention only a few) utilizing different forms of content sharing and crowdsourcing[1] to communicate, promote, enrich and sometimes create exhibits.

However, if we think about participation in a more encompassing way, it is clear that visitors are only one of the communities to be involved: there is also a multiplicity of staff roles (from curators and archivists to guides, educators, etc.) and stakeholders (from funding bodies to consultants, designers, etc.) that can contribute to the co-creation and sharing of heritage. All of these groups have invested values and interests in cultural heritage institutions; they can bring unique perspectives and ideas, and contribute to increased social interaction around the sharing of heritage.

Heritage sites, as they are experienced by different communities of visitors and stakeholders, become inscribed with *social traces*: ideas, opinions, physical trajectories and collaborative practices that embody the presence, activity and agency of multiple participants, and that can be represented in perceivable traces (e.g. visitor comments), in curatorial choices, and in the information on display. Social traces are derived from people's practices, values and understandings, but are often 'invisible', that is to say, not represented in the way heritage is displayed and communicated.

The interaction design process for introducing novel ways to enable participation in heritage through technology can play a significant role to highlight social traces from different stakeholders, and thus enrich a site with a perceptible representation of the different communities involved. This function of design as a support for expressing and representing the social nature of heritage is key in facilitating the creation of shared heritage through active participation.

I will describe a number of projects undertaken by the Interaction Design Centre with this goal, and I will show how different social players were involved and how their contributions have shaped our designs. Although most of these projects predate the emergence of social media as it is known today, the technologies that were employed and the functionalities supported were to a large extent precursors of contemporary social media. A reflection on their design can be of guidance and support for what we believe is an inclusive and sustainable application of social media in heritage settings.

Enabling social traces: case studies

The set of projects I describe here feature different heritage sites, different communities and different design briefs. I have chosen to use these cases because they all represent examples of a process where a number of different stakeholders were engaged in contributing to the exhibit and in other forms of active participation. The sites involved represent a broad range of heritage settings: from traditional art museums, to city spaces, to open-air exhibitions and historical landmarks. Table 4.1 provides a brief description of these settings.

TABLE 4.1 Summary of case studies from the Interaction Design Centre, Limerick (Ireland)

	Re-Tracing the Past	The Shannon Portal	The Recipe Station	Reminisce
Years of work	*2001–2003*	*2004–2007*	*2004–2008*	*2008–2010*
Site/ institution	The Hunt Museum, Limerick	Shannon International Airport, Co. Clare	The Milk Market, Limerick City	Bunratty Folk Park, Co. Clare
Designed piece	Interactive rooms: 'The Study Room' and 'The Room of Opinion', radio frequency identification (RFID)-tagged cards trigger interactive behaviours in each (Figure 4.1)	Interactive standalone installation, the Portal Dolmen, and motion-activated Image Wall; website (Figure 4.2)	Station for browsing and printing recipes, operated by RFID cards; website (Figure 4.3)	Mobile application following a fictional character, coupled with standalone installations (Figure 4.4)
Contributions enabled	Recordings of opinions about the nature of mysterious museum objects	Annotated images with messages representing people's journeys	Recipes based on the Market's produce	Recordings of memories and reminiscences of old Ireland, and of comments and impressions
Design objectives	Involving participants in discussing the collection and creating new knowledge	Enabling participants to use the airport as a hub for communication as well as travel; connecting the airport with the region	Enhancing the traditional food culture of the Market with community building around produce and recipes	Helping visitors find connections with the buildings and artefacts on display, putting them into a real-life context
Stakeholders (other than visitors)	Museum management, curator, volunteers (i.e. docents), teachers, educators	Airport management, security staff, retail personnel	Market stallholders, market board of trustees, managers	Folk Park management, human animators and impersonators, groundskeepers, retailers

FIGURE 4.1   Re-Tracing the Past at the Hunt Museum, Limerick. Photo © Luigina Ciolfi

Although different design projects derive from different briefs or agendas, it is of general importance to establish a positive relationship with the institutions involved. The terms and practical articulation of this relationship have an important role in shaping an interaction design solution that is fitting for a setting and offers meaningful interactions for participants.

At the Hunt Museum the design team established close connections with the museum staff and volunteers and conducted in-depth studies of visitor activities (Ferris *et al*. 2004). This small and eclectic museum was formed originally as a private collection of art and antiquities by a local family, and we felt that the traces of such personal and close involvement of individuals in museum objects should be highlighted (Figure 4.1). The Hunt Museum employs a small staff, but its most interesting feature from the point of view of interpretation and access is the docent programme, seeking enthusiastic volunteers who are willing to lead guided tours and engage with visitors in hands-on workshops and other activities. This programme is unique in Ireland. Another interesting aspect of the museum is that curators have knowledge of the objects but also of the family history, thus allowing visitors to experience the collection from the point of view of the collectors' personal histories. Although a relatively small institution, the presence of these different communities of stakeholders means that the Hunt Museum is enriched by lively dialogue between curators, visitors, schools and educators, and volunteers.

The education officer (very keen to encourage personal interpretation and connection with the museum's holdings) had an active role in the design process we led. The docents were also consulted regularly, and we had the opportunity to join them in some of their activities, witnessing the rich social interaction within the group and with the visitors.

At Shannon Airport, we faced a project with a completely different set of concerns, including security measures, rules of behaviour and safety regulations (Ciolfi *et al*. 2007). Shannon Airport is a historic landmark for the West of Ireland and for the history of aviation: it has played a significant role in establishing the importance of the local area within Ireland. It has historical relevance and an immense community value, as it has been operational since the 1940s as the obligatory refuelling airport

FIGURE 4.2   The Portal at Shannon Airport. Photo © Luigina Ciolfi

for all transatlantic flights, the home of the first ever duty-free shop, and a hub of activity for the region ever since. As a setting, it embodies many contrasting interests and manifold practices: from passengers and staff, to security, management and visitors (Figure 4.2).

During our studies, it became clear that the airport houses a strong community of workers: they feel that they 'belong' to Shannon even if some workers are mainly hired by contracting firms rather than by the airport itself. They are proud of the place and of its unique role in recent Irish history and economy. Local passengers are also strongly tied to it, which is really surprising for an airport – a space that is normally thought of as alienating, or a 'non-place' (Augé 1995). During the design process, we paid particular attention to these different communities, and we sought the constant feedback of the airport management on the design scenarios we produced.

In the Milk Market (Deshpande 2007; McLoughlin 2008), it is the civic community aspect that is the most striking: the Market is a Limerick institution and takes place weekly in a historic building, where people go for socializing and connecting, and not only for shopping. There is a 'light' management structure in place, and the ties between the Market and its patrons are strong and well established through the years. Patrons, vendors and local residents are all highly involved with the Market, not only through buying and selling, but also by promoting the event and choosing it as a meeting and entertainment venue (Figure 4.3). These communities are also involved in creating the multisensory experience of the Market: from the elaborate displays of foodstuffs, to the playing of live music and the cooking demonstrations. Our design had to be mindful of this richness and of the

FIGURE 4.3 The Recipe Station at the Milk Market, Limerick. Photo © Marc McLoughlin

connection between the Milk Market and the history of the city. We were keen to create an interactive experience that could involve vendors as much as patrons and visitors, and a physical design that would represent the warm, 'organic' atmosphere of the place.

Finally, at Bunratty Folk Park we have worked in the context of a living-history museum, collecting buildings, artefacts and landscapes of Ireland's past within a large outdoor park (Ciolfi and McLoughlin 2011b). The Bunratty Folk Park houses an impressive collection of original buildings, nearly all of them reconstructed after being moved stone by stone to Bunratty from locations all around the island of Ireland (Figure 4.4), and fitted with period-appropriate furnishings and decorations. A team of professional animators enacts traditional activities such as baking and butter making at different sites in the Park. They are the primary medium of communication between the Folk Park and the visitors, and play a crucial role in keeping visitors engaged and in bringing the buildings to life through the performance of traditional activities.

Bunratty Folk Park is one of the most important tourist attractions in Ireland (with numbers in excess of 300,000 visitors per year) and the management there includes a large number of marketing and communication experts. Therefore, the site offers facilities of entertainment value (such as banqueting facilities, a fully licensed pub and several shops) in addition to the historical content on display. In this work, we had to bring together the concerns of marketing as well as those of visitor engagement. We also involved one of the senior animators as 'key-informant' (Willis 2000) so that the concerns of the staff would be constantly on our mind when developing ideas, and could be represented in the design solution.

FIGURE 4.4   Reminisce at Bunratty Folk Park. Photo © Marc McLoughlin

This overview highlights how, in each project, the involvement of a different set of stakeholders was important for the final design. Each case study is different and influenced by different objectives, goals and practical constraints. However, for each project, we had to become aware of the complex social relationships among communities of visitors, managers, staff and other stakeholders. This enabled us to produce design ideas that would enable open participation by all players, the representation of traces of their involvement with the site, and the creation of shared contributions. Each community involved in a project was acknowledged and listened to, and the development of the design was influenced by the ideas, roles and contributions that all participants provided, thus engaging in a design process necessarily open, participative and social. Given the common traits of this design approach and the explicit focus on inclusion and participation brought to bear in all our practice, I will now point out and discuss further a number of themes linked to the presence of different social traces that have emerged in our designs.

Heterogeneity of stakeholders and actors

We observed that a range of different roles characterize each institution: from the curators (who are in charge of how the museum and its holdings are communicated and represented and are responsible for preserving and sharing the knowledge of the collection or site), to management (concerned with the smooth running of the site), to other members of staff deeply involved in the life of the institution with their own specific tasks. This acknowledgement is important not only in terms of the different activities that need to be taken into account, but also in terms of different understandings of both the institution itself (managerial, curatorial, infrastructural, etc.) and the design project.

The heterogeneous mix of backgrounds, competencies, expertise and interests that distinguishes each institution means that involving stakeholders will create different roles within the project itself. It is not uncommon to encounter difficulties when dealing with the heterogeneity of actors involved and reconciling their agendas. In the projects mentioned here, this negotiation took place successfully thanks to a substantial effort in team coordination, and because our design had deep connections with important communities of stakeholders. One example is the guidance staff that act as a point of contact with visitors, such as the Hunt Museum docents and the animators in Bunratty Folk Park. These groups are often the actors who bring the exhibit, literally, 'to life', although usually get little representation in curatorial choices. The installations we designed for the Hunt Museum and Bunratty Folk Park had the clear goal of both supporting and representing their role. In the exhibition Re-Tracing the Past at the Hunt Museum, the docents were invited to put on record their theories and studies of the mysterious artefacts featuring in the exhibition: objects of the Hunt collection that have never been conclusively identified. In the Reminisce tour at Bunratty Folk Park, the storyline of the installation was inspired by the presence of animators such as the *Bean An Ti*'s (Irish for 'woman of the house'): the content provided to visitors at each site of the installation could be used by the animators as prompts for their own conversations with the visitors as well as support to the visit when animators were too busy with other activities such as baking and building the fires.

We wanted our designs to highlight the connections that these informal guides spontaneously establish with visitors, and that sometimes management staff lack. Their experience from daily interaction with the visitors, and their understanding of what entices and engages visitors were of great inspiration to us in the phase of concept generation, and the design process was enriched by the complex understandings and stories that animators shared with the project team.

In the Hunt Museum case, the education officer was also heavily involved in the project, and offered us full participation in project activities, including design sessions, formal presentations, documentation, etc. Of course, different sites are characterized by different 'ethos': for example, the Milk Market and Bunratty Folk Park have a clear business focus, and this also has to be taken into account when shaping a design solution. It is impractical to demand the same degree of participation, and at the same stages of the interaction design process, by all the communities involved in a project. Each contribution though leaves a trace in the design decisions well before visitors are able to interact with the installation. Those groups that can actively participate in the installation leave more visible traces; although these may be different and more or less prominent in the installation, it is important to communicate to stakeholders that there is an underlying will to represent them somehow. Truly social design (including that which is realized through social media) needs to allow space for these groups of stakeholders to provide a contribution in order to make the heterogeneity of communities surrounding heritage a feature and not a hindrance.

Community engagement

Heritage institutions are not isolated, and they reach out to a wider community beyond that of visitors. Broader community engagement is another 'social' feature of designing interactive installations that needs to be taken into account. Our installations Re-Tracing the Past, the Shannon Portal and the Recipe Station all included components that allowed remote participants to interact somehow – thus making connections with a greater community beyond the 'walls' of the installation.

As part of Re-Tracing the Past we offered a specific education programme to Limerick schools, including pre- and post-visit workshops (Hall and Bannon 2006). The Recipe Station included a web resource for contributing and finding recipes that people interested in the Market could access remotely, outside trading days. In the case of the Milk Market, there was a strong emphasis on making our design intervention something to support the wider Limerick City community, and not just the regular patrons of the Market, thus attracting new visitors and attention from outside the site itself. Similarly, the Recipe Station design included also a role for the Market's stakeholders, who were asked to hand out the radio frequency identification (RFID)-tagged ingredient cards to customers who bought their produce; in this way, they were a part of the interactive experience and could benefit from it by encouraging people to purchase more items from them. Finally, it is worth noting that the Shannon Portal's online gallery was used widely as a means to outreach to the local community and communicate the importance of the airport to local residents. This compensated for the fact that the Portal itself was located in the departures lounge of the airport, and only passengers in possession of a boarding pass and staff members could access this area.

These features made the sites of the museum, of the city market and of the local airport connect with the broader community beyond the exhibition, thus to some degree also involving in the installations people who were physically removed from the site and allowing them to contribute.

Designing engaging activities

Making good design decisions revolves around creating detailed scenarios and envisioning an engaging activity that the installation should offer to participants. The final solution is usually the product of design work balancing possibilities and constraints, but one of the most important features to be decided are the *modalities* of participation that the interactive installation will offer.

Some of our examples allow for graffiti-style forms of participation, encouraging the reaction to an opportunity for visual interaction: for example, the Shannon Portal supported this type of participation without the need to buy into a long storyline, thus making it easier for people with limited time to engage with the installation.

Another modality is supported by embedding a unique story into a sequence of activities that the installation offers to visitors and by opening a space where participants can contribute: for Bunratty Folk Park, for example, we created a fictional storyline with characters that people could follow in a modular fashion and to whom they could respond with their own opinions and personal reminiscences.

Finally, participation can be encouraged as a means of enriching existing knowledge: in Re-Tracing the Past, participants were involved in the task of using known information to generate possible interpretations of mysterious objects in the Hunt Museum. We focused on a particular subset of the Hunt collection and encouraged people to populate the information space around these objects. Similarly, with the Recipe Station, we concentrated on a particular market activity, i.e. shopping for ingredients, and asked participants to contribute to a shared repository of culinary knowledge with original recipes.

Different components to the activity that is offered to visitors can mediate different forms of participation and social interaction: for example, in Re-Tracing the Past all the components of the Study Room installation enabled collaborative interaction while participants were researching the mysterious objects, thus becoming hubs for social exchange during the initial part of the activity. Similarly, in the same exhibition, the Interactive Radio that was playing back visitors' opinions about the mysterious objects triggered discussion about the 'findings' recorded and shared by visitors.

All our designs also allowed for multiple forms of interaction: from onlooking to full-on active participation. For example, airport passers-by could enjoy the Shannon Portal's Image Wall at a distance as an interesting dynamic visual display as well as interact with it directly through bodily movements. On the other hand, the other component of the Portal, the interactive Dolmen (replicating the shape of ancient Celtic monuments built for marking a community hub) required further active interaction in the form of selecting and annotating photos to the benefit of subsequent visitors. All these levels of engagement led to different forms of participation and of social interaction. In defining the overall activity that interactive technology supports, all these nuances of social behaviour and how they connect to the activity itself must be taken into account.

Overall, an engaging participatory activity should be embedded in the social dimension of other activities taking place onsite. At the Hunt Museum, the docents' recordings in Re-Tracing the Past connected to the stories they told visitors on their guided tours through the Hunt Museum and resonated with the docents' unique style of communicating the collection. At Shannon Airport, the annotated images related to passengers' physical journeys, with their destinations and points of departure. At Bunratty Folk Park, the recorded memories describing past ways of domestic life and the traditionally baked goods that the animators left in the houses mutually enriched each other.

Soliciting contributions and enabling multiple traces

As well as the modality of participation, it is important to consider the form that contributions to an installation can take. By evoking a reaction, or stimulating further imagination through stories, the visitors can leave a trace in several ways, thus helping to create different configurations of shared heritage.

It is important to consider the temporal aspects of participation on either a synchronic or diachronic dimension: participants can be encouraged to make a contribution in the here and now – something that can be shared instantly and quickly leads to reactions and more interactions – or contribute something after the visit (for example, the visitors' own memories recorded in real time in Reminisce versus the recipes for the Recipe Station that could only be uploaded through the web portal). Another temporal aspect is the persistence of the traces left by visitors: for example, the Shannon Portal's Image Wall was updated constantly so that only the last 60 images or so could be seen at any time; on the other hand, the Recipe Station's database was left to grow over time so that more and more content would be available at every market day. These different levels of permanence influence the social interactions that emerge: for example, some recipes had become favourites by returning participants to the Recipe Station, and were recommended to newer visitors through the recounting of participants' own experiences in experimenting with cooking.

Different forms of contributions often represent different voices from different communities involved in a heritage site. For example many of the docents in the Hunt Museums recorded their detailed theories regarding the mysterious objects, making their recordings easily identifiable with their role within the museum and with their belonging to the group of docents. Similarly, local residents of Shannon Town and airport staff members using the Shannon Portal tended to choose photographs of the locality (such as historic photographs of the airport itself), whereas visitors from other parts of Ireland or from abroad often chose images of more recognizable locations in the region. These different types of contributions identified unique backgrounds, interests and motivations. Therefore, the discussions and reactions that ensued after the sharing of different photographic traces were tightly connected to how these traces represented a certain community of stakeholders, and this often enabled dialogue between different groups of participants (for example, between local staff and passengers at Shannon Airport).

As mentioned earlier, the involvement of each group of stakeholders leaves certain traces in the design: we designed to allow for the heterogeneous nature of such traces to emerge.

Design innovation and technology

The design projects described in this chapter used a broad technology platform. The choices regarding technological infrastructure and specific devices followed the development of an appropriate design concept and scenario. In order for interactions to happen collaboratively, it is important to inscribe social elements into the architecture of the system, from the creation of ad hoc networks to the use of multiple displays (visual, auditory and tangible).

Additionally, we have used a variety of technological artefacts: from tangibles (e.g. the RFID-tagged ingredients in the Recipe Station) to mobile devices (e.g. the phone application in Reminisce), to standalone artefacts (e.g. the dolmen in the

Shannon Portal). We have also used 'low-tech props' such as the tangible tokens of Reminisce providing clues as to where to continue the trail around the Park, and the replicas of mysterious objects in the Hunt Museum. These components were crucial in engendering social interaction and participation as they often provided easily recognizable 'access points' to the interactive experience, and they also worked very effectively as triggers for informal conversations and collaborations among participants (Ciolfi and McLoughlin 2011a).

Finally, we have chosen multiple interaction styles for the creation of contributions: drawings, audio recordings, written notes and photographs. This choice was informed by the activities that characterized each site and by the understanding of the communities involved. The photographs in Shannon resonated with the photo taking and postcard writing that people do while travelling; the audio recordings in the Hunt Museum and at Bunratty reflected the stories told by docents and animators; the printed recipes in the Milk Market were informed by the idea of a 'modular' recipe book that visitors build week by week.

In general, the choice of a technical solution needs to be informed by the overall activity that is to be supported and by the goals of facilitating participation: not all technologies will work effectively in all contexts, nor will all of them support visitor activities adequately. In the context of using readily available social media tools and services (such as Twitter, Flickr, Facebook, etc.) that can be configured to work in conjunction with different platforms (e.g. mobile phones, standalone installations, websites, etc.), it is important to design such configurations on the basis of the interaction scenario that is guiding the installation, and to adapt them to the context and scope of the installation itself.

Conclusions: Towards social media, truly

In this chapter I have presented reflections on the multilayered ways in which social traces pervade the process of interaction design for heritage sites. From the composition of the design team, to the development of ideas in collaboration with different stakeholders, to the deployment of installations involving active participants, the social dimension of heritage work has been a constant aspect of our interaction design experience thus far. The actual installations that our group has built and exhibited were created with the contributions of many participants to the design process, and were experienced by different communities of stakeholders at each site. This has always been done intentionally to let the different voices surrounding heritage be heard: curators, visitors, volunteers, but also other stakeholders and wider communities of interest. Throughout the chapter, I have indirectly referred to all the phases of the interaction design process while outlining salient themes related to idea of 'social traces'. How are these examples useful in the context of social media for cultural heritage?

I would argue that considering media for heritage as socially inscribed by diverse communities is of extreme importance: it is sometimes tempting to plug in social media components without recognizing the role that multiple stakeholders have in shaping the design of heritage experiences from the very start. One risk here is that by packaging the social into the box of social media, this dimension could become paradoxically less attended to. For example, a still only relatively small number of heritage institutions have social media strategies inclusive of not only curators/ educators and visitors, but also of volunteers and other stakeholders. These voices are often not represented, yet they could add significant value to the role of social media in facilitating the creation of true forms of shared heritage. Participation strategies that are sensitive to this are currently being developed, with the goal of supporting the use of social media in heritage as added value for visitors (Chan 2008), and of enhancing the civic and political role of heritage institutions (Russo, this volume). Still all too often, the recommendations on how social media strategies should be embraced by heritage organizations exclude certain social traces, and focus only on enticing visitors instead of multiple communities (cf. Allen-Greil *et al.* 2011).

Another risk is that of making social media stand against other technologies and platforms: by identifying these as two different categories, the possibilities offered by other technologies to engender social interaction and promote active participation could be forgotten. As shown for example by studies of smartphones (Burnette *et al.* 2011) and web portals (Grabill *et al.* 2009), social media platforms certainly offer interesting possibilities for design. What I argue here is that conventional social media tools might not provide the right or sole solution for every design case. Through the cases discussed in the chapter, I have shown how components of installations that are not 'functionally' collaborative per se did foster significant patterns of participation and collaboration. In order to think of solutions that can make interaction truly 'social', it is important to consider technology as something that is shaped by the concerns of different communities as well as by the designers' intent, not just in terms of applications.

In our interaction design projects we did not make use of mainstream social media platforms: some projects were realized when such tools were not yet available, others were led with an explicit intention to realize ad hoc technical solutions to support active participation rather than adding external plug-ins such as 'like' or 'share' buttons. However, I believe these projects can provide valuable lessons for current and future research involving the design and use of social media for heritage purposes. They illustrate and discuss a range of possible supports to the perceivable representation of social traces in design and the creation of shared heritage – particularly advocating community engagement, enabling multiple traces to be represented, and embracing innovative combinations of both high and low tech solutions to facilitate open and active participation.

Acknowledgements

The projects mentioned in this chapter were funded by: EU-FET 'The Disappearing Computer', Science Foundation Ireland, Fáilte Ireland and the University of Limerick Seed Funding initiative. Thanks to all the partners in the SHAPE Project, and to all the staff, management and visitors at the four exhibition sites. The installations would not have been realized without, first and foremost, Liam Bannon,

IDC Funding Director, who also gave valuable feedback on this chapter, Mikael Fernström, Parag Deshpande, Marc McLoughlin and many other IDC colleagues and students who have worked on the projects through the years.

Notes

1 Crowdsourcing is the process of gathering information, skills or particular solutions to a problem through a community effort and by means of an open call for participation, rather than by recruiting specific individuals (Howe, 2006).

References

Allen-Greil, D., Edwards, S., Ludden, J. and Johnson, E. (2011) 'Social media and organizational change', in J. Trant and D. Bearman (eds) *Museums and the Web 2011: Proceedings*, Toronto: Archives & Museum Informatics. http://conference.archimuse.com/mw2011/papers/social_media_organizational_change (accessed 16 August 2011).

Augé, M. (1995) *Non Places*, London: Verso.

Balka, E. and Wagner, I. (2006) 'Making things work: Dimensions of configurability as appropriation work', in *Proceedings of CSCW 2006*, 229–238. New York: ACM Press.

Bannon, L.J. (2005) 'A human-centred perspective on interaction design', in A. Pirhonen, H. Isomäki, C. Roast, and P. Saariluoma (eds) *Future Interaction Design*, London: Springer.

Bannon, L.J. (2011) 'Reimagining HCI: Toward a more human-centred perspective', *Interactions*, 18 (4): 50–57.

Bannon, L.J., Benford, S., Bowers, J.M. and Heath, C. (2005) 'Hybrid design creates innovative museum experiences', *Communications of the ACM*, 48 (3): 62–65.

Burnette, A., Cherry, R., Proctor, N. and Samis, P. (2011) 'Getting on (not under) the mobile 2.0 bus: Emerging issues in the mobile business model', in J. Trant and D. Bearman (eds) *Museums and the Web 2011: Proceedings*, Toronto: Archives & Museum Informatics. http://conference.archimuse.com/mw2011/papers/getting_on_not_under_the_mobile_20_bus (accessed 10 May 2011).

Chan, S. (2008) 'Towards new metrics of success', in J. Trant and D. Bearman (eds) *Museums and the Web 2008: Selected Papers from an International Conference*, 13–22. Toronto: Archives & Museum Informatics.

Ciolfi, L. and Bannon, L.J. (2007) 'Designing hybrid places: Merging interaction design, ubiquitous technologies and geographies of the museum space', *Co-Design*, 3: 159–180.

Ciolfi, L. and McLoughlin, M. (2011a) 'Physical keys to digital memories: Reflecting on the role of tangible artefacts in *Reminisce*', in J. Trant, J. and D. Bearman (eds) *Museums and the Web 2011: Proceedings*, Toronto: Archives & Museum Informatics. http://conference.archimuse.com/mw2011/papers/physical_keys_digital_memories (accessed 15 November 2011).

Ciolfi, L. and McLoughlin, M. (2011b) 'Challenges for the technological augmentation of open-air museums: Bridging buildings, artefacts and activities', *Nordisk Museologi*, 1 (1): 15–34.

Ciolfi, L., Fernström, M., Bannon, L.J., Deshpande, P., Gallagher, P., McGettrick, C., Quinn, N. and Shirley, S. (2007) 'The Shannon Portal installation: An example of interaction design for public places', *IEEE Computer*, July: 65–72.

Ciolfi, L., Bannon, L.J. and Fernström, M. (2008) 'Including visitor contributions in cultural heritage installations: Designing for participation', *Museum Management and Curatorship*, 23 (4): 353–365.

Desphande, P. (2007) *Analyzing Urban Spaces for Design of Interactive Installations From Architectural Design Perspective*, Technical Report UL-IDC-10-07. Limerick: Interaction Design Centre.

Dix, A. (2007) 'Designing for appropriation', in *Proceedings of HCI 2007*, 27–30. Swindon: British Computer Society.

Dodd, J. (1994) 'Whose museum is it anyway? Museum education and the community', in E. Hooper-Greenhill (ed.) *The Educational Role of the Museum*, London: Routledge.

Ferris, K., Bannon, L., Ciolfi, L., Gallagher, P., Hall, T. and Lennon, M. (2004) 'Shaping experiences in the Hunt Museum: A design case study', *Proceedings of DIS04*, 205–214. New York: ACM Press.

Giaccardi, E. (2005) 'Metadesign as an emergent design culture', *Leonardo*, 38 (4): 342–349.

Giaccardi, E. (2011) 'Things we value', *Interactions*, 18 (1): 17–21.

Giaccardi, E. and Palen, L. (2008) 'The social production of heritage through cross-media interaction: Making place for place-making', *International Journal of Heritage Studies*, 14 (3): 282–298.

Grabill, J.T., Pigg, S. and Wittenauer, K. (2009) 'Take two: A study of the co-creation of knowledge on museum 2.0 sites', in J. Trant and D. Bearman (eds) *Museums and the Web 2009: Proceedings*, Toronto: Archives & Museum Informatics. http://www.archimuse.com/mw2009/papers/grabill/grabill.html (accessed 10 May 2011).

Greenbaum, J. and Kyng, M. (1992) *Design at Work: Cooperative Design of Computer Systems*, Hillsdale, NJ: L. Erlbaum Associates.

Hall, T. and Bannon. L.J. (2006) 'Designing ubiquitous computing to enhance children's learning in Museums', *Journal of Computer Assisted Learning*, 22 (4): 231–243.

Hooper-Greenhill, E. (1992) *Museums and the Shaping of Knowledge*, London: Routledge.

Howe, J. (2006) 'The rise of crowdsourcing', *Wired Magazine*, 14 (14): 1–5.

Kyng, M. (1991) 'Designing for cooperation: Cooperating in design', *Communications of the ACM*, 34 (12): 65–73.

McLoughlin, M. (2008) 'The Recipe Station: Technology facilitating social interaction in a public environment', in *Proceedings of Create 2008*, 34–40. London: British Computer Society.

Salgado, M. (2009) 'Designing for an open museum: an exploration in content creation and sharing through interactive pieces', PhD dissertation, Helsinki, Finland: Aalto University.

Simon, N.K. (2010) *The Participatory Museum*, Santa Cruz, CA: Museum 2.0.

vom Lehn, D., Heath, C. and Hindmarsh, J. (2001) 'Exhibiting interaction: Conduct and collaboration in museums and galleries', *Symbolic Interaction*, 24 (2): 189–216.

Walker, K. (2008) 'Structuring visitor participation', in L. Tallon and K. Walker (eds) *Digital Technologies and the Museum Experience*, Plymouth: AltaMira Press.

Willis, P. (2000) *The Ethnographic Imagination*, Cambridge: Polity Press.

PART II
Public formation

5

REMEMBERING TOGETHER

Social media and the formation of the historical present

Roger I. Simon

It has become commonplace to comment on the fact that the posting of images, documents, experiential testimony and informative analysis on highly accessible and freely available forms of social media has enhanced the collective social memory of particular historical events. Yet more is at play in the changing landscape that informs cultural memory than an increase in the number of social media sites dispensing and/or distributing information about particular historical events. Starting from the premise that social media platforms offer new ways in which heritage practices constitute an arena of participation in the formation of collective memory, this chapter is concerned with the social implications of the digital technologies that offer a productive space for assembling diverse groups of people to engage in an interactive practice of *'remembering together'*. Such a practice is constituted as more than the sharing out of information. It also includes the public posting of (and response to) various experiences and understandings of, interests and investments in and questions and concerns about an event considered to be of historical significance. In this respect, practices of remembering together are indicative of what José van Dijck (2011: 402) calls 'the culture of connectivity . . . where perspectives, expressions, experiences and productions are increasingly mediated by social media'. As van Dijck has stressed, in this networked techno-culture, social norms manifest in patterns of interactions are inseparably enmeshed in technological systems commonly designed to inscribe particular legal and economic interests. Given the increasingly pervasive character of this culture of connectivity, it has become commonplace for people to use social media such as Facebook, Flickr and blogs to offer others (who are mostly strangers to each other) links, stories, comments and questions all addressed to the memory and legacies of a particular event. My concern in this chapter is to consider what such practices accomplish from the perspective of remembrance as a social process.

The social, educative and political implications of bringing of people to participate in practices of remembrance within digitally constituted public settings is still much understudied and consequently so is the development of future technologies designed to support or foster such activity (Lindley *et al.* 2009). In this respect, what I offer here is modest beginning of a critical approach to questions of the design of social media platforms, one that fully recognizes that the use of social media involve complex imbrications of historically, materially, embedded norms and desires with technologies designed to foster the possibility of new or renewed forms of human connection. The development of this approach necessitates an empirical and judicious consideration of how through social media people express and remake their relation to distinct historical events while coming to recognize not only their differences in regard to how an event is being remembered but, as well, how previously unacknowledged complementary interests and affinities are forged in shared practices of social memory. A basic premise of the considerations elaborated throughout this text is that the social realm of norms and desires does not entirely pre-exist actual practices of remembering, but in part is constituted in the very possibility of various modes and methods of remembrance. Remembrance is then not only a set of practices that reinforce existing social relations but also may alter them instantiating a transformation through the ongoing interchange of thoughts and affects, opinions and beliefs, attachments and antipathies (Simon and Ashley 2010).

In what follows I first give some attention to the outlines of a conceptual and methodological framework within which one might address the practice of remembering together. Then drawing on posts to sites devoted to the remembrance of the ongoing disaster of the Union Carbide gas leak in Bhopal on 3 December 1984, I provide examples of differing practices of 'remembering' along with a discussion of what these practices differently accomplish from the perspective of remembrance as a social process. Finally, I discuss what might one envision as to future possibilities of memory-work not only in regard to the disastrous Bhopal gas leak but other significant historical events. In this regard, attention will be given to several features that the design of future digital technologies might address in order to enhance these possibilities.

The practice of remembering together

It is important to distinguish the approach taken to the study of 'remembering together' from a significant strand of existing research in the area of human–computer interaction (HCI). Within this research framework, remembering together is construed as a practice through which a cluster of people collectively archive material that when subsequently retrieved might serve future purposes. Conceiving of remembering together on such terms is clearly consistent with the quite significant notion that every act of remembering is always already about a particular conception of the future. This idea is evident in the work of Nancy Van House and Elizabeth Churchill (2008) regarding the development of systems for digital memory capture, storage and retrieval. Their concerns are rooted in the evident point that what we will 'remember' (that is, retrieve) individually and collectively is primarily a matter of the choices made at the point of digital archiving. As there are limitations to what can be stored and what can be indexed and searched, decisions must be taken not only about what is to be archived (or not) but, as well, the technical and organizational procedures that will be used for accessing archival records. In this context, what is particularly important to note is that both the design of such storage and retrieval systems and the decisions made at the point of archiving are memory practices dependent on the anticipation of future needs. As Churchill and Ubois (2008:10) argue, the meaningful construction of collective and cultural memory depends on a curatorial logic of a 'prospective retrospective' understood as 'imagining now what we will want to remember in the future'. For designers of information systems, this translates into the challenge of anticipating and discerning in the present what set of memories will have future use value and what consequent processes will preserve and manage these memories so as to realize this value.

While the approach taken in this chapter is centrally concerned with the relation of remembrance and the future, it diverges considerably from the concerns of this 'prospective retrospective' logic. While the substance of this divergence will become evident as the argument unfolds, at this juncture there are a few points that should be kept in mind. While information systems designers typically focus on anticipating and discerning what set of memories need to be preserved, I am concerned with remembering as embodying more than a storage and retrieval problem. In this respect, it must be emphasized that remembering through digitally mediated platforms is a lived social practice that puts people in relation as they express and remake their connections to specific historical events and each other. How this remembering is done very much influences the form of collectivity constituted by these practices. In addition to this, it is crucially important to underscore that digital practices of remembering together constitute a collectivity that publically displays its own process of formation. On websites through which remembering together takes place, it is common to find displayed a record of – more or less – interactive posts that constitute an evolving public representation of the social syntax organizing this practice. Thus digital practices of remembering together have to be understood as productive of both a form of collective sociality *and* a visible scene of sociability. The importance of this duality will become evident in the analysis below. For the moment, I only wish to make the point that remembering together needs to be framed as a socially productive process that requires attention to how (within a particular technological apparatus) specific practices come to reflexively influence the future character of relations among those who collectively engage in this process. Attending to this reflexivity means considering how existing norms and desires structure practices of digital remembrance as well as how such practices structure these norms and desires. To engage in a critical study of remembering together so as to shed light not only on existing social media practices but as well on future possibilities, one must interweave two distinct but complementary lines of inquiry. The first of these is the empirical study of the character and implications of the forms of sociality dialogically produced by various practices of publically posting contributions to a site as well as reading and reflecting on a display of posts that have been made over a period of time. Such an inquiry is substantially different from studies of social media that focus on understanding individual user behavior in the context of group activity (Sas *et al.* 2009). It is grounded in a consideration of the way an assemblage of people and interactive technologies bring into presence the dissemination of and engagement with images and texts; in the process, forging a particular sense of collectivity and social solidarity. More precisely, what is at stake in such inquiry is an understanding that when practices of remembering together are extensive enough they constitute the *social accomplishment* of the formation of a public understood as a site of recognition, acknowledgment and reflection.[1] This notion of a public is a somewhat open, discursively informed, affectively charged scene of lateral identification among strangers. As such, it 'promises a certain experience of belonging and provides a complex of consolation, confirmation, discipline and discussion' about how to live in relation to the memory of a particular event whose collective significance is subject to continuous transformation (Berlant 2008a:viii). Taking this as a starting point, the initial empirical focus of a critical inquiry into such practices must be to document and clarify differences in the substance and character of the social accomplishments achieved by remembering together. But more is at stake than such an analysis. Needed as well is a form of immanent critique that would assess the implications of different forms of remembering together. This critique would not just register the contradictions and limitations of any given practice, but would also shed light on what it might mean to evoke the normative notion of remembering well in the face of demands made on collective practices of remembrance. While I will consider what such demands might be, at this juncture it is important to underscore that the intention of such an immanent critique is to address the question of what the practice of remembering could accomplish at the level of the social. More specifically, it is intended to address how diverse people might be with one another in the context of practices enacting a heightened attentiveness to the realities of past events and the consequences they have had on the lives of others both living and dead.

    If 'remembering together' is to be more than a collective archiving of personal experiences of those caught up in specific events, we must concern ourselves with its potential for being a digital space where diverse people address the significance of how various histories might dwell within their current and future ways of being together in the world. On such terms, remembrance is a question of history as a force of inhabitation, as stories we live with, that intertwine with our sense of limits and possibilities, hopes and fears, identities and distinctions (Simon 2005). This is why such an inquiry must proceed from the recognition that through the articulation of socially produced meanings and the expression of affective investments, when 'remembering together', social media participants are not only articulating personal encounters with the traces of a particular history but, as well, collectively redefining what might be understood as the temporal and spatial parameters of a historical event (Simon 2008). In this respect, a practice of 'remembering together' may be said to restructure historical consciousness, instituting a viscerally felt 'historical present'. Following Lauren Berlant (2008b), this historical present is not something constituted in the idiom of pasts and futures. It is not about 'the past's presence as *revenant*' (2008b: 858), a return of the past that haunts the present. Rather, as Berlant has noted, such a historical present resides as a core aspect of the present's ongoing condition and, as such, is 'a thing being made [and] lived through' (2008b: 848). It is not only infused with particular interests, emotions and desires but as well questions pertaining to ethics and politics.

Particularly if one is concerned with how people located differently, with very different histories, interact with each other when attending to memories of social injustice and mass violence, not only do we need to study various ways that practices of 'remembering together' preserve traces of the past but, as well, how they bear on the obligations inherent within the work of remembrance. In this magisterial work *Memory, History, Forgetting*, Paul Ricoeur (2006:89) argued that the 'duty of memory is the duty to do justice, through memories, to an other than the self'. While Ricoeur was clear that the virtue of justice necessitates turning toward otherness, he knew full well that coming to terms with what this actually meant for remembrance was no easy matter and certainly open to rhetorical abuse. I do not intend to settle the issue as to what would establish a 'just remembrance' nor will I be mapping the terrain of its possible alternatives. However, I want to adopt at least one tentative approach to thinking through how the demand for such a remembrance might be envisioned, working with the notion of remembering together as a practice subject to this duty of memory. This means I will be attentive to the degree to which particular forms of remembering together incorporate an interactive regard for the non-equivalent, singularity of others, particularly those who have been subjected to the violence of injustice. As Jean-Luc Nancy (2000) has emphasized, a sociality which respects the notion of the singularity of others (what he calls 'being-in-common' or 'being-with-one-another') is not something that can be totalized into union. In pursuit of the possibilities of a 'just remembrance', I will be concerned with how remembering together might do justice to the lives of people subjected to the actualities of injustice and systemic violence as these are made present through practices attentive to the thoughts and feelings of those attempting to understand the significance of such events.

Studying practices of remembering together it is not a matter of marking out a collective memory that defines what everyone should remember in order to ground a specific communal ethos in a particular set of memories. Rather it is to study remembering together so as to open the possibility of a transformative critique of existing remembrance practices. Such a critique would assess the way such practices limit possibilities as well as gesture toward future different ways of being with one another within a co-produced historical present. When applied to practices of remembering together through social media this means developing a critical understanding of the milieu of information systems and collectivized habits that structure the regularities of how social media are currently being used as well as the possibilities left unrealized by such practices.

Remembering together – The Union Carbide gas leak in Bhopal

To illustrate the issues discussed above, consider the social media practices through which people have attended to the event of the devastating, deadly gas leak that took place in a Union Carbide plant in Bhopal in the Indian state of Madhya Pradesh. This is an event that began over twenty-five years ago and that is still continuing today. Its trail of corporate culpability, inadequate attention to the medical and environmental consequences and government incompetency is the focus of an international solidarity movement drawing participation from people in India, Europe and North America. These transnational practices of remembrance and advocacy involve a quest for productive forms of sociability across political distances that carry the weight of colonialism and the reality of quite disparate material conditions. As such they present substantial challenges for an emergent cosmo-political social movement. Indeed, the digital practices of 'remembering Bhopal' are exemplary of a situation where in confronting the realities of difficult knowledge, various actors participate in acts of remembrance within divergent embodied histories and consequent different perspectives and interests (Lehrer et al. 2011).

During the evening of 2–3 December 1984, forty tons of lethal methyl isocyanate gas leaked from the Union Carbide plant situated in the densely populated old sector of the city of Bhopal. Over the twenty-five years since that evening, websites providing documented information and images addressing the causes and immediate and ongoing consequences of the leak have continued to proliferate. An example of such a site is the current entry for 'Bhopal disaster' on Wikipedia,[2] the first search result one would find using Google to locate information on the gas leak. This entry states that, initially, the official death toll was 2,259 but that subsequently the government of Madhya Pradesh confirmed a total of 3,787 deaths related to the gas release. The Wikipedia page also notes that other government agencies estimate 15,000 deaths, while still other estimates state that 3,000 died within weeks and that another 8,000 have since died from gas-related diseases. In addition, the entry references a 2006 government affidavit that stated the leak caused 558,125 injuries including 38,478 temporary partial and approximately 3,900 severely and permanently disabling injuries. Many of the websites providing basic information about the causes and effects of the gas leak also post images documenting the consequences of the deadly dispersion of methyl isocyanate. Additionally, these sites provide information regarding various and ongoing attempts over the last three decades to hold to account those responsible for the loss of life, the infliction of infirmities and the continuing pollution of the environment of old Bhopal. Information is often furnished about the non-governmental organizations that are providing ongoing support for those still suffering from the initial exposure to the lethal gas as well as well as to the toxic environment surrounding the adjacent, abandoned chemical plant. Taken together what these Internet sites clearly instantiate is that the disaster of the Union Carbide gas leak is ongoing and very much a part of historical present lived by a very large number of people even if, at times, some have attempted to render it a tragedy that one can securely place in 'the past'.

While a discussion of the manifold curatorial differences that exist among the various websites providing information about the Bhopal gas leak would be of interest in and of itself (for such discussion see Liu, this volume), my concern here is the social media practices that facilitate and encourage a variety of people to engage in an interactive process of 'remembering Bhopal'. Most commonly these practices have been instituted in the name of demanding and/or supporting efforts to afford justice to the victims and force action on cleaning up the toxic environment of the plant and the surrounding area. A prime example of such an effort has been that coordinated by the International Campaign for Justice in Bhopal (ICJB)[3] that has brought together Bhopalis with other Indians as well as people worldwide. In September of 2006, ICJB created a Facebook group called Students for Bhopal (later abbreviated SFB).[4] Reading the posts currently available on this site, one can consider how and with what consequences participation in this Facebook group instantiates a particular form of a practice of remembering together.

As of 18 January 2011, the SFB Facebook Group had 1,851 members. Between 11 October 2010 and 12 January 2011, the 'Wall' of the group's Facebook page contained a modest 29 posts.[5] As one might expect for an organization that is part of the ICJB, the substance of these posts contained information items informing people about upcoming activist events, exhortations intended to spur participation in ICJB activities and links to relevant print and video news items or newly released documentary material. There were a few comments on specific posts but these were primarily limited to brief expressions of 'thanks' or short statements of affirmation (e.g. 'Justice delayed is justice denied'). In the 'Discussion' section of the group's Facebook page there were eleven topics listed but only one with more than two posts, this being the topic 'Getting Involved'. It is worth considering the substance of the exchange in this thread. This discussion produced nineteen posts, three of which had been deleted. Of the remaining sixteen, one person contributed five times, the other eleven contributed one post each. These posts consisted of brief statements as to how they first heard about Bhopal disaster and what their response was when they did, what forms of actions are needed in the present in order to pursue justice and provide help for survivors, statements of what they intend to do in this regard in the near future, and suggestions as to how to raise awareness in others. There were also two posts providing personal stories regarding experiences in Bhopal, one told by a survivor of the gas leak. None of these posts replied to any other except for the person who contributed five posts, each of which was a response that provided advice and encouragement intended to foster activism.

What might we make of this activity? If we understand the character of the participation on this site as a set of social practices structured through a set of systematic relations among partial knowledges, investments, affects, norms and technologies, what specific notions of collectivity might these practices be accomplishing? It is evident that taken together these practices constitute a sequence of thematically related but relatively independent statements. The content of the majority of these posts are not contingent on the substance of previous ones. The result is a collection of material that lacks the interpersonal contingency of a conversation. Furthermore, given the relative paucity of information that the architecture of Facebook makes available about individuals who post comments to this site and given the character of the posts whether on the 'Wall' or in the thematic discussions, for the most part it doesn't particularly matter who said what. With a few exceptions (the convener of the site as well as the one individual who retells his experience of living through the gas leak), what is said on the SFB site could in principle be said by anyone participating in the evolving series of posts. While not holding identical views, from the point of view of the social practices that generate this collectivity, the individuals participating on this site could be seen as interchangeable as they remain dialogically independent of each other.

The above observations do not invalidate nor diminish the importance of the form of remembering together constituted by the practices on the Facebook pages of SFB. Despite the sequential, non-contingent collection of posts, this activity constituted the co-production of an attempt at a 'just remembrance' and its concomitant work of transforming the future in solidarity with the survivors of the industrial disaster in Bhopal (as well as interested members of a wider international community working toward similar ends). No doubt the SFB site has operated as a technology of 'affiliation, alignment and identification' (Dourish 2010:7). Most of the participants on the SFB site would recognize themselves and one another as participants in a common project that is best accomplished by 'remembering together' and 'standing with others' who, while not participating on the site, are committed to the goals of the ICJB. While such recognition is meaningful in and of itself, it is also carries considerable consolidating affect. This is affect mobilized in a setting that constitutes its own process of sociality as a locus of desire.

The sense of the sociality appearing on the SFB Facebook site publically foregrounds the affective attachments located in the sensibility of 'the common' produced by use of social media. Here is made manifest the importance of understanding practices of remembering together as productive of a visible scene of sociality whose relations are structured in a quite specific way. As the social syntax organizing this scene becomes apparent to all who access a site, in this respect the display of the practice of remembering together assumes the phantasmatic character. To evoke the notion of 'phantasy' here is not to suggest that remembering together is a site of illusion. Rather, the conception of phantasy I am referring to draws from Laplanche and Pontalis' (1986) elaboration of Freud's writing on this subject. Within the desire at work in this specific notion of fantasy (often demarcated by the 'ph' spelling), one does not pursue a particular object or sign but is caught up in the desire that underwrites an imaginative representation of oneself as participating in a scene (even if one cannot be assigned any fixed place in it).[6] What this means is that as remembering together manifests an evolving practice publically represented through social media, it develops into a scene that is itself the referent of a desire that is immanent in its sequence of contributions. For this reason the emotional world of the SFB is heightened not only by its subject matter but also its own process of formation. Given the extent of emotional continuity circulated in this always-in-formation public, it is clearly an intimate sphere that not only aspires to be a moral place but feels like one as well. The notion of the phantasmatic located in this sphere offers the position of a general subjectivity that serves the unifying convergence of collective social, legal and economic objectives. While this phantasmatic investment in the production of a particular sense of commonality may all too easily be disrupted by posts that introduce difference and disagreement, the non-contingent character of postings to the site strongly mitigates against such disruption.

What is socially accomplished by the posts on the SFB page is thus considerable. No doubt, such a practice of remembering together helps to secure the meaning and desire that informs aspects of the solidarity necessary for the articulation and pursuit of a set of common objectives. Nevertheless, it is important to consider in what ways this particular form of collective remembering might limit what stands as remembrance, particularly when such a practice is subjected to Ricoeur's aforementioned 'duty of memory'. Certainly one can consider the participants on the SFB site as an online community understood as a digitally interconnected group of people who recognize themselves as engaging in a shared, purposeful relation with one another (Kraut 2010). Most SFB participants would likely acknowledge that together they are undertaking a more or less common project pursuing a just remembrance of the Bhopal disaster. What remains to be considered, however, is the modality of being together constituted by participation on the SFB site. As I have indicated above, key in this respect is the non-contingent, relatively interchangeable character of the vast majority of the posts to this site. The significance of these characteristics can be more sharply drawn through an adaptation of aspects of Jean-Paul Sartre's (1976) notion of seriality. Sartre employed the term 'seriality' to designate a particular quality of social life and action. In considering this idea, Sartre's focus was various *forms* of collective experience and their implications for social and political life. This is quite different from seriality understood as a temporal framework such as that organizing a sequence of posts to a social media site. In Sartre's conception of a serial social form, individuals minimally relate to one another while pursuing habitual patterns of participation in regard to an object or institutionalized structure that brings them together. In such a form, each person acts more or less independently, pursuing one's interests and expressing one's thoughts, but always within a taken for granted milieu of action constituted by particular technologies as well as the collectivized habits that normalize specific ways of employing these technologies. While one's actions may take into account expectations of the behavior of others, in a serial social form people rarely if ever encounter and respond to each other. To borrow a phrase from Sherry Turkle's critique of HCI applications (2011), as a way of being-in-common, participants in a serial social form are 'alone together'.

In regard to any given set of normalized practices, practices that are usually taken for granted, one must consider not only what they socially accomplish but what social possibilities are occluded or constrained by them. Thus the importance of considering what a serial form of sociality closes off in regard to possible modes of 'being-in-common'. Given the clear marginalization of responsive, dialogical discourse within a serial form of communication, strikingly apparent in the sequences of SFB Facebook posts is the absence of the expression of uncertainty that might serve as an invitation to a collective exploration of a concern. There are no posts that express a sense of anxiety, ambivalence or curiosity, no problems are posed and no questions are articulated. One may certainly argue that on a site whose purpose is the evocation of the remembrance of the disaster of the gas leak and the mobilization of support of the ICJP, such expressions of uncertainty would be out of place. Perhaps this is just the point. There is a taken-for-grantedness to the form of communication on the SFB site produced within the seriality evident in its archive of posts. Indeed, to insert a sense of uncertainty in this evolving form of a public would likely disrupt the particular phantasmatic quality the space has generated. I am not at all suggesting that the expression (or, alternatively, 'confession') of various uncertainties is a prerequisite for acting in the service of justice. However, I do think it worth considering how various expressions of uncertainty might alter what a practice of remembering together might collectively accomplish.

To make in clear what is at stake in pointing to the absence of uncertainty on the SFB site, consider the contrasting interchange offered on a the blog 'Yes!' between the author of the blog 'marginalien' and someone variably posting as 'anonymous' or 'gt'.[7] The blog entry is dated Tuesday, 1 December 2009 and entitled 'Remembering Bhopal'. Below this title there appears a short text and a graphic image created by the blog's author (Figure 5.1).

The following exchange begins immediately below the image in Figure 5.1.

Anonymous: hi ms.mp thanQ 4 shaking [sic] us back to these sordid times. it infuri8s me to read all this – but what can we really do now to make a difference? gt

marginalien: I know what you mean about the helplessness and believe me, I am no cause-chasing candle-vigilista. But here are two thoughts: (1) remembering is the very least we can do. If we do nothing else, we must (I think) pass on links, post comments and share the memory of the horror of that time. (2) We can donate and inspire others to donate. I nearly always only do (1). That's what I've done this time too, i.e., by creating and posting my graphic. But every so often, a tipping point will be reached and I cross over into donation. So I figure it really does help to do (1) – because there will be others who have a similar life-cycle. Everyone needs a push. So the take home message here is: BE A PUSHER!!! At the very least.

Anonymous: ranting and raving helps no one except perhaps oneself – in the allusion that something has been done. donations – gosh 90% or even more of all donations never even reach the intended parties! i think one needs to garner support from some powerful international corporate lawyers who can chase the dow chemical scoundrels, make them pay the victims – and circumvent the greedy corrupt political bastards who always stay in the interception pathways gt

Remembering Bhopal

Please visit REMEMBER BHOPAL to leave your thoughts, your comments, your reminiscences of the Bhopal Gas Tragedy. The 25th anniversary of the world's worst industrial disaster starts on the night of the 3rd and continues for 72 hours.

Posted 1st December 2009 by marginalien

FIGURE 5.1 'Remembering Bhopal': blog entry from marginalien (posted on 1 December 2009)

marginalien: Nothing gets done when the culprits are wealthy and powerful. I believe it's important to realize that forgetting is part of how they get away with what they do. The least one can offer is the memory of an atrocious misdeed. What is happening with Bhopal is that it's been gradually forgotten under the slush of all the other misdeeds that have followed it and the numbing of our sensibilities as the daily accounts of fresh horrors build up. Today's newspaper (we get the Asian Age) did not so much as feature a headline on Bhopal on the front page!

marginalien: to add to what I said in my previous comment: gt, post the link to the I AM BHOPALI to as many people as you can.[8] And leave comments there (or at any of the other related sites). And don't forget.

Anonymous: have alerted a few folks. even got feedback. haven't 4go10. gt

marginalien: There's been so little traffic at that website … it's very sad. This is where I think we've got to recognize the worth of raving and ranting – in a world where the squeaking wheel gets greased, they are the squeakers. I am NOT good at raving/ranting and I resist 'hearing' those who do. So I guess I'm not good at either end of the spectrum. I think it's atrocious that Bhopal gets so little attention. Why is it so? In my opinion it's because there's a deep-seated cultural abhorrence towards criticizing 'home' and 'family'; many Indians transpose their feelings towards HOME/FAMILY onto the country they belong to – without thinking their feelings through. There has to be SOME reason why so few writers/artists/film-makers have chosen Bhopal as their subject! …

gt: i suppose there is a sense of apathy that you feel – and try to not let it ooze out. but certainly you are right in that it seems to be a 4go10 tragedy…… and the poor victims suffer doubly – with their afflictions and the fact that we, their brothers and sisters 4get them. i was alerted to a front page write up in the london times a few says [sic] ago – and i have also seen write ups in CNN – but shamefully very little in domestic indian papers. you might be correct in noting that indians dont feel com4table in openly criticising this…or is it in recognizing the futility of complaining? collective guilt? i cant get the london times link but the write up follows – i put it here because of its unusual nature and belief in humanity (something i don't share) gt

[At this point in the post gt places excerpt from the London *Times* which offers a story of a Bhopali family affected by the gas]

marginalien: Thanks for that gt – I think every little bit DOES make a difference. For instance, responding to your comments caused me to continue to think about and react to the situation – as a result of which I posted another item at that site. Like the writer of your London Times piece says, we just have to keep putting out messages. The item won't appear right away, maybe in a day.

The first thing one might notice about the above interchange is that when constrasted with the serial comments posted to the SFB site, it appears as a more dialogical sequence. While declarative statements are certainly made, there is a reflexive, responsive tone to the exchange in which problems are posed and uncertainties are expressed. What we see in this discourse is a scene in which two people, using a form of social media, publically engage each other through reflectively discussing practices of remembrance, asking questions, telling stories and rethinking not only what they know of an event but also how they have come to those understandings. Within the social syntax displayed by this exchange, one is offered a glimpse of a form of remembering together that accomplishes a quite different mode of social and political engagement. What organizes this engagement is something substantially divergent from the collective affirmation of a definite and distinct understanding of the disaster of the toxic gas leak and demands for justice in the wake of its consequence. And what makes it different is that what organizes the practice in the above dialogue is the sharing out of concerns, questions and perspectives. Unmistakably, this dialogue attends to the memories of a complex multifaceted event in way that presents remembrance as tied up with actions that address the demands for corporate accountability and the mitigation of suffering. Yet in doing this, the conversation cultivates a complex spirit of clarity and determination mixed with ambivalence and modesty. It is such complexity that makes it possible to pursue the remembrance of the event while initiating an ongoing reflective reconsideration of what remembrance might mean. In this regard, the practice of remembering together on marginalien's blog illustrates the accomplishment of a social form in which there is a mode of reading and responding that fosters a reflexive recognition of the limits of one's own knowledge and the ethically grounded acknowledgment of and curiosity about perspectives and experiences that are quite different from one's own. This dialogical social form of 'being-with' is no less phantasmatic than the seriality discussed earlier, although the phantasy presented in the syntax of this conversation is clearly of a different order from the desire embodied in a non-contingent, serial formation that evinces a greater degree of cohesion.

As stated above, the SFB site can be legitimately considered as a politically efficacious attempt at a 'just remembrance' and its concomitant work of transforming the future. Nevertheless, if we want to think through how one might foster practices of remembering together subject to the duty of memory, it is worth considering the terms on which the SFB site attempts to render a just remembrance. In saying this, I am underscoring the premise that justice is to be apprehended as something done (or is to be done). When Ricoeur (2006) writes that 'the duty of memory is the duty to do justice, through memories, to an other than the self', the central question becomes how others (particularly those who have died or continue to suffer) are addressed within practices of remembrance. As I have argued, a serial collectivity is realized in a way that diminishes the distinct character of those making up its composition. To the degree to which individual, non-contingent posts on the SFB site are functionally interchangeable, their difference from each other is inconsequential. What this non-contingent character of seriality means is that individuated posts are situated in relation to each other only to the extent that they posit a relation to corporate entity that constitutes the very reason for being of the SFB group: the collective figure of the dead and suffering of Bhopal. This form of remembrance is similar to the way national rituals constitute the memory of those, who in the service to their country, have been killed or maimed. A community of the living, dead and disabled is hailed in such a way that all its elements are representations of its national substance (Coward 2009:255). Such a corporatization of who and what is being remembered, while an emotionally powerful representation facilitating identification with those memorialized, risks a forgetting of the complexities of an event that has established the grounds for memory in the first place. This process of the simplification of memory allows singular death and suffering to be appropriated as symbolic elements in and for other collective struggles.

The remembering together evident on marginalien's blog constitutes very contrasting terms on which to pursue the possibility of a 'just remembrance'. What we glimpse on the blog is the prospect of a sociality constituted as a form of 'being-with' in which division and sharing, difference and relation are immanent to the form. To the extent that this is the case, remembrance is less unified. On these terms, what constitutes a just remembrance of the gas leak and its consequent devastation is somewhat less certain and certainly less easily appropriated as symbolic resource for other interests. In this sense it points us to a notion of remembrance that attempts to do justice by placing memory in the service of the singularity of the experiences of those who died in Bhopal or are still struggling to live in the aftermath of the exposure to toxic gas and the environmental contamination traceable to the decaying remains of the Union Carbide plant. This is not a matter of individuating either those being remembered or those doing the remembering. Rather, it is enacting a remembrance of what makes and preserves the singular as historically specific and, in doing so, illuminating the human dilemmas of a shared world. This necessary tension between the specific and the universal is inherent to a practice of just remembrance, a remembrance that necessarily must remain open to conversation and transformation.

Designing social media for a practice of remembering together

To this point, I have considered contrasting serial and dialogical modes through which the practice of remembering together may take place. These practices can be understood as differing ways of accomplishing the production of particular forms of sociality and their corresponding phantasmatic scenes embodying the desire manifest in one's imaginative projection into a given scene. Furthermore, as argued above, each practice of remembrance enacts the duty of memory in very different ways. Given the necessary circumscription of this text, I cannot provide an adequate account of the complex of factors determinative of these differences. However, it is important to note that the SFB Facebook page and marginalien's blog provide relative simple formats for receiving and displaying a sequence of posts (at best, allowing their segmentation into discussion topics). Given the sharp differences between the remembrance practices on each of the sites, it is clear that in this instance, differences in social media design did not account for the evident differences in use. Yet this observation in no way cancels the significance of the project of considering how digital and social technologies might encourage and cultivate particular ways of being-in-common, particularly if one views it as desirable to expand the range and complexity of the possible forms through which remembering together might take place. The significance of the differences in the modes of participation noted above underscore the importance of thinking through what is at stake in such differences and how technology might enhance the prospect of remembrance practices that enact what Hannah Arendt called 'the perspectival density of our shared world' (Curtis 1999:17). While the formation of memory structured by digital networks is infrangibly personal, social and technological, there is little question that thought should be given to how future software design might render a structure of possibility with the potential to support more dialogical forms of memory work. At the very least, this would entail developing software that would enhance the potential for practices of remembrance through which people might work through the significance of the past, sharing divisions and agreements, and informing and (re)forming their social and affective connections through a dialectical engagement with each other. The following is a brief indication of some of the concerns important to such considerations.

Certainly one implication of the discussion above is that the future design of social media that support remembering together could productively consider how such technologies are implicated in the participatory articulation of specific phantasmatic scenes. If the mode of remembering together on marginalien's blog is understood as exemplary of at least one desirable form of collective remembrance, design considerations might attend to the ways social media could draw out the specific phantasmatic character of this scene so as to enhance the desirable character of such participation. For instance, it is possible that the desire inherent in such a phantasmatic scene would be enhanced by practices of 'acknowledgment' (Cavell 2002) in which the conversation on a site displayed an openness and acceptance of the exposure enacted by others. Such acknowledgment would resist the temptation of immediate judgment as well as the tendency to all too quickly reduce another's experience as something graspable on the terms of one's own, habituated ways of viewing the world. Given that such social syntax would be desired and desirable, design considerations might explore ways of enhancing the possibility that posts to a site be attended to in way that makes it clear that the singularity of one's perspectives, interests, uncertainties and questions are genuinely considered and taken into account in the context of an evolving dialogical archive of contributions. Consider some of the design features that might be addressed in this regard.

When people engage in the practice of remembering together, conversations may be enriched by each participant having access to a multi-modal archive of relevant material that could be flexibly tagged, cross-referenced and queried. A social media site articulated with such an archive could be designed so that material was easily citable within the context of any individual post making it possible to refer to and access specific texts, images, audio files or videos. Further, since contributions to remembering together often include substantial expressions of affect, one might explore new ways of enhancing the capability of digital platforms in regard to communicating and storing multi-modal contributions wherein text would be supplemented by images and sound (including, for example, voice and/or music). With such capability, affect might be elicited that would enrich the communicative capacity of dialogue enacted on any given site. As well, given any archive of posts to a site, digital conversations could be enriched if the contents of these posts were meta-level and content searchable.

In addition to enriching the substance, searchability and range of materials on any given site, it would be interesting to consider how a phantasmatic scene of remembering might be enhanced by an application capable of fostering the specificities of acknowledgment. Design consideration could be given to software that would recognize when a given previous contribution was being referenced in a new post (even when not in a directly threaded response) and a notification of this sent to the person who posted the cited contribution. Furthermore, the phantasmatic character of a scene might be enhanced if people were able to express something of the questions and confusions they may have as they engage myriad narratives and images that pertain to a past event. Thus it would be worth exploring the possibility of semantic web applications to help fashion a platform that would aid people in recognizing what it is that they do not know about either a given event and/or the perspectives and experience of others in regard to this event. Drawing on archival sources, such an application could explore the absences in any given person's contributions to a site by placing the substance of these contributions into a relation with archived texts and images that would extend the information and understanding expressed by any one person's posts. This could be a way of legitimating the recognition of the limits of one's own knowledge and the importance of curiosity as well as the subsequent questions that might be pursued by responding to invitations to read or view new material pertinent to the thoughts a person had previously expressed. Another possibility would be to explore utilizing a form of human aided algorithmic curation that could recognize the similarities and differences between the informative and emotional substance of posts of various contributors. If this were possible, such an application could make this relation visible to an emergent digital public engaging in the work of collective remembering. Not only might such juxtapositions help provoke and inform thought regarding the integration of the past in the historical present but they also might serve as a basis for sending invitations to specific members to elaborate on the similarity or distinctiveness of their contributions.

What the cluster of design considerations above make clear is that to confine an understanding of social media to its existing forms limits the notion of how digitally mediated interactions might bring people together to work through how the past is to be made present in their lives. Collective remembering through social media holds the potential to be much more than the documenting and sharing of experiences in the aftermath of specific events and/or promoting actions in the face of events that have left a wake of suffering and death. This chapter has attempted to move the discussion of the importance of digitally mediated collective remembering in a different direction by considering what practices of remembrance might look like that encourage an ongoing conversation as to how and why past events still matter in our lives and how they form the very conditions for our actions in the present. To this extent, perhaps the designation of a digital platform as a form of 'social media' is beside the point. Much more significant is the question of how new information technologies can transform the question of 'heritage' into a practice of enacting an ongoing, informed conversation about how to fulfill Ricoeur's notion of the duty of memory.

Notes

1 The notion of public referenced here is taken from Warner (2002). For a recent paper applying Warner's notion of publics and counter-publics to social media practices see Lindtner *et al.* 2011.
2 Wikipedia entry on the 'Bhopal disaster': http://en.wikipedia.org/wiki/Bhopal_disaster (accessed 24 July 2011).
3 International Campaign for Justice in Bhopal (ICJB): http://bhopal.net/ (accessed 24 July 2011).

4 SFB   Facebook   group: http://www.facebook.com/group.php?gid=2206855545
   (accessed 24 July 2011).
5 As I began writing this chapter in mid January 2011, I decided to focus on the prior
   three months of regular postings to the SFB Facebook site. A 19 November 2011 visit to
   the site found that the discussion section had been removed.
6 As Laplanche and Pontalis state: 'The subject does not pursue the object or its sign: he
   appears caught up himself in the sequence of images. He forms no representation of the
   desired object, but is himself represented as participating in the scene although … he
   cannot be assigned any fixed place in it' (1986: 26).
7 marginalien's blog: http://marginalien.blogspot.com/2009/12/remembering-bhopal.
   html (accessed 18 July 2011).
8 marginalien is referring to the solidarity website *I Am A Bhopali*: http://rememberbhopal.
   wordpress.com/ (accessed 24 July 2011).

References

Berlant, L. (2008a) *The Female Complaint: The Unfinished Business of Sentimentality in American
   Culture*, Durham, NC: Duke University Press.
Berlant, L. (2008b) 'Intuitionists: History and the Affective Effect', *American Literary History*
   20 (4): 845–860.
Cavell, S. (2002) 'Knowing and Acknowledging', in S. Cavell, *Must We Mean What We Say?*
   Cambridge: Cambridge University Press.
Churchill, E. F. and Ubois, J. (2008) 'Designing for Digital Archives', *Interactions* 15 (2): 10–13.
Coward, M. (2009) 'Jean-Luc Nancy', in J. Edkins and N. Vaughan-Williams (eds) *Critical
   Theorists and International Relations*, London: Routledge.
Curtis, K. (1999) *Our Sense of the Real: Aesthetic Experience and Arendtian Politics*, Ithaca, NY:
   Cornell University Press.
Dourish, P. (2010) 'HCI and Environmental Sustainability: The Politics of Design and the
   Design of Politics', *Proceedings of DIS 2010*, 1–10. New York: ACM Press.
Kraut, B. (2010) 'Designing Online Communities From Theory', ICWSM online lecture.
   http://videolectures.net/icwsm2010_kraut_doc/ (accessed 24 July 2011).
Laplanche, J. and Pontalis, J.B. (1986) 'Fantasy and the Origins of Sexuality', in V. Burgin, J.
   Donald and K. Cora (eds) *Formations of Fantasy*, London: Methuen.
Lehrer, E., Milton, C. and Patterson, M. (2011) (eds) *Curating Difficult Knowledge: Violent Pasts
   in Public Places*, New York: Palgrave MacMillian.
Lindley, S.E., Durrant, A., Kirk, D. and Taylor, A.S. (2009) 'Collocated Social Practices
   Surrounding Photos, *International Journal of Human–Computer Studies*, 67 (12): 995–1004.
Lindtner, S., Chen, J., Hayes, G. R. and Dourish, P. (2011) 'Towards a Framework of Publics:
   Re-encountering Media Sharing and Its User', *ACM Transactions on Computer–Human
   Interaction*, 18 (21): 1–23.
Nancy, J.-L. (2000) *Being Singular Plural*, Stanford, CA: Stanford University Press.
Ricoeur, P. (2006) *Memory, History, Forgetting*, Chicago, IL: University of Chicago Press.
Sartre, J.-P. (1976) *Critique of Dialectical Reason, vol. 1, Theory of Practical Ensembles,* tr. Alan
   Sheridan-Smith, London: New Left Books. Reprinted in 2004, foreword by Fredric
   Jameson. London: Verso.
Sas, C., Dix, A., Hart, J. and Su, R. (2009) 'Emotional Experience on Facebook Site', *Proceedings
   of CHI EA 2009*, 4345–4350. New York: ACM Press.
Simon, R.I. (2005) *The Touch of the Past: Remembrance, Learning and Ethics*, New York: Palgrave
   Macmillan.

Simon, R.I. (2008) 'Altering the "Inner Life of the Culture": Monstrous Memory and the Persistence of 9/11', *The Review of Education, Pedagogy and Cultural Studies*, 30 (3): 352–374.

Simon, R.I. and Ashley, S. (2010) 'Heritage and Practices of Social Formation: Introduction', *International Journal of Heritage Studies*, 16 (4–5): 247–254.

Turkle, S. (2011) *Alone Together: Why We Expect More From Technology and Less From Each Other*, New York: Basic Books.

van Dijck, J. (2011) 'Flickr and the Culture of Connectivity: Sharing Views, Experiences, Memories,' *Memory Studies* 4(4): 401-415.

Van House, N. and Churchill, E.F. (2008) 'Technologies of Memory: Key Issues and Critical Perspectives', *Memory Studies*, 1 (3): 295–310.

Warner, M. (2002) *Public and Counterpublics*, New York: Zone Books.

6

HERITAGE KNOWLEDGE, SOCIAL MEDIA AND THE SUSTAINABILITY OF THE INTANGIBLE

Dagny Stuedahl and Christina Mörtberg

Introduction

The writing of this chapter started without a power adaptor. Being in a cottage in the mountains, hours away from the next Mac store, this loss of electrical power prompted a series of reflections on sustainable design of digital technologies for cultural heritage knowledge. The loss made it clear how knowledge creation is closely related to the physical tools used as well as to the whole apparatus of knowledge connected to these tools: the reflexive acts of cutting and pasting, the dynamics of using document map to keep track of the story told, the word check, spelling and grammar functions integrated in the software, and so on. Without power, can the digital and creative dynamics of cutting and pasting, changing sentences and swapping paragraphs be replaced with the diameter and the shape of the pen, and the hardness or softness of the lead in relation to the friction of the paper material?

The struggle to overcome the beast of the material is embedded in craft as well as in the knowledge traditions on which craft skills build. The translation of the craft of research writing from digital into physical form, which we experienced, builds an analogy to the translation of physical craft into digital forms when traditional boatbuilders are using digital technologies and social media to communicate their craft – the subject of this chapter.

Social media are expected to support online participation for co-creation and reflection on cultural heritage knowledge (Russo *et al.* 2010). Not only amateurs but also professionals are increasingly embracing social media places to strategically and discursively negotiate issues of authenticity, trust and power (Waterton 2010). With the advent of digital technologies and social media, it becomes crucial to understand if and how digital technologies and social media may sustain the negotiating with the material embedded in craft. This negotiation is connected to a vast amount of techniques and skills that distinguishes between alterations of the material in various variables and in relation to diverse contexts. We have to ask in what ways social media make visible in digital form how communities build and form the dynamics of traditional craft. Also, if and how digital technologies and social media may be designed to sustain the dynamics of continuity and change embedded in traditional craft knowledge.

Questioning the role of digital technology and social media to sustain the intangible heritage of traditional craft knowledge goes beyond issues of preservation and documentation. When digital technologies are introduced into the cultural heritage field, we are presented with a variety of questions that transgress questions of technology durability and maintenance into issues of continuity of heritage practices in digital forms. While the role of continuity is well known in heritage practices, we still need to understand the role that durability and maintenance of the technology might have for a sustainable design of digital cultural heritage. A craftsman's performed knowledge activities with materials and tools builds a good example of how the translation of traditional craft needs to address issues of durability, maintenance and continuity when craft knowledge and activities are represented, reorganized and shared in digital form.

Our studies are based on longitudinal collaboration with individuals and communities of traditional boatbuilding in Norway. In this chapter we describe two case studies that focus on translation of practical knowledge of traditional craft related to building wooden boats. Both cases are based on physical reconstructions of replicas of traditional Norwegian boats, one from Viking times and one from the Renaissance. Video recording and photo documentation are used in combination with social media communication to document the construction of the boat, the craft processes involved, and the questions and findings produced during the reconstruction process. The documentation captures how contemporary knowledge of traditional boatbuilding is used to interpret the excavated fragments from archaeological findings, and to build a hypothesis of the fragments missing. The cases demonstrate the cultural–material relations (Latour and Weibel 2005) in which traditional crafts, intangible knowledge traditions, and analogue and digital tools are entangled. While digital technologies and social media both provide new forms of interpretation and participation, these technologies also present challenges and limitations in regard to communicating and understanding the processes of continuity in the performances of making that are involved in craft. This is the tension we illustrate and discuss in this chapter.

Sustaining traditions and craft digitally

Craft has attracted a growing attention from researchers of history, anthropology and design, and has been the centre of recent discussion on experimental knowledge in creative disciplines (Niedderer 2009). We have currently seen a powerful re-emergence of craft especially in the young generation, whose 'net -political' tendencies provide craft to be distributed, molecular, appropriational and interconnected (von Bush 2010). An example is the 'technophilic' movement in the crafts, where crafters combine century-old techniques with digital technology (Shales 2008). Another example is the cultivation and intensification of skills and engagement of communities that emerges into forms such as 'craftism' (Greer 2008), where craft combines with activism by means of wikis and YouTube for sharing. There is a ongoing shift from positioning craft as a mode of education and paradigm of working (Dormer 1997; Greenhalgh 1997; Risatti 2007) to focusing on the individual skills of craft practices (Sennett 2008), its elusiveness and flexibility to create a relation between manual skills and the understanding of making, and relations between personal value and the hand and mind of the maker (Niedderer and Townsend 2010).

While not especially focused on safeguarding cultural heritage tradition *per se,* this re-emergence of craft does happen in parallel with a shift in the cultural heritage field. A former emphasis on conservation and preservation of architectural remains and physical artifacts is increasingly supplemented by recognition of the value of intangible traditions and a shift of focus towards understanding heritage as a totality of social activities and interpretation (Kirschenblatt-Gimblett 2004; Silberman 2008; see also Silberman and Purser, this volume). With this follows a growing acknowledgement of the claims of non-academic, non-governmental heritage stakeholders, such as community groups, indigenous people and ethnic minorities (Isar 2006; Berkaak 2010; Boswell 2011; Labadi 2011; Truscott 2011).

Issues of digital media related to these themes are labeled in two ways. The first label is 'digital cultural heritage' (Cameron and Kenderdine 2007; Brown 2007), and points to the challenges of digital technology when recreating cultural heritage in digital forms in different kinds of communities. Another label is 'new heritage' (Kalay *et al.* 2008), which points to the new practices that emerge with digital technologies, and the need to broaden the definition of the field to encompass the complexity of the social, political and economic issues that comes into play in contemporary heritage practices. The idea of new heritage points to production and reproduction of cultural heritage in the shift between analogue and digital media, and refers to Walter Benjamin's characteristics of mechanical reproduction as a removing of the objects away from their embeddedness within 'the fabric of tradition' (Benjamin 1969). As remarked by Jeff Malpas (2008), the recording and representation of cultural heritage artifacts, stories, tools and sites bring 'enormously increased reproductive and productive capacities' and alter the thing reproduced.

Several projects and research initiatives explore how databases and online archives may support communities to record and document intangible heritage such as oral traditions of indigenous knowledge (Witcomb 1997, 2003; Brown 2007; Cameron and Robinson 2007). Meanwhile, critical voices have pointed to the ways digital systems fail in allowing communities to make explicit its own context and knowledge – since digital systems are in danger of imposing a single unifying ontology rather than supporting diversity (Turnbull 2007). Further, several digital community projects build on traditional models of encyclopedic archives, which positions the presumption that knowledge can exist and be located through a priori ontological structure of metadata (Verran *et al.* 2007; van der Velden 2011).

To design digital technologies in ways that sustain communities and their intangible heritage of craft knowledge, therefore, requires taking into account a broad spectrum of cultural dynamics of communities as well as issues of the translation of practices from analogue into digital. This includes the heterogeneity of reflection, creativity and social activities involved in the entwined interpretation and reinterpretation of tangible and intangible cultural heritage (Kirschenblatt-Gimblett 2004). It also requires designing digital systems that sustain intangible heritage as whole systems of knowledge and reproduction (Kirschenblatt-Gimblett 2004; Giaccardi 2008). With this follows the need to provide a way for communities to make explicit interpretations and reflections in autonomous ways and in their own context (Turnbull 2007). To this goal, we need to ask what is created and what is lost when people use digital and social technologies as tools to sustain and share their cultural heritage practice, knowledge and traditions.

Cultural sustainability: durability, maintenance and continuity

The definition of sustainable development formulated in *Our Common Future* as a process 'that meets the needs of the present without compromising the ability of future generations to meet their own needs' (World Commission on Environment and Development 1987:43) has lost the powerful idea of intergenerational responsibility, or what Yudhishthir Raj Isar calls 'cultural learning' (Isar 2006). This has been reflected in the report *Our Creative Diversity* (World Commission on Culture and Development 1996) with an emphasis on the twofold process of discovery and understanding of cultural selves. Rather than asserting that cultures are fixed identities, Isar points out that people today are negotiating the boundaries of fluid, changing cultures. There is an imperative for a more active 'interculturalism' that provides opportunities for critical, even conflicted, exchanges between communities. Equally vital is also to articulate and mediate a sense of separate as well as shared spaces, where the relational and collective aspects of culture may be transformed and reconstructed (Isar 2006). Thus the notion of sustainability in the cultural heritage field addresses the ways we configure participation and communities as well as the way we configure sustainability.

The Brundtland Commission's focus on environmental responsibility, economic health and social equity has been criticized for its failure to take into account the cultural and spiritual dimensions of human life, as well as 'its lack of clarity about how an individual fits in the model as an active player' (Worts 2006: 157; see also Braidotti 2006). To meet with this ambiguity, cultural sustainability has been emerging as the fourth pillar of sustainable development (Hawkes 2001, 2006). Cultural sustainability emphasizes well-being, creativity, diversity and innovation, and the role of cultural vitality in communities as part of sustainable development. This cultural dimension is closely related to engagement, expression and dialogue, and focuses on diversity, creativity, expression as well as cultural practices, values, norms and beliefs as configured into models of community participation (Duxbury and Gillette 2007). Cultural sustainability of community participation in heritage matters is therefore highly dependent on how effectively the community functions as a centre for common, reciprocal reflection, self-assertion, productive questioning and historical awareness (Silberman 2007; see also Silberman and Purser, this volume), rather than on professional competencies, technology and rational planning. Sustainable forms of participation are therefore both a political challenge and a cultural process requiring continuity and perseverance among all actors involved. Their objectives of preservation, transmission and enrichment of cultural heritage have to be consciously shared by the active groups of a community (Varine 2006).

Barbara Kirchenblatt-Gimblett (2004) describes an example of this in the Japanese *shikinen sengu* tradition, where the reconstruction of the sacred shrine of Ise Jingu is performed every twenty years. In the process 'master carpenters pass on to apprentices their expert knowledge of how to put together the complex joint, using ancient and unfamiliar tools' (Kirschenblatt-Gimblett 2004: 59). This demonstrates how intangible cultural heritage is fundamentally based on cultural learning processes that involve people sharing their knowledge, skills and practice. While it may not be even necessary to preserve such cultural manifestations, Kirschenblatt-Gimblett argues that 'it is necessary to support the continuity of knowledge and skills, as well as the conditions for creating these objects' (Kirschenblatt-Gimblett 2004: 61).

When translated into digital representations, intangible heritage takes new forms that introduce new aspects of sustainability. We have to ask if the discussion of sustainable cultural heritage in digital forms is related to the durability of the digital technology, and the way software and systems preserve cultural heritage digitally. Or if sustainable design of digital cultural heritage also concerns the ways digital technologies may support maintenance of participation in communities of practice. We also see a third issue related to sustainability in digital cultural heritage, which brings focus to the way digital media support the dynamics of continuity and negotiation of tradition of cultural heritage knowledge. Our argument here is that in order to open a discussion on cultural sustainability in relation to digital and social technologies meant to support new heritage practices, we need to keep in mind all three aspects: durability, maintenance, but also continuity, and how they are related to each other.

Sustainability in design of digital technology

Discussions of sustainability in design have been given particular attention in relation to architecture and urban planning, industrial development, development of energy systems, and the exploration of novel research perspectives in interaction design. In these fields, sustainability has been usually discussed with a focus on social design and ecological design (Papanek 1972). In addition, sustainability has been discussed in relation to use, reuse, disposal and the material effects of interaction design (cf. Blevis 2006, 2007) as well as on concerns of facilitating the durability of information technology (IT) systems (cf. Braa *et al.* 2004; Byrne 2005). While the core focus for these discussions has been on material and technological principles, several alternative movements propose different perspectives and frameworks. One such movement is the 'slow design' movement (Hallnäs and Redström 2001; Redström 2001; Fuad-Luke 2002), which approaches issues of sustainable design by way of alternative commercial processes and ways of living. Another one is 'participatory design', where sustainable design is often defined as issues of balancing development, use and protection of a company's resources, goals and needs while accommodating future development potential (see Bødker et al. 2004).

We have in earlier research focused on the cultural dimension of sustainable design by arguing that aspects of continuity need to be considered in our understanding of how the designed artifacts are involved in meaningful practices (Mörtberg et al. 2010). In this chapter we build on this argument in our discussion on how the sustainable design of digital and social technologies can enhance intangible knowledge of traditional craftsmanship. As we will argue, the notion of cultural sustainability calls for sustainable development of documenting, archiving, sharing and negotiating heterogeneous heritage interpretations and embodied practices. A thoughtful approach to design (Löwgren and Stolterman 2005) would align such interpretations in ways that support the inherent dynamics of continuity as well as change. This approach to sustainable design goes beyond issues of preservation and safeguarding, and aims also to sustain negotiations of interpretation and reconstructions of cultural continuity in support of people's everyday heritage practices.

Making and passing on cultural patterns

Thinking about intangible heritage holistically rather than as an inventory brings forth several conceptual models. One is to frame cultural heritage as an ecology or a systemic living entity (Kirschenblatt-Gimblett 2004). This model captures intangible heritage, earlier called folklore, as existing in versions and variants rather than single, original and authoritative forms, and defines intangible heritage as created in performance rather than in tangible forms. This approach also points out that UNESCO's focus on vitality as the main criterion for designating heritage masterpieces can in fact pose a problem: 'if the phenomenon in question is truly vital, it does not need safeguarding; if it is almost dead, safeguarding will not help' (Kirschenblatt-Gimblett 2004: 56). Kirschenblatt-Gimblett's comment emphasizes the inherently procedural nature of culture, and that of people as performers and conscious, reflexive subjects. From this perspective, intangible heritage is not only embodied, but also inseparable from the dynamics of people's material and social worlds.

To point to objectives of designing digital and social technologies that support performative and reflexive aspects of traditional craft practices in sustainable ways, we need a framework that gives a space for technology in relation to heritage intended as living entity.

A useful framework is provided by Donna Haraway, which focuses on the material-semiotic character of 'collaborative practices for making and passing on culturally interesting patterns' (Haraway 1994: 70). She uses the cat's cradle string game as an active metaphor for her perspective on the performative relation between human and non-human actors that are relevant for our discussion. Cat's cradle has been played in numerous cultures and has a vast number of pattern variations. It starts with one player creating a string figure that is handed over to the next player to develop. The play continues by mutual constructions and reconstructions of patterns with the string, passed on between the players in co-creative ways, which emphasizes that knowledge is not a once-and-for-all given, but rooted somewhere and dependent of the embodied practices in which it is produced. The metaphor also points to knowledge as partial and inherently based on interpretation and reuse of physical, social and cultural elements. This approach is relevant for understanding digital cultural heritage knowledge as intersecting in negotiations, translations and production of knowledge that transgress the human and the technological as thought in isolation.

Digital sustainability of collaborative practices of interpretations

We contrast two cases of collaborative practices in Norwegian boatbuilding communities to discuss how digital and social technologies have been used in forms that cradle with durability, maintenance and continuity in different ways. In both cases digital and social technologies are used to document the craftsmen's knowledge, techniques and use of tools in ways that sustain and at the same time renew aspects of the craftsmen's knowledge in reconstructing boats from the past. The first case reveals the cradle of using and sharing video recording and photos as a means to capture and store community perspectives from diverging boat traditions and harness them for solving problems concerning a Viking boat reconstruction. The second case describes the use of mainstream social media, in this case blogging, as an alternative platform to invite communities to discussions concerning the reconstruction of a cargo boat from the fifteenth century. Both cases demonstrate how traditional craft tools and intangible heritage knowledge get entangled with digital and social technologies in different types of peer-to-peer sharing activities. The case studies also show how different publics are forming in the sharing of videos and photos versus the sharing taking place on a blog, and how these publics address issues of durability, maintenance and continuity in different ways.

Case 1: digital recording to capture and share community discussions of how to build a Viking boat replica

The first case concerns the reconstruction of the one of the three Gokstadboat found in the 1880s, together with the renowned Gokstad ship, in one of the biggest excavations from the Viking times in Norway. The ship was found with other two smaller boats similar to boats still used in western and northern Norway. These two boats were reconstructed in the 1930s, and since then have been exhibited in the

Viking Ship Museum in Oslo. The 150 pieces of the third boat have meanwhile been stored at the museum because of the many missing pieces and its incompleteness. The reconstruction of the third boat aimed at discussing the archaeological perspectives on which the former two reconstructions were based, and introduce craft knowledge of traditional wooden boats found in craftsmen communities today as an alternative departure point for understanding the boat. It also examined central presumptions in archaeology and ethnology related to the form and function of Viking boats. For example, one assumption was that boats in Viking times were symmetrical, with the same shape both front and back. Another assumption was that boats were constructed either to slide easily through water or to provide a large carrying capacity.

Terje, the ethnologist responsible for the reconstruction of the third Gokstadboat, emphasized the interpretative work that he and his boatbuilder had to perform while building first a cardboard model and then a full-scale replica of the boat (Figure 6.1). Terje defined this reconstruction as making a hypothesis in oak. The boat as hypothesis, rather than as a cultural heritage object to be interpreted as a text, is an assemblage of present activities and interpretations of traditional knowledge in craftsmanship as well of rowing and sailing (Planke 2005). The aim of using digital media to document the process was to record the discussion of alternative hypotheses, where the argument for the present understanding of traditional craftsmanship came to the fore. This interpretative level of reconstructions is normally lost when replicas are finished. Therefore, the aim of the reconstruction project was precisely to archive and communicate the negotiation of intangible heritage knowledge involved in understanding Viking boats.

We used video and audio recording to support the documentation of the physical activities of craftsmanship involved in the building of the boat and to find ways to communicate the process both online and in a museum exhibition (Stuedahl and Smørdal 2010, 2011). The first challenge was to adjust the use of digital media in order to successfully capture the activities performed in the reconstruction. Placing the video camera in one corner of the working zone, as we did initially, missed the details of handling the tools in relation to the wood. The best solution would have been to give the boatbuilder and Terje helmet-mounted video cameras that could record their hands while using the tools. However, we failed to find a solution that could capture the details of crafting activities and could work over the six months of the project. Additionally, we experienced challenges in finding audio recording methods that prevented the noise of the ax and the tools drowning out the discussions between the ethnologist and the craftsman. Terje, therefore, had to plan themes and discuss these with his partners relating to the camera, positioning the recording equipment, planning the activities, and forcing the discussion and decision-making process of the reconstruction to happen in front of the camera (Figure 6.2). All these adjusting and translating activities provide concrete examples of how digital media impact the content they purport to preserve in the reconstruction. The examples also emphasize how important parts of the performative and live interpretations of

FIGURE 6.1   Details of the reconstruction of the third Gokstadboat (cardboard and full-scale replica in oak). Photo © Terje Planke, Gokstadbåtprosjektet

traditional craftsmen's knowledge are lost when translated into digital forms (see also Bidwell and Winschiers-Theophilus, this volume).

In the end, we had to make a decision on whether the recordings should mainly document the collaborative process of reconstruction of the boat or the details of crafting activities. We decided to use the video documentation to focus on the trajectory of the reconstruction. We started with documenting the construction of the initial model by means of a translation of the original fragments of the excavated boat into cardboard pieces and then the filling out of the missing parts. In doing this, we documented the initial hypothesis of how the shape of the boat may have been. Later, we documented the process of using traditional craftsmanship to build the boat in oak and in full scale. For Terje, the use of digital video recording made it possible to fully concentrate on the reconstruction process, without having to make notes during the process. As the reconstruction was part of his own research on the dynamics of craft knowledge in Norwegian boatbuilding tradition, Terje used the

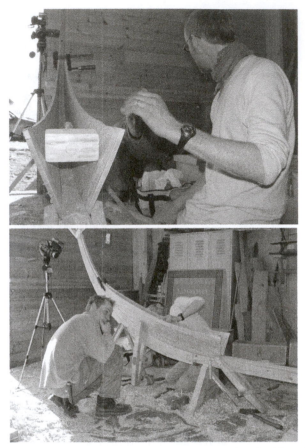

FIGURE 6.2   Video recording of the discussions between boatbuilders from different traditions. Photo © Terje Planke, Gokstadbåtprosjektet

video recordings as empirical research material. The dated recordings worked well as a visual diary of the reconstruction process, supplemented by photos of problems that emerged in relation to specific parts of the boat during the building process.

While the photos seemed to be used to cover the details of problems that appeared during the process, the video and audio recordings documented the negotiation of diverging craft interpretations between Terje and the boatbuilder, and between other boatbuilders invited from northern and west coast communities during the reconstruction. While the fifty hours of recordings reveal the slow and collaborative development of an understanding of the third Gokstadboat, it was difficult at times to properly document such a process. A good example is the four-hour recording of a discussion that took place when Terje and the boatbuilder brought the boat model to a well-known, elderly boatbuilder versed in the western boatbuilding tradition. The recording shows the three men pointing at different spots on the cardboard model and discussing themes that were difficult to understand for external listeners. However, the camera was too far from the model and failed to capture what they were indicating with their hands, and the sound was poor and did not help make sense of their gestures.

More significant problems surfaced when we attempted to store the digitally recorded material from the reconstruction process in durable ways and use it to communicate the reconstruction online and in an exhibition. We wanted to adopt the CIDOC Conceptual Reference Model (CRM), developed by the International Council of Museums (ICOM) Data Model Working Group. This metadata categorization standard is based on a large group of object-oriented categories describing the implicit and explicit relations of an item in a general semantic framework for cultural heritage information. Our idea was to use this standard to tag the recorded video material with themes and categories that would store the recorded material in relation to the issues and challenges of the craftsmen's knowledge that came into play in the reconstruction. For Terje, the object-oriented character of CIDOC and the event-based focus of this standard were quite challenging when used as framework for archiving fifty hours of video material. Categorizing the video recordings with CIDOC metadata demands that the reconstruction process is defined in discrete events – a demanding task since the reconstruction was based on ongoing interpretations based on 'trajectories' of events as well as sustained argumentations concerning the continuity of boatbuilding traditions (Stuedahl and Smørdal 2010; Mörtberg *et al.* 2010). As a solution, even though not optimal for search purposes, we decided to tag the video material with Terje's own categories.

Terje's endeavor to use the CIDOC CRM ontology to translate and communicate the fluid negotiation of intangible heritage interpretations is an example of how a cat's cradle interaction with digital technologies can freeze such negotiation. While digital recording supported Terje's cradle in discussing aspects of continuity with different communities, the CIDOC standard was going to introduce practices that did not support the game of his cradle. The framework of durability and maintenance embedded in CIDOC introduced a pattern that Terje could not relate to his practice.

Case 2: blogging to build open dialogue with communities

In this case we describe how the social features of blogging were explored to broaden participation of the communities involved in another reconstruction. The context of this reconstruction was a boatbuilding workshop organized at the Norwegian Maritime Museum with the goal of exhibiting the reconstruction activities of the boat as part of the museum exhibition program. The museum had the responsibility for an archaeological excavation in 2009 where fourteen boats from the fifteenth century were found in central Oslo. The reconstruction of the most complete boat, a cargo boat called Barcode 6 (BC6), was used by the museum to publicly demonstrate the importance of Norwegian boatbuilding traditions for understanding maritime history. This reconstruction was structured in very much the same way as the Gokstadboat reconstruction – involving local communities in workshops and visits, traveling between different regional traditions to explore different perspectives about the cargo boat, and discussing materials, methods and tools used in the Norwegian

FIGURE 6.3 Boatbuilder Lars writes a blog diary to communicate the reconstruction process and open a dialogue with communities of amateur and professionals in traditional boatbuilding and sailing. Photo © Idunn Sem, InterMedia

maritime Renaissance period. However, in this case, because the reconstruction was physically situated within the museum, communicating effectively with audiences and communities was particularly important.

The direct verbal communication with museum visitors in the open workshop was critical, but Terje (now working as conservator at the Norwegian Maritime Museum) was well aware of the potentials of using digital technologies to communicate with a wider audience as well as for involving geographically spread communities. In collaboration with him, we decided to open a blog as an online space for the activities occurring in the boatbuilding workshop. Lars, the boatbuilder engaged to build BC6, configured the blog into serving as a personal online dairy that documented the steps and challenges of the reconstruction and also as a place where to pose questions (Figure 6.3).

Lars wrote daily on the blog during the one-year process of building BC6. He used the blog to upload photos, videos and daily descriptions of the reconstruction process, and to articulate the puzzles, open questions and hypotheses that he encountered during the process (Figure 6.4). His texts were closely related to the published photos; sometimes he published a photo series that captured problems related to the boat or to the traditional tools he was using. Some video recordings show special events, such as the preparation of the tree trunks into sections as part of the preparation for building the boat. The blog entries were tagged with keywords related to the phases of the reconstruction; these tags coincide with parts of the boat (e.g. 1st–9th tables, nails, keel, sail) and with reflections, interpretations, questions to be answered, etc.

NORSK MARITIMT MUSEUM

BåtLab'en - for dokumentasjon, rekonstruksjon, og båtbygging

Stevner og kjøl fra BC-6 er prøvemontert i felt, etter at hele skroget er dokumentert og fjernet. Arkeologer ved NMM poserer

Start

Om Barcode 6

I båtlaben ved Norsk Maritimt Museum rekonstruerer vi arkeologiske funn og arbeider med dokumentasjon av norsk tradisjonsbåtbygging.

Båtlab'ens første prosjekt er å rekonstruere Barcode 6; et båtvrak som nylig ble gravd opp i Bjørvika i Oslo. Båten er fra slutten av 1500tallet, den er typisk østnorsk i formen, og båtene fra funnet kan betegnes som et "missing link" i vår forståelse av båtutviklingen i Norge.

Bloggen følger båtbyggerens arbeid med å rekonstruere båten som skalert modell og gjennom en fullskala rekonstruksjon. Båten skal sjøsettes sommeren 2011.

Siste kommentarer

Jørn Løset wrote...
Etter å ha sett på det bildet, så må jeg vel si meg enig i at det mest trolig er øksespor. Det ser...
Continue >>

Lars Stålegård / NMM wrote...
Det er ingen tvil om at fellingene er laget med øks, det ser vi på sporene. I et tidligere innlegg...
Continue >>

Jørn Løset wrote...
Hvordan vet dere at fellingene er gjort med øks, og ikke et annet redskap som f.eks. bandekniv...

torsdag 5. mai 2011
Mer om 3. omfar -problem, løsning og metode

Sitt ned, konsentrer deg og følg med nå:

Under arbeidet med 3. omfar hadde jeg noen problemer med legget ved målestasjon 2 og 3 (i baugen i føren). Målene - legg og bredder - er tatt ut fra modellen og tegningen, som er basert på 3D-oppmålingen av modellen. Ved stasjon 2 hadde vi notert oss et legg på 53 grader og ved stasjon 3, 80 cm bak stasjon 2, var legget 36 grader. Altså en forskjell på 17 grader på en strekning av 80 cm. Problemet var at jeg hadde vanskeligheter med å vri bordet så kraftig at jeg fikk riktig legg ved begge stasjoner. Spørsmålet ble : er målene riktige, er modellen korrekt tolket , eller er det jeg som må gjøre noe annerledes for å få det til i full skala ?

Vi startet med å dobbeltsjekke våre mål: Først kikket vi på modellen. Da vi har tatt vinkler direkte fra modellen har vi brukt en liten digital vinkelmåler som vi har plassert direkte på pappbordene. Det er relativt uproblematisk midt i båten, der bordene ikke skrår inn mot stevn. Men mot stevnene (som ved stasjon 2 og 3), der bordene skrår kraftig inn, er det ikke lett å plassere vinkelmåleren korrekt. Den skal stå eksakt i 90 graders vinkel mot kjølen, rett over målestasjonen, som er markert på kjølen. Ved oppmålingen har vi gjort dette på skjønn, men nå da vi ville sjekke at vi hadde gjort riktig la vi opp til en mer omfattende operasjon. Vi la opp en

FIGURE 6.4 Writing the blog gives boatbuilder Lars the opportunity to share his reflections during the reconstruction process. Photo © Idunn Sem, InterMedia

Lars openly invited visitors to the blog to become involved in conversation, commenting on the reconstruction development and decisions made in the workshop. Visitors to the blog also posed questions that either Lars or the community around the blog would answer. In short, the blog facilitated an exchange of ideas and interpretations with craftsman practitioners and with other involved communities, and it also offered insights into the interpretative reflections that a craftsman makes when handling fragments from former times.

On the blog, for example, Lars reflects on whether the boatbuilder from 1595 might have used templates to handle the strakes, since the timber seems to be sawn both by hand and by using some technical device. The following is an excerpt from the blog on 21 May 2011 (translated from Norwegian):

> 4th table is finished!
> The fourth strake is finished and we have started the fifth. Something worth mentioning from the 4th strake is that I now am aware of a problem that the builders for the BC6 probably had to handle in 1595. Either they had to do like I do today – by some extra effort working on the strakes. Or maybe this was no problem for them – if they built by using templates? Yes, that's right. I now keep the door open for the possibility that templates were used, as I wrote in some entries ago…

Understanding Lars' process of interpretation during the reconstruction of the boat requires some knowledge. As the excerpt demonstrates, the reader of the blog has to understand what a template is and how it may influence the sawing process, to make sense of Lars' reflections in shadowing the boatbuilder from the fifteenth century in his present reconstruction. The embodied knowledge to which the excerpt directs is easy to understand for those in the blog community that possess a similar practical knowledge. However, to non-professional but interested visitors, Lars' reflections reveal how he is using his own sense of craft continuity in exploring possible craft techniques in the past by reconstructing not only the boat, but also the professional rationales and decisions the craftsmen of the past probably made while building.

The blog built a public event around the activities in the workshop and the BC6 reconstruction, while at the same time creating a space for the community involved in the reconstruction to negotiate on continuity. From a perspective of durability and maintenance of the material documented and shared on the blog, the blogs helped understand the context of the reconstruction, showing the relation between archeological treatment of the pieces of the shipwreck, the conservation of the wooden pieces and the building of the replica. All these phases inform the craftsmanship knowledge that comes into play in the building of the boat. While much of this is covered by Lars in his writing, the blog entries do not always capture the conclusions that Lars initially made when he was inspecting the original wooden fragments, discussing with the archaeologists and the conservator, and building his preliminary interpretation of how the boat might have looked and functioned.

After BC6 was finished and launched on its maiden voyage, we have observed that the activity on the blog has now decreased dramatically. It is now time to solve the challenges of maintenance and durability of the dialogues and the documentation material on the blog. We see several challenges to maintain the blog and to reorganize the blog material into durable forms for future use. First, the blog is creating a timeline function that translates the process of the reconstruction mainly in relation to chronology. Using the blog as a documentation tool poses questions concerning temporality and durability of the documentation material: what kind of documentation material should be preserved? In what context should it be searchable? How should the temporal sequence of blog entries be archived?

The blog gives us a direct medium to communicate the boatbuilder's reflections and explorations of continuity during the reconstruction process as well as to involve participants and communities on several levels. But once the public event of the reconstruction is concluded, the temporality and day-to-day narrative fostered by the blog features introduce us to a new cradle. This cradle has to do with the durability and maintenance of event-based activitites, such as in our case. The social format of the blog gave an open space for communities to participate into the details of the reconstruction, but makes it harder to connect several entries and reflect upon their relations. This gives the reader of the BC6 blog just an oversight of the reconstruction process in the form of procedural documentation, and less insight in the knowledge building debates related to the continuity of boatbuilding craft.

Discussion

Social technologies are challenging traditional notions of how cultural heritage could and should be represented, interpreted and disseminated, and question what affordances and impact digital media offer to the content they purport to preserve and communicate (Kalay 2008). We also have to ask whether, and in what way, digital technologies and social media can have a role in providing tools for sustainably negotiating the cultural continuity of people's learned and developed knowledge, skills and creativity. In this context, the challenge for sustainable design is to create technologies that bring continuity to the negotiated, performed and changing character of intangible cultural heritage when re-manifested in digital forms. As we have seen in the two cases, craft people can easily configure video recording, online photography and blogging into their practices of sharing knowledge and skills. But they are also faced with the limitations of such technologies in that they only tenuously support the capturing of their performed skills (continuity), and because they require an extra level metadata annotation and editing (durability and maintenance) that calls for digital competencies outside their craft. The two case studies demonstrate how using different technologies provide diverse opportunities for physical, social and cultural interpretations, and thus for knowledge sharing and building. The cases also show that the rootedness and cultural embeddedness of the craftsman's knowledge about traditional boats is no longer 'within the fabric of tradition' when translated into digital form, because it is separated from its place of practice. However, social media tools in particular (in our case, blogging) seem to have the potential to contribute to cultural sustainability as long as they are used to explore, negotiate and reflect upon the continuity and dynamics of intangible heritage.

Our aim in this chapter has been to open a discussion on how issues of cultural sustainability can be addressed in the design of digital and social technologies. We have discussed notions of sustainability in relation to the use of technologies for the documentation and sharing of the intangible heritage of traditional craftsmanship. We have focused on the role of durability and maintenance of digital technologies as well as the importance of social media in supporting processes of continuity. We have questioned the practices that emerge from digital and social technologies when used to sustain intangible heritage knowledge, and highlighted the affordances and constraints that such technologies bring to the translation of intangible heritage into digital forms.

When talking about sustainable design of digital and social technologies for cultural heritage, we must ask how the intersection between the durability and maintenance of technology can be considered in relation to the continuity of cultural heritage practices as well as in relation to the revitalization and enhancement of cultural heritage participation. When we observe craftsmanship in action and we see how craft cradles can be translated into digital form, it seems that important elements of the whole system of knowledge performed through craft activities are lost. The two cases demonstrate that designing for the cultural sustainability of intangible heritage is primarily an issue of sustaining the social dimension of heritage practice through shared spaces for negotiating interpretations. Even though translation into digital forms (i.e. through video recording) fragmented and narrowed the process of reconstructing boats, blogging built a social space where the community might reflect on aspects of the reconstruction processes, to the benefit also of the general public. Sustaining the continuity of embodied knowledge, the place-based traditions, and in our cases the relationships between the logics of diverse traditions of boats, also entails non-digital ways. While the blog offered a tool to chronologically access the details and interpretations concerning the reconstruction process, continuity seemed to take place somewhere else. This temporal character of social media communication poses a challenge to the durability and maintenance of intangible heritage. Being aware of and accountable for these limits is fundamental to the sustainable design of digital technologies for cultural heritage.

Social media have a role to play in supporting the social dimension of sustaining and renewing cultural heritage continuity. But they require thoughtful and honest design. Social media cannot substitute the embodied performance of intangible cultural heritage practice, but can involve stakeholders from different communities and audiences in the revitalization of heritage by providing a space for communication, dialogue and negotiation. This requires an approach to the design of digital and social technologies that focuses on sustaining both the continuity and vital diversity of people's intangible heritage practices, while taking into account the entanglements of online and offline technology in producing and reproducing embodied heritage knowledge.

References

Benjamin, W. (1969; orig. pub. 1936) *The Work of Art in the Age of Mechanical Reproduction*, in W. Benjamin, *Illuminations*, New York: Shocken Books.

Berkaak, O. (2010) *UNESCOs konvensjon om vern av den immaterielle kulturarven – en analyse [UNESCO's Convention for the Safeguarding of the Intangible Cultural Heritage – An Analysis]*. Oslo, Norway: The Norwegian UNESCO Commission.

Blevis, E. (2006) 'Advancing Sustainable Interaction Design: Two Perspectives on Material Effects', *Design Philosophy Papers* #04, Crow's Nest, Queensland: Team D/E/S. http://www.desphilosophy.com/dpp/home.html (accessed 21 November 2011).

Blevis, E. (2007) 'Sustainable Interaction Design: Invention & Disposal, Renewal and Reuse', in *Proceedings of CHI 2007*, 503–512. New York: ACM Press.

Bødker, K., Kensing, F. and Simonsen, J. (2004). *Participatory IT Design. Designing for Business and Workplace Realities*, Cambridge, MA: MIT Press.

Boswell, R. (2011) 'Challenges to Sustaining Intangible Cultural Heritage', *Heritage & Society*, 4 (1): 119–124.

Braa, J., Monteiro, E. and Sahay, S. (2004) 'Networks of Action: Sustainable Health Information Systems Across Developing Countries', *MIS Quarterly*, 28 (3): 337–362.

Braidotti, R. (2006) *Transpositions on Nomadic Ethics*, Cambridge: Polity Press.

Brown, D. (2007) 'Te Ahu Hiko: Digital Cultural Heritage and Indigenous Objects, People and Environments', in F. Cameron and S. Kenderdine (eds) *Theorizing Digital Cultural Heritage: A Critical Discourse*, Cambridge, MA: MIT Press.

Byrne, E. (2005) 'Using Action Research in Information Systems Design to Address Change: A South African Health Information Systems Case Study', in *Proceedings of the 2005 Annual Research Conference of the South African Institute of Computer Scientists and Information Technologists on IT Research in Developing Countries SAICSIT '05*, White River, South Africa: 131–141.

Cameron, F. and Kenderdine, S. (eds) (2007) *Theorizing Digital Cultural Heritage: A Critical Discourse*, Cambridge, MA: MIT Press.

Cameron, F. and Robinson, H. (2007) 'Digital Knowledgescapes: Cultural, Theoretical, Practical, and Usage Issues Facing Museum Collection Databases in a Digital Epoch', in F. Cameron and S. Kenderdine (eds) (2007) *Theorizing Digital Cultural Heritage: A Critical Discourse*, Cambridge, MA: MIT Press.

Dormer, P. (ed.) (1997) *The Culture of Craft*, Manchester: Manchester University Press.

Duxbury, N. and Gillette, E. (2007) *Culture as a Key Dimension of Sustainability: Exploring Concepts, Themes, and Models*, Working Paper No 1, Creative City Network of Canada, Centre of Expertise on Culture and Communities. http://www.cultureandcommunities.ca/downloads/WP1-Culture-Sustainability.pdf (access 21 November 2011).

Fuad-Luke, A. (2002) '"Slow Design": A paradigm Shift in Design Philosophy?' in *Proceedings of Developments of Design*, Bangalore: Thinkcycle.

Giaccardi, E. (2008) 'Cross-Media Interaction for the Virtual Museum: Reconnecting to Natural Heritage in Boulder, Colorado', in Y.E. Kalay, T. Kvan and J. Affleck (eds) *New Heritage: New Media and Cultural Heritage*, London: Routledge.

Greenhalgh, P. (1997) 'The History of Craft', in P. Dormer (ed.) *The Culture of Craft*, Manchester: Manchester University Press.

Greer, B. (2008) *Knitting for Good; A Guide to Creating Personal, Social and Political Change, Stitch by Stitch*, Boston, MA: Trumpeter.

Hallnäs, L. and Redström, J. (2001) 'Slow Technology: Designing for Reflection', *Personal and Ubiquitous Computing*, 5 (3): 201–212.

Haraway, D.J. (1994) 'A Game of Cat's Cradle: Science Studies, Feminist Theory, Cultural Studies', *Configurations* 1: 59–71.

Hawkes, J. (2001) *The Fourth Pillar of Sustainability: Culture's Essential Role in Public Planning*, Melbourne: The Cultural Development Network.

Hawkes, J. (2006) 'Why Should I Care?' *Museums & Social Issues*, 1 (2): 239–247.

Isar, Y.R. (2006) 'Sustainability Needs Cultural Learning', *Museums & Social Issues*, 1 (2): 219–223.

Kalay, Y.E. (2008) 'Introduction: Preserving Cultural Heritage Through Digital Media', in Y.E. Kalay, T. Kvan and J. Affleck (eds) *New Heritage: New Media and Cultural Heritage*, London: Routledge.

Kalay, Y.E., Kvan, T. and Affleck, J. (2008) *New Heritage: New Media and Cultural Heritage*, London: Routledge.

Kirschenblatt-Gimblett, B. (2004) 'Intangible Heritage as Metacultural Production', *Museum International*, 56 (1–2): 52–65.

Labadi, S. (2011) 'Intangible Heritage and Sustainable Development: Realistic Outcome or Wishful Thinking?' *Heritage & Society*, 4 (1): 119–124.

Latour, B. and Weibel, P. (eds) (2005) *Making Things Public*, Cambridge, MA: MIT Press.

Löwgren, J. and Stolterman, E. (2005) *Thoughtful Interaction Design*, Cambridge, MA: MIT Press.

Malpas, J. (2008) 'Cultural Heritage in the Age of New Media', in Y.E. Kalay, T. Kvan and J. Affleck (eds) *New Heritage: New Media and Cultural Heritage*, London: Routledge.

Mörtberg, C., Stuedahl, D. and Elovaara, P. (2010) 'Designing for Sustainable Ways of Living with Technologies', in I. Wagner, T. Bratteteig and D. Stuedahl (eds) *Exploring Digital Design: Multi-Disciplinary Design Practices*, London: Springer Verlag.

Niedderer, K. (2009) 'The Culture and Politics of Knowledge in Design Research: How to Develop Discipline Specific Methodologies', paper presented at Design & Cultures. 5th Annual Design Research Conference, Spokane, WA: Washington State University.

Niedderer, K. and Townsend, K. (2010) 'Craft Research and Its Context: Editorial', *Craft Research* 1: 3–10.

Papanek, V. (1972) *Design for the Real World*, London: Thames & Hudson.

Planke, T. (2005) 'Feltarbeid I fortiden' ['Fieldwork in the past'], in *Kulturvitenskap i felt. Metodiske og pedagogiske erfaringer* [*Cultural Science in the Field. Methodological and Pedagogical Experiences*]. Kristiansand. Høyskoleforlaget.

Redström, J. (2001) 'Designing everyday computational things', PhD dissertation, Department of Informatics, Gothenburg University, Sweden.

Risatti, H. (2007) *A Theory of Craft: Function and Aesthetic Expression*, Chapel Hill, NC: University of North Carolina Press.

Russo, A., Watkins, J., Kelly, L., Chan, S. (2010) 'Participatory Communication with Social Media', *Curator: The Museum Journal* 51(1): 21–31.

Sennett, R. (2008) *The Craftsman*, London: Penguin Books.

Shales, E. (2008) 'Technophilic Craft', *American Craft Magazine*, 68: 2. http://www.americancraftmag.org/article.php?id=1615 (accessed 22 November 2011).

Silberman, N. (2007) 'Sustainable Heritage? Public Archaeological Interpretation and the Marketed Past', in Y. Hamilakis and P. Duke (eds) *Archaeology and Capitalism: From Ethics to Politics*, Walnut Creek, CA: Left Coast Press.

Silberman, N. (2008) 'Chasing the Unicorn? The Quest for "Essence" in Digital Heritage', in Y.E. Kalay, T. Kvan and J. Affleck (eds) *New Heritage: New Media and Cultural Heritage*, London: Routledge.

Stuedahl, D. and Smørdal, O. (2010) 'Design as Alignment of Modalities', in A. Morrison (ed.) *Inside Multimodal Composition*, Cresshill, NJ: Hampton Press.

Stuedahl, D. and Smørdal, O. (2011) '"Designing for Young Visitors": Co-composition of Doubts in Cultural Historical Exhibitions', *Computers and Composition*, 28 (3): 215–223.

Truscott, M.C. (2011) 'Peopling Places, Storying Spaces: Heritage Sustaining Human Development?' *Heritage & Society*, 4 (1): 125–134.

Turnbull, D. (2007) 'Maps Narratives and Trails: Performativity, Hodology and Distributed Knowledges in Complex Adaptive Systems – An Approach to Emergent Mapping', *Geographical Research*, 45(2): 140–149.

Varine, H. (2006) 'Ecomuseology and Sustainable Development', *Museums & Social Issues*, 1 (2): 225–233.

Velden, M. van der (2011) 'When Knowledges Meet: Wikipedia and Other Stories from the Contact Zone', in G. Lovink and N. Tkacz (eds) *Critical Point of View: A Wikipedia Reader*, Amsterdam: Institute of Network Cultures.

Verran, H., Cristie, M., Anbins-King, B., van Weeren, T. and Yunupingu, W. (2007) 'Designing Digital Knowledge Management Tools with Aboriginal Australians', *Digital Creativity*, 18 (3): 129–142.

von Bush, O. (2010) 'Exploring Net Political Craft: From Collective to Connective', *Craft Research* 1: 113–124.

Waterton, E. (2010) 'The Advent of New Digital Technologies', *Museum Management and Curatorship*, 25 (1): 5–11.

Witcomb, A. (1997) 'On the Side of the Object: An Alternative Approach to Debates About Ideas, Objects and Museums' *Museum Management and Curatorship*, 16(4): 383–399.

Witcomb, A. (2003) *Re-Imagining the Museum: Beyond the Mausoleum*, London: Routledge.

World Commission on Culture and Development (1996) *Our Creative Diversity*, Brussels: UNESCO Publishing.

World Commission on Environment and Development (1987) *Our Common Future*, Oxford: Oxford University Press.

Worts, D. (2006) 'Fostering a Culture of Sustainability', *Museums & Social Issues*, 1 (2) 151–173.

7

CONNECTING TO EVERYDAY PRACTICES

Experiences from the Digital Natives exhibition

Ole Sejer Iversen and Rachel Charlotte Smith

Introduction

Museums have traditionally been seen as formal places for heritage preservation and displays that connect us to history. They provide the public with authoritative historical and cultural knowledge and act as civic educational spaces of reflection about the past, made meaningful in the present (Macdonald 2003; Bennett 2004). While these cultural institutions have acted as important 'bearers' of heritage and identity, they often ignore the dialogical aspects of people's social practices that take place inside and indeed beyond their walls (Handler and Gable 1997). Our approach sees the mission of a museum as one fundamentally concerned with transforming and enriching our understandings, perspectives and visions of the world as they relate to past, present and future experiences. We are particularly concerned with the role of the museum as a connector, creating meanings between contemporary cultural practices and people's everyday lives. Embedded in this mission is the fundamental challenge of bringing together, exploring and harmonizing what arise at the intersection between audiences' everyday practices and what people experience, value and construct as heritage. We see this challenge as one of exploring connections – that is, addressing the potential issues and designs that may link heritage matters to the everyday lives of particular audiences through concrete exhibition projects.

These connections between heritage and audiences' everyday lives are neither given nor stable, rather they emerge through dialogue and interaction. In this chapter, we suggest that mainstream social media services for user generated content and social networking sites can contribute to reconnecting audiences' everyday practices to heritage matters in the museum, reinforcing the museum as a place for ongoing reflections on the past and novel understandings of the present and future. We present experiences from a research project, the Digital Natives exhibition held at the Aarhus Centre for Contemporary Art in December 2010, in which social media was designed as an integral part of the exhibition to connect the museum space with audiences' everyday practices and experiences. Findings from Digital Natives provide new insight into the qualities of social media in support of heritage dialogue in museum spaces. These findings challenge conventional conceptions of the museum institution, and encourage us to rethink understandings and constructions of cultural heritage through new paradigms of communication and interaction.

Technology-supported heritage communication

The study of digital technologies in cultural heritage communication is a well-established research field. Concerned with issues of interactivity in exhibition spaces, numerous studies within the area of Computer-Supported Cooperative Work (CSCW) have addressed the role of digital technologies in shaping the museum visit, and explored such issues as visitor participation (Heath and Lehn 2008), learning (Pierroux et al. 2007) and social interaction (Heath et al. 2005). These contributions reflect the wider concern for providing new ways for visitors to engage with exhibition spaces. Part of this challenge is to create exhibition spaces based on dialogue, which frame the visitors as resourceful individuals and groups that can be invited to participate actively in the museum (see Hooper-Greenhill 2001). In this respect, a number of contributions have explored the potential of ubiquitous technologies in exhibition spaces, in the form of augmented reality (Woods et al. 2004; Wojciechowski et al. 2004), context aware museum guides (see Raptis et al. 2005; see also Wakkary et al. this volume), and various forms of mixed reality that blend physical and digital materials inside the exhibition space (Hall et al. 2002; Sparacino 2004; Ferris et al. 2004) as well as outside the museum (Dähne and Karigiannis 2002).

Recently, researchers have explored the potential of social technology frameworks for supporting intangible cultural heritage.[1] Dynamic expressions of traditional and contemporary 'living heritage' have been achieved through supporting collective memories (Taylor and Cheverest 2009), storytelling (Leder et al. 2010; see also Speed, this volume), crisis related grassroots heritage (Liu, this volume), and shared experiences of heritage sites (Giaccardi and Palen 2008). Research in social media within the heritage sector, however, has been conducted mostly in relation to institutional heritage practices (Giaccardi, this volume). A large of body of research on new media in museums is concerned, for example, with identifying how museums can use social technologies as new virtual and distributed platforms of communications, connecting and engaging with audiences outside these institutions, thereby extending the museum space (Deshpande et al. 2007; Arvantis 2010; Galani and Chalmers 2010; see also Russo, this volume).

While we acknowledge these characteristics of social technology in support of an extension of the museum space, we are more focused on exploring how the use of social media inside the museum space can create a renewed 'connectedness' between audiences' everyday practices and matters of heritage in the context of particular exhibitions. Our emphasis is on the living, intangible aspects of contemporary cultural knowledge, skills and practices in combination with a sensitivity to the physical and anchored space of the museum. Ciolfi (this volume) describes how she has facilitated visitors' personal contributions to an interactive exhibition at the Hunt Museum, Limerick, by combining interactive media and social technology in the unique context of the physical space of the museum. Her aim was to create opportunities for visitors' to shape the content of the exhibition and offer their personal interpretations of museum objects, thus facilitating audience participation and reflection. Following this line of work, we perceive the central role of new media technologies in museums not merely as a means of creating audience engagement in curated narratives. Rather, our concern is the extent to which social technologies can vitalize and renew the role of the museum as a hub for reflecting and constructing a sense of heritage, by connecting people's everyday lives and experiences to concrete exhibition spaces.

(Re)connecting audiences and the museum through social media

By social media we refer to digital technologies that support online and user-generated content, ranging from social networking, online media sharing and locative media to social tagging, microblogging, etc. These media are by definition participatory and dialogical forms of communication and engagement that create social interaction and co-create cultural meanings in intersections between virtual and real, local and global environments (Kaplan and Haenlein 2010). According to Castells (2010), museums in the information era can act as important cultural connectors of time and space. By using information and communication technologies, museums have the capacity to articulate fragments of real and virtual environments, and develop hybrid forms of cultural communication. As such, social media in particular, in their capacity of cultural 'connectors' of social practices that take place across different times and spaces, can play a vital role in transforming the museum into a place of dialogue and interaction. These 'connectors' can have several dimensions: in time (they can support either synchronous or asynchronous forms of communication and dialogue) and in space (they can be either socially and physically co-located or distributed). Hence, the forms of social dialogue that we refer to can take various forms, but are all characterized by being established through emergent and transient social spaces and dialogue. And here the museum can play a role as a connector of these various forms of times and spaces, and of the cultural knowledge and practices they represent.

As Giaccardi (2011) argues, social media are having a profound impact in terms of social practice, public formation and sense of place, creating new opportunities for people to experience and engage with both historical matters and emerging practices of heritage. Social media and networked forms of communication reflect social practices that *already exist* as part of people's everyday lives and experiences. People actively create everyday experiences within and through the communication paradigm of social media. This creates a model of communication based on engagement and dialogue that is rooted in particular and situated everyday practices. Thus, social media can be actively used as both a means for and a model of communication and interaction emphasizing engagement and dialogue. Social media are dialogic by nature and allow for meanings and experiences to be co-created and recreated within and through ongoing dialogues. This can forge new connections between museums and audiences, and break down the formal dichotomies between 'official' and 'living' expressions of heritage by acknowledging people's authority in co-creating and defining what is exhibited. Ultimately, this use of social media creates a framework in which we can bring the 'connectedness' *from* our everyday social and living heritage practices *into* the museum, and create new dynamic spaces for cultural experiences and communication.

The institutionalization of cultural heritage has a profound impact on our sense of heritage. Intangible cultural heritage *per se* connects everyday social practices and heritage matters within ongoing cultural processes. But whereas these connections are subtle, informal and emerging processes of shared meaning-making that extend over time and space, formal heritage representations in museums tend to carve out more formal and authoritative knowledge and stories, freezing the emerging and co-constructed nature and experience of cultural heritage (Kirschenblatt-Gimblett 1998; West 2010). Thus, the space for living heritage inside the museum traditionally has been limited, restricting visitors' practices and engagement with broader matters of heritage. Our goal is to shift this dynamic to create extended spaces and experiences of living heritage in the exhibition space of the museum.

Because we consider the exhibition as a specific space for creating dialogical experiences and connections between matters of heritage and audience's everyday lives, in our work the intersections between heritage, exhibition space and audience's social practices no longer rely on linear models of communication about the past. On the contrary, they depend on ongoing dialogue, negotiation and social participation in the present, with each exhibition becoming a vehicle for creating and transforming new understandings and experiences of ongoing cultural processes and connections. In this way, the exhibition space becomes a place for creating two-way connections between *heritage matters* and *exhibition space* on one side, and between *exhibition space* and *audiences' everyday social practices* on the other side. The 'connectedness' and dual process of communication between these three elements allow for a strong focus on the role of the audience, with the goal of enriching their situated engagement, their contribution to meaningful experiences in the exhibition space, and their extended role in defining, negotiating and co-creating understandings and conceptions of cultural heritage. This expanded role of the audience revitalizes the connection between institutionalized and living forms of heritage, and underlines the dialogical and negotiated nature of all cultural processes. In this way, active audience engagement is not the end goal in itself, but merely a means in the process of renewing the connection between audiences' everyday practices and matters of heritage.

Social media can serve the purpose of reconnecting everyday life and heritage matters inside the museum space, by reinforcing the everyday practices and experiences that people bring to the exhibition space. In its capacity of involving people in situated, dialogic micro-acts of communication and activity, social media can contribute to enriching the qualitative relations between audiences, exhibition space and heritage. In other words, the overall challenge is not so much how to use social or interactive technologies in support of institutional museum practices, but rather to rethink the language, design and conception of cultural heritage communication in relation to digital technologies and contemporary digital cultures. In the following sections, we will describe the Digital Natives exhibition, and how we used social media as a means of creating novel connections between audiences and matters of heritage inside the museum space.

The Digital Natives exhibition

Digital Natives is a research and exhibition experiment exploring the intersections of cultural heritage, participatory design and new interactive technologies. The project experimented with possible new futures and innovations of cultural heritage communication. It involved creative collaboration between a group of young people, anthropologists, architects and interaction designers through an extended period of nine months. The project focused on 'digital natives', the new generation of people born in the digital era, who are surrounded by new media and information technologies, and whose life worlds are said to depart from that of previous generations both mentally, socially and culturally (Prensky 2001; Ito 2009). The aim of Digital Natives was to create an exhibition in collaboration with a group of digital natives to explore and express their lives and cultures in a local museum setting. The resulting exhibition explored these young people's everyday cultures, identities and communication practices, and also experimented with new ways of representing and interacting with them in the context of a concrete museum exhibition.

The project was explorative in nature, actively interweaving understandings and boundaries between cultural heritage, contemporary digital cultures and new interactive technologies through the design process as well as in the final exhibition. The aim was to create new modes of communication and engagement that would create dialogical spaces and novel connections between museum space, exhibition and audiences. For this mission, it was central that the possible statements or arguments concerning the exhibition subject(s) emerged *through*, not prior to, the collaborative design process and the dialogical exhibition format. Therefore, we were concerned with integrating the voices, concerns and perspectives of our exhibition subjects (i.e. the digital natives), academic researchers, museum and design professionals, and audiences through the entire process up to the closing of the exhibition. The Digital Natives project was carried out by the Center for Digital Urban Living,[2] Aarhus University, Denmark, in collaboration with a number of external partners, including the Center for Advanced Visualization and Interaction (CAVI), The Alexandra Institute, Innovation Lab and the Moesgaard Museum. The Digital Natives exhibition was held at Aarhus Center for Contemporary Art in December 2010. Four interactive installations were created for the exhibition, which focused on the everyday lives and social practices of the seven young natives (aged 16–19) variously involved in the project. All installations had a strong focus on social media and interaction design, and on crossing the boundaries between art, culture, technology and people. In this chapter, we describe the four installations of the exhibition: Google My Head, DJ Station, Portraits and Digital Sea to illustrate by examples how we used social media to create new experiences and dialogic connections through the exhibition.

Google My Head

Google My Head is an interactive tabletop installation connected to a 72" Evoluce One liquid crystal display (LCD) multi-touch display (Figure 7.1). In the Google My Head installation, audiences were encouraged to browse in a repository of digital natives' online and mobile updates, pictures and videos continuously posted and displayed on the multi-touch display.[3] While browsing through the digital traces from various social media services, audiences were confronted with the task of completing the sentence 'Digital Natives are: ...'. They could choose up to four utterances, pictures or videos that caught their interest and supported the completion of their argument or sentence. The chosen samples were stored in a docking placed at each narrow end of the table. When clicking on a small icon on the dock, an onscreen keyboard would display and allow the audience to complete the sentence with statements such as 'Digital Natives are "creative"', 'Digital Natives are

FIGURE 7.1   The Google My Head installation, Aarhus Center for Contemporary Art, Denmark. Photo © Matthew Charnock

"egocentric and spoiled"', 'Digital Natives are "no different than others"', 'Digital Natives are "gorgeous"' or 'Digital Natives are "belligerent"'. These statements were stored in a database and displayed as a part of the Digital Natives exhibition on two 22" touch screens located near to the interactive tabletop. Here, visitors could see the utterances made by themselves as well as others, and explore the kind of digital material that had been associated to support the statement. Moreover, visitors could respond to the statement by pushing a 'like' or 'dislike' button on the touch screens, adding their score to the total number of likes and dislikes for each utterance.

Google My Head illustrates and represents the vast amounts of fragmented information and communication that exist in the lives of digital natives. The social traces in the repository were selected by the young natives themselves, as were the visible tags combining these elements across various media platforms. Audiences were able to browse and select these materials following their personal interests and to create new connections and statements about digital natives. In this way, using the form and language of social media, audiences were invited to explore the everyday life and cultures of digital natives, and to contribute to their emerging understanding through the exhibition.

DJ Station

DJ Station is an interactive audiovisual installation using on a tangible user interface based on fiducial tracking[4] (Figure 7.2). DJ Station allowed audiences to interact with the musical universe of the seven digital natives involved in the project, while getting

FIGURE 7.2   The DJ Station, Aarhus Center for Contemporary Art, Denmark. Photo © Matthew Charnock

first-hand experience with the remix and mash-up cultures that are hallmarks of the new digital generations. Each young native was represented in the installation by a cube with visible fiduciary markers, which played musical loops when placed on the table surface. Each cube represented one digital native's musical taste, and each side of the cube contained a unique loop co-produced with the person in question. Flipping the cube to a new side played a new loop, while rotating the cube controlled the volume of the loop. Another range of coloured cubes contained unique audio effects that could be applied to the musical loops. The closer an 'effect cube' was placed to a 'loop cube', the more reverb would be applied to that loop. By placing more musical cubes on the table and applying effects to them dynamically, the user could combine and alter loops and create complex mash-ups. In addition to these features, visual images depicting the seven digital natives gathered around their respective musical cubes on the table surface and interacted with images from the other cubes. The tracks created by the audience were streamed live on the exhibition's website.[5]

DJ Station created an audiovisual universe for exploring and interacting with the digital natives through their personal musical landscape. The language built into the installation was based directly on the remix and mash-up cultures of social media. It also focused on the profound importance of music for digital generations, who continuously stream, modify and reproduce music through online services such as YouTube, iTunes, MySpace, GrooveShark and music-producing software. The installation invited audiences to take part in cultural constructions and appropriations of digital music by encouraging them to actively engage with the cubes, mixing and remixing unique tracks from the existing loops and materials. Each visitor became his/her own DJ, creating music both singlehandedly and socially (while engaging with other visitors), and contributing to the global production and distribution of music.

Portraits

Portraits is an artistic interactive video installation that invites participants to explore the world of a girl and her passion for books, and a boy and his fondness for photography (Figure 7.3). The films were personal and aesthetic accounts created by two young girls from the Digital Natives project, and gave an intimate glimpse into the dreams, values and self-representations of the young digital generation. Visual representations were not represented as a forward-moving timeline. Rather they were accessible as fragmented clips with which audiences could interact. Tracking the audience with infrared cameras, the intensity of their movements controlled the timing and selection of clips, playback speed and coloring of the visuals. Thus, from an experiential perspective, Portraits provided a dynamic range of possibilities for audiences to explore the visual portraits of the installation.

Portraits was back-projected onto a large 2 × 3 metre semi-transparent alto-glass screen.[6] A subtle poetic soundtrack accompanied the visuals. A mirror was mounted opposite the screen, and high black walls surrounded the installation. This

FIGURE 7.3 A still image from Portraits, Aarhus Center for Contemporary Art, Denmark. Photo © Stine Nørgaard Andersen

constructed a secluded and intimate area allowing the audience a private experience of the visual portraits. With minimal guidance or explanation, the room became an experiential pocket feeding upon the engagement and curiosity of the audience. What audiences were able to explore were not merely aesthetic representations of the digital natives. Rather they explored the ongoing digital and visual practices of production, reproduction and consumption in which young digital generations are involved – practices in which self-expression, identity and meanings are constantly negotiated, constructed and reworked. Being a direct visual representation by and of the 'natives' themselves, the installation thus opened additional, possible nuances and interpretations.

Digital Sea

Digital Sea is an interactive floor-projection installation allowing audiences to explore digital materials from various media and mobile platforms that, like in Google My Head, represent the young digital natives in the project (Figure 7.4). Facebook updates, photos, short message service (SMS) messages and videos linked to the Google My Head installation float randomly on the floor, and the audience can activate fragments according to their interest by physically standing on them. Audience movements are tracked with ceiling mounted cameras and chosen materials are enlarged on the floor, with related materials from the 'sea' surfacing at the same time and surrounding the visitor. With its blue graphical shades, swivels and well-effects, the 5 × 3 metre Digital Sea was visually and aesthetically prominent and functioned as the physical and 'virtual' center of the exhibition. It was connected

FIGURE 7.4 The Digital Sea installation, Aarhus Center for Contemporary Art, Denmark. Photo © Matthew Charnock

to the other installations, with activity in other parts of the exhibition influencing what would appear in the sea. When audiences were active in Portraits, images from the films would surface on the floor. Likewise, materials used in Google My Head would be flushed into the sea for other audiences to explore.

Digital Sea represented the infinite grid of digital connections constructed across various media platforms in the daily lives of digital generations. Fragmented materials were preselected by the young natives and placed in different categories (my pictures, family, school, Roskilde Festival, Japanese manga, demonstration, random, etc.) to represent their personal interests, values, experiences and digital practices. When activating specific images on the floor, audiences could access fragmented narratives about the everyday lives of the young digital natives involved in the project, as they were represented through and distributed across the social media and digital platforms used.

Experiences from the Digital Natives exhibition

All four installations in Digital Natives invited audiences to explore and interact through individual experiences as well as social engagement. In Google My Head, people browsed the large amounts of digital materials by playing with the multi-touch function of the table, becoming acquainted with the opportunities created through the interface. Visitors selected materials according to their personal interests, and gradually became more focused in their search when prompted with the question 'Digital natives are ...'. The selection process forged a kind of in-situ curation, where audiences created their own micro-stories about the exhibition subject. Whether they commented on a particular image from someone's computer game, a text message concerning fascination for Japanese manga, or saw several materials as reflecting characteristics of a whole digital generation, was entirely up to them. However, being prompted to make a statement on the basis of authentic materials made them reflect upon the 'natives' as well as their own relation to digital 'nativeness' in new ways.

Once statements were sent to the two screens, they were made visible to other audiences who could respond to their argument. In this manner the communication and dialogue was instantaneous and collective, creating social engagement between the participants at the installation, who were able to negotiate what characterized the exhibition subject(s) and how to capture this in brief comments. The situated concern of the audience was no longer the museum's authored narrative to them as audiences, but rather visitors' own stories, contributions and reflections about the subject of the exhibition and their relations to them. Through a series of actions, selections, reflections and communicative acts, audiences related the specific content and issues of the exhibited materials to their personal understandings and everyday lives, and then contributed these reflections to the collective narrative of the exhibition. In this way, Google My Head created modes of engagement and interaction that encouraged participation and dialogue between individual visitors as well as with potentially much larger and unknown audiences. Using and mimicking the language of social media – browsing, selecting, commenting and posting – the installation created hybrid and living connections between the exhibition subject(s) and the audiences' everyday lives.

Whereas Google My Head was reflective and intellectual in focus, DJ Station was playful and creative in its expression (Figures 7.5 and 7.6). People explored the DJ Station by placing different cubes on the table, turning and adjusting them, while gradually making sense of the various functions combining the musical loops and the visual universe of the installation. Creating their own tracks and music, visitors playfully mixed, sampled and explored various unique strands and styles of music. The loops on each cube contained musical styles, from techno to ambient beats, rock, heavy metal and acoustic sounds. This variation allowed audiences to reflect upon contemporary musical trends and to choose and navigate in the materials according to their own taste, while experimenting with combinations and mash-ups of otherwise disparate musical genres. Many audiences spent extensive time at the installation – often more than thirty minutes – creating music in small groups of two to three people, but also often engaging with up to six or eight people at a time. As the functions and possibilities of the installation were discovered, they were shared among fellow visitors or passed on to new arriving guests, thus creating dialogue and transfer of personal experiences between various groups of audiences. Audiences enjoyed the explorative and creative freedom that the installation afforded them and the feeling of creating something both unique and cool. In this way, DJ Station allowed the audience to gain insight into the contemporary musical life of young people, and offered an opportunity to experience and become part of the social and cultural processes and practices surrounding these musical universes.

FIGURE 7.5 The DJ Station emphasizes playful interaction. Photo © Matthew Charnock

FIGURE 7.6 The Google My Head installation prompts reflection among visitors. Photo © Stine Nørgaard Andersen

Entering the Portraits installation was in many ways a different experience from the other installations. Audiences expected to be able to assess the function and rationale of the installation almost immediately, but its more hidden agenda prompted another type of visitor exploration. Some explored the visuals on the screen, while others faced their own image in the mirror. Some were disorientated by the subtle means of interaction and feedback. However, most audiences took time to gradually explore the space and the clues they received from their own physical movements and interactions. As a result of this process, and due to the secluded layout of the installation, many visitors experienced an unexpected closeness with the personal universe of the girl and the boy, and the possibility of almost physically entering into their world. When facing the mirror, they could actually experience themselves *as part of* this other universe – a world they could affect and that allowed their own experiences and movements to be included into it.

The Portraits installation challenged the audience, questioning their personal boundaries and relationship with the two characters represented. The fragmented visuals and the hidden technological means of engaging with the installation both contrasted stereotypical conceptions of 'digital natives' and challenged conventional uses of computer interaction. Here, the subtle use of technology afforded a reflective and artistic experience of the exhibition subject. What did it mean to be a digital native? Did they exist at all, or where they just like the rest of us? How did a girl's passion for books represented in a dream-like universe fit into the picture at all? The voices and personal perspectives of the young creators were implicitly moulded into the installation, giving the audience an intimate window into their private spheres. On the other hand, audiences became situated curators of the representations as well as subjective co-creators of their own experiences. This created a range of personalized experiences that were both emotional and reflective, and for many gave a sincere and 'unfiltered' feeling of connecting directly with the universe and characters in the installation.

Digital Sea also used the physical space and layout of the exhibition. But in contrast to the secluded experiential space of Portraits, Digital Sea was open, inclusive and explorative. Audiences were immediately attracted to and curious about the sea, and gathered around it both before and after exploring the rest of the exhibition. Many audiences walked, danced and jumped on the floor, showed each other images and materials that caught their attention, and commented on their experiences. Visitors experienced the floating materials and their own physical interaction with the sea as a novel way of representing and gaining insight into the world of other people. The connections of Digital Sea to the other installations (created through images from other installations reappearing in the sea) gave the audience a subtle sense of familiarity and overarching coherency in the exhibition. The visual aesthetics of the installation attracted audiences into the centre of the exhibition, while the physicality of walking on the installation prompted a relaxed and informal atmosphere between audiences. Audiences related not only to the tracing of materials on the floor, but also to their own actions in relation to other audiences. This transformed the space of Digital Natives into a social arena for interaction and dialogue between audiences.

Again, the language, layout and physicality of the installation created the experience of being an expressive part of the exhibition.

Through Google My Head, DJ Station, Portraits and Digital Sea, audiences connected with the cultural universe of a specific group of people through their physical, social and emotional engagements. In each case the underlying language, or DNA, of social media was the key to creating the connections and dialogical spaces between contemporary matters of heritage and the everyday lives and practices of particular audiences. This intertwined space for co-creation and experience clearly allowed the audience to gain an important role in the exhibition, revealing new personal perspectives, narratives and connections through physical gestures, individual choices and social engagement. Formal or authoritative knowledge about the exhibition subjects was never constructed through the exhibition design. Rather, sporadic fragments, possible connections and arbitrary meanings were ingrained in the actual installations and the representations of materials – materials that the exhibition subjects themselves had a decisive role in framing, selecting and co-producing.

Each installation demanded the involvement and reflections of the audience in order to create meaningful experiences. These experiences were created precisely at the meeting point between matters of cultural heritage, the language and design of the installation, and the active involvement of the audience. Those visitors who did not involve themselves, but relied on traditional conventions of distanced gaze in the museum space, experienced difficulties in engaging with the installations and the potential meanings and experiences they contained. As a result, some visitors experienced the technology as a barrier for getting *inside*, *behind* or *beyond* the surface of the installations. But framed within the language and experience of social media, and in Bakhtin's (1981) sense of dialogical communication, there was no experience *outside* this engagement and involvement, and each experience was created in unique moments of dialogue and interaction inside the actual exhibition space.

Expanding understanding and use of social media in exhibitions

An important aim of the Digital Natives project was to investigate how the use of social media and interactive technology could support 'connectedness' between audiences' everyday practices and heritage, at the museum. The four installations were developed on the premises that all of them should promote participation and forge co-experiences and co-creation within the physical space of the museum exhibition. In doing so, we expanded the conventional qualities of social media by exploring different combinations of 'modes' of engagements (i.e. the way audiences engage in the museum experience) and the 'means' of engagements (i.e. the way audiences interact with social media), thus leading to four different applications of social media in each of the installations.

Google My Head and DJ Station illustrate two ends of a continuum in the mode of engagement, ranging from reflective engagement to playful engagement. Whereas Google My Head encouraged audiences to reflect on the material shown on the tabletop and select different utterances and materials to support personal statements,

DJ Station encouraged audiences to play with the digital cubes in a trial and error activity that explored possible musical loops and effects as they were placed on the table. Both Google My Head and DJ Station are installations in which symbols and representations were manipulated to spur either reflection or playfulness. In contrast, Portraits and Digital Sea explored how a different approach to the audiences' means of engagement would affect the use of social media. In both installations, kinesthetic interaction played an important role in the audience's experience and conception of the museum exhibition and space. In Digital Sea, audiences were encouraged physically to browse through different materials using their feet to select among the materials in the sea. In Portraits, the interaction between the audience and the installation was reconciled in the body movement that took place in front of the projection screen. The dialogue between audiences was conducted as performative acts in which different body movements articulated an experience and interpretation of the installation. But whereas Portraits spurred a reflective mode of engagement, Digital Sea was a walk-up-and-use installation that encouraged the audience to playfully interact with it. In this way, each installation represents a unique take on the interrelation and connectedness between the heritage subject, audiences' involvement, and the exhibition space.

The four installations provide valuable insights into the potential role of social media in opening up and shaping new audiences' roles and experiences at the museum. In the Digital Natives exhibition, the language and nature of social media transformed conventional museum communication into interaction and dialogical acts. Social media can resourcefully support diverse individual and social experiences – from playful and reflective, to kinesthetic and intellectual – and it can forge dialogic participation and engagement in the museum space. Integrating social media with interactive technologies in exhibitions can create more inclusive and non-hierarchical spaces for cultural experiences and expressions. This prompts both curators and audiences to constantly challenge and contribute to emerging constructions and conceptions of cultural heritage, and questions the role of museum institutions and their connection to people's everyday lives.

Conclusion

As we have demonstrated, social media can support various types of dialogic and co-created engagement between audiences and exhibitions. The focus on connectedness between audiences' everyday practices and heritage in dialogical exhibition spaces does not merely concern questions of how museums can effectively use new technological platforms, but more importantly how the generic language and culture of social media can initiate a transformation of the museum *per se*. From our experiences with the Digital Natives exhibition, this transformation is particularly evident in three areas.

First, the use of social media to emphasize audiences' everyday practices brings about a shift in perspective from communicating authored narratives of heritage, to designing frameworks and media platforms for collective reflection and dialogue.

This promotes novel ways of constructing knowledge about the past, and new ways of including cultural issues and fragmented storytelling into ongoing experiences and constructions of cultural heritage. Our experiences from Digital Natives show us that the transformation of museum communication from more or less linear knowledge transfer to more exploratory and collective micro-interpretations is promoted by the dialogical, situated and interactive qualities of social media – speaking *with* and *between,* rather than *to* the audience.

Second, our experiences from the Digital Native exhibition also show that the use of social media is not just a matter of virtualizing and distributing museum knowledge to larger audiences through new Internet-based social communication channels or platforms. Rather, social media can reconnect audiences' everyday practices to the museum through *co-located* experiences, and emphasize the importance of physical presence for audiences' experiences of and contributions to the exhibition. Adding kinesthetic interaction to social media interaction by grounding such interaction in a physical setting, fundamentally challenges the museum space from one of appreciation and one-way communication to one of dialogue and active engagement. In this sense, social media transforms the museum space from a curated, highly facilitated and predictable experience to an emerging cultural space for collective interaction and dialogue.

Third, the use of social media in the museum transforms the processes through which we traditionally curate and design museum exhibitions. Dialogical exhibitions and the ensuing democratization of the museum space call for a higher degree of user involvement and interdisciplinary collaboration in the exhibition design process (see also Ciolfi, and Russo, this volume). In the Digital Native project, designers, anthropologists, digital natives and museum curators worked together in a design laboratory, exploring and negotiating cultural agendas as well as design possibilities and physical layout of the exhibition. It was through this integrated and iterative design process that the dialogical nature and social communicative language of the exhibition and museum space were developed and created.

In conclusion, social media can help constitute the museum space as one of dialogue; a dialogue that emerges between and among audiences' everyday practices and particular heritage matters in the exhibition space. In this perspective, audience involvement and contributions become an integral part of the framing, design and experience of the exhibition, dissolving dichotomous conceptions of curators and audiences into new relationships and co-created partnerships. As shown by the Digital Natives project, this transformation dispels the conventional challenge of 'how to engage audiences in museum exhibitions', to give attention to the 'unfinalizability' ingrained in social and cultural performances. There simply is no exhibition separate from audiences' engagement and contributions. Or said differently, the audience engagement *is* the exhibition, and the construction and representation of heritage matters.

Social media forge both individual and collective experiences in the ongoing construction, reproduction and distribution of cultural heritage meanings. Their generic language and structure can allow contributing, modifying and sharing heritage 'content' from audiences inside the exhibition space beyond the walls of the museum. Using social media in the design of exhibitions dissolves the boundaries between institutionalized and living forms of heritage, and connects museum spaces with audiences' everyday practices in new ways. This bears a resemblance to the use of crowdsourcing and crowd-curating by mainstream museums (e.g. Power Museum, Brooklyn Museum of Art, and projects such as Europeana), where audiences and communities are invited to either contribute content to collections and exhibitions or to offer knowledge and discussion about them. But whereas these initiatives often create dialogue as a *consequence* of an already existing collection, meaning or historical argument about the world, we argue for modes of communication that reach beyond such modes of engagement. As such, the end goal is the dialogic mode of engagement itself, and the ongoing and emergent creation of meanings and experiences in the present. For the museum, this means a turn away from paradigms of linear communication and formal knowledge production, to new dynamic and dialogical ways of connecting with the fragmented and intersecting social practices and cultural flows of meaning. In this sense, we not only need to develop and rethink social technologies in support of the museum as a dialogical space. We also need to rethink museums through social media and digital cultures, and align the potential of physical exhibition spaces with the inherent qualities of social media in order to create environments that encourage audiences to participate, reflect, co-create and engage.

Notes

1   We refer to UNESCO's definition of intangible cultural heritage focusing on knowledge, practices and skills covering forms of traditional, contemporary and living heritage (see UNESCO 2003).
2   The Center for Digital Urban Living is funded by the Danish Council for Strategic Research, grant number 2128-07-0011.
3   The materials were created in and drawn from a Redia Gallery © database.
4   Fiducial markers are unique identifications (usually images) that can be used to computationally track an object.
5   DJ Station uses reacTIVision for fiducial tracking, Ableton Live for audio processing and Unity for visuals. The installation was inspired by Reactable.
6   The software used for video-replay was Max/Msp while the infrared tracking was programmed in Community CoreVision (CCV).

References

Arvantis, K. (2010) 'Museums outside walls: Mobile phones and the museum in the everyday', in R. Parry (ed.) *Museums in a Digital Age*, London: Routledge.
Bakhtin, M.M. (1981 [1930s]) *The Dialogic Imagination: Four Essays*, Austin, TX: University of Texas Press.
Bennett, T. (2004) *Pasts Beyond Memory: Evolution, Museums, Colonialism*, London: Routledge.
Castells, E. (2010) 'Museums in the information era: Cultural connectors of time and space', in R. Parry (ed.) *Museums in a Digital Age*, London: Routledge.
Dähne, P. and Karigiannis, J. (2002) 'Archeoguide: System architecture of a mobile outdoor augmented reality system', *Proceedings of ISMAR 2002*, 263–264. Washington, DC: IEEE Computer Society.

Deshpande, S., Geber, K. and Timpson, C. (2007) 'Engaged dialogism in virtual space: An exploration of research strategies for virtual museums', in F. Cameron and S. Kenderdine (eds) *Theorizing Digital Cultural Heritage*, Cambridge, MA: MIT Press.

Ferris, K., Bannon, L., Ciolfi, L., Gallagher, P., Hall, T. and Lennon, M. (2004) 'Shaping experiences in the Hunt Museum: A design case study', *Proceedings DIS2004*, 205–214. Cambridge, MA: ACM Press.

Galani, A. and Chalmers, M. (2010) 'Empowering the remote visitor: Supporting social museum experiences among local and remote visitors', in R. Parry (ed.) *Museums in a Digital Age*, London: Routledge.

Giaccardi, E. (2011) 'Things we value', *Interactions*, 18 (1): 17–21.

Giaccardi, E. and Palen, L. (2008) 'The social production of heritage through cross-media interaction: Making place for place-making', *International Journal of Heritage Studies*, 14 (3): 281–297.

Hall, T., Ciolfi, L., Bannon, L., Fraser, M., Benford, S., Bowers, J., Greenhalgh, C., Hellström, S.O., Izadi, S., Schnädelbach, H. and Flintham, M. (2002), 'The visitor as virtual archeologist: Exploration in mixed reality technology to enhance educational and social interaction in the museum', *Proceedings of VAST'01*, 91–96. New York: ACM Press.

Handler, R. and Gable, E. (1997) *The New History in an Old Museum*, Durham, NC: Duke University Press.

Heath, C. and Lehn, D.V. (2008) 'Configuring "interactivity": Enhancing engagement in science centres and museums', *Social Studies of Science*, 38 (1): 63–91.

Heath, C., Lehn, D.V. and Osborne, J. (2005) 'Interaction and interactives: Collaboration and participation with computer-based exhibits', *Public Understanding of Science*, 14 (1): 91–101.

Hooper-Greenhill, E. (2001) 'Communication and communities in the post-museum – from metanarratives to constructed knowledge.' Paper delivered to the Nordic Museums Leadership Programme, Copenhagen, June.

Ito, M. (2009) *Hanging Out, Messing Around, and Geeking Out: Kids Living and Learning with New Media*, Cambridge, MA: MIT Press.

Kaplan, A. and Haenlein, M. (2010) 'Users of the world, unite! The challenges and opportunities of social media', *Business Horizons* 53 (1): 59–68.

Kirschenblatt-Gimblett, B. (1998) 'Destination museum', in B. Kirschenblatt-Gimblett (ed.) *Destination Culture: Tourism, Museums and Heritage*, Berkeley, CA: University of California Press.

Leder, K., Karpovich, A., Burke, M., Speed, C., Hudson-Smith, A., O'Callaghan, S., Simpson, M., Barthel, R., Blundell, B., De Jode, M., Lee, C., Manohar, A., Shingleton, D. and Macdonald, J. (2010) 'Tagging is connecting: Shared object memories as channels for sociocultural cohesion', *M/C Journal of Media and Culture*, 13 (1). http://journal.media-culture.org.au/index.php/mcjournal/article/viewArticle/209 (accessed 4 December 2011).

Macdonald, S. (2003) 'Museums, national, postnational and transcultural identities', *Museums and Society*, 1 (1): 1–16.

Pierroux, P., Kaptelinin, V., Hall, T., Walker, K., Bannon, L. and Stuedahl, D. (2007) 'MUSTEL: Framing the design of technology-enhanced learning activities for museum visitors', *Proceedings of ICHIM'07*, Toronto, Canada, October 2007. http://www.archimuse.com/ichim07/papers/pierroux/pierroux.html#ixzz1PjHF53sS (accessed 4 December 2011).

Prensky, M. (2001) 'Digital natives, digital immigrants', *On the Horizon*, 9 (5): 1–6.

Raptis, D., Tselios, N. and Avouris, N. (2005) 'Context-based design of mobile applications for museums: A survey of existing practices', *Proceedings of Mobile HCI*, 153–160. New York: ACM Press.

Sparacino, F. (2004) 'Scenographies of the past and museums of the future: From the *wunderkammer* to body-driven interactive narrative spaces', *Proceedings of the 12th Annual ACM International Conference on Multimedia (MM 2004)*, 72–79. New York: ACM Press.

Taylor, N. and Cheverest, K. (2009) 'Social interaction around a rural community photo display', *International Journal of Human-Computer Studies*, 67 (12): 1037–1047.

UNESCO (2003) Convention for the Safeguarding of Intangible Cultural Heritage. http://www.unesco.org/culture/ich/index.php?lg=en&pg=00006 (accessed 22 November 2011).

West, S. (ed.) (2010) *Understanding Heritage in Practice*, Manchester: Manchester University Press.

Wojciechowski, R., Walczak, K., White, M. and Cellary, W. (2004) 'Building virtual and augmented reality museum exhibitions', *Proceedings of the Ninth International Conference on 3D Web Technology (Web3D 2004)*, 135–144. New York: ACM Press.

Woods, E., Billingshurst, M., Aldridge, G. and Garrie, B. (2004) 'Augmenting the science centre and museum experience', *Proceedings of the Second International Conference on Computer Graphics and Interactive Techniques (GRAPHITE '04)*, 230–236. New York: ACM Press.

8

THE RISE OF THE 'MEDIA MUSEUM'

Creating interactive cultural experiences through social media

Angelina Russo

Introduction

The contemporary museum is a media space. The ways in which audiences engage, participate, review and critique museum practices increasingly occur within the realm of online media. The notion of a *media museum* comes about from the rise in the use of new media technologies within the museum environment. As online audience experience becomes increasingly important in the development of museum communication, digital media and social networking technologies provide complementary platforms through which to engage with and create new cultural content.

This chapter describes the contemporary museum as a *media museum* – one which is situated within a historical understanding of the formation of the museum, the spaces it creates, the fields it presents and the media it uses. The idea of media museum looks at the transformation of display spaces, fields of practice and use of media, as the museum moves from its traditional base as a social and educational institution based on collections, to an experiential model based on knowledge exchange and active cultural participation.

The chapter contends that while technological stimuli have previously driven forms of display and interpretation, the creation of online cultural interactive experiences has yet to be articulated as a framework for audience engagement, participation and co-creation in relation to the notion of media museum. If the media museum is to provide a trusted, authoritative source through which to create new types of active online cultural participation, then we must look at how to situate traditional museum roles within the social media environment. This chapter goes some way to providing a framework for such engagement.

A potted history of Western museums...

Many of the principles and processes which underpinned the formation of the *modernist museum* were established in the nineteenth century. The modernist museum attempted to merge knowledge and education in a constructed environment which held an unalterable sense of refinement, authority and power. In the twentieth century, the histories, stories and policies of the museum were inculcated through the practices of museum curators. Curators were responsible for disseminating complex stories and information to a broader public through research, exhibition and advocacy. Technologies of communication were developed in tandem with the disciplinary practices of the curator who translated the myths and meanings surrounding collections and their stories, and disseminated them using the media technology of the day. Over time the curator's role acquired greater authority through their manipulation of technologies of display. Since then, exhibitions have been an integral, though often uncited tool for the museum in general and curators in particular to establish and maintain an expert position in the knowledge exchange of the institution. At the same time, the reach of this expertise was often restricted to peers rather than the visiting public. This created a lack of understanding of the value of interpretation to a broader audience.

From the 1960s onwards museum discourse began to acknowledge that visitors brought their own experiences, knowledge and responses to exhibitions to frame the meanings that they derived from the collections on view. Eventually, this acknowledgement resulted in established forms of museums, including interpretive centres, theme parks and zoos, being viewed as significant sites of knowledge and communication of community histories. As museum discourses broadened, structured educational programs became integral to museums, and distributed networks such as heritage trails and urban museums were added to the growing architectures of museum exhibition site.

In the late twentieth century, changes to the modernist museum program occurred as a social shift from education to entertainment began in cultural institutions. By the late 1990s, institutional websites and virtual community sites were added to already well-established modes of communication such as exhibitions, interactive kiosks, educational, public and outreach programs. These changes in visitor status and community engagement laid the groundwork for engaging with broader social changes in the notion of museum consumption as active and creative work (Miller 1998; Abercrombie and Longhurst 1998).

The past ten years have seen a rise of interactive technologies in the rhetoric of museum programs, with a number of major museums placing 'technology' at the heart of their future agendas (see for example the National Museum of Australia[1]). Yet, across the sector, there has been very little critical literacy for describing the functional link between technology and the experience it can afford the audience. Therefore, while it has become increasingly common for audiences to expect to view and engage with content online, the way in which experiences are formulated and designed have changed very little (Hooper-Greenhill 2000).

Social media, that is, media that enables audiences to critique, converse and create content and distribute it publicly, has offered a new platform for partnerships between audiences and cultural organizations. The wave of non-professional content resulting from social media activity (unpaid but not 'amateur' in the old-fashioned sense) has provided a unique environment to create online cultural interactive experiences that encourage active audience engagement, participation and co-creation.

The first half of this chapter contends that experience-focused online cultural communication can maintain the museum's traditional remit as an authoritative source while enhancing the relationship between institutions and audiences by means of new forms of cultural participation.

The second half of this chapter explores the rise of non-professional, user-generated content and the ways in which this content adds to the mission of the museum. Social networking and media technologies supporting this phenomenon are discussed in relation to the experiences they enable. This second half of the chapter emphasizes how social media is unique in its ability to both draw networks together in collaboration with the museum and to have the products of that collaboration distributed to a wider audience.

Media museum: the next wave

In the 1990s museum content began to emerge from behind the walls of institutions and to appear on distributed websites. The Internet was increasingly becoming a common medium for institutions to display, in a limited way, their cultural knowledge. This movement 'beyond the walls' brought about a rise in debate around notions of deterritorialization (where the museum was no longer bound by a single built entity) and dematerialization (where the relationship between audience and institution became more malleable) (Silverstone 1994; Kenderdine 1996). At the same time, critique around the experience of visiting 'real', physical sites versus 'virtual' experiences became topical (Pearce 1995; Trant 2010 [1997]). Since that time, debate has continued to range over the value of online display, the effect that it has on the 'aura' of the museum object, the authenticity of experience and the power/knowledge relationships between audience and museum.

While the dominant discourses that surrounded early Internet interaction were played out in opposition between 'the real' and 'the virtual', the critique implicit in such opposition was centered around how virtual experiences might undermine the expertise and social standing of the museum. In contrast to this critique, Trant (2010 [1997]) suggested that the use of the Internet to deliver museum content could be viewed as a potentially powerful networked system, which provided greater authority to the museum by creating 'trusted cultural networks'. While there were some early Australian programs that encouraged cross-institutional content sharing (such as the Australian Museums and Galleries Online (AMOL) Task Group[2]), there was little agreement among museums on the development of user-centered or user-generated content sharing. This was partly a result of the limited interactivity afforded by early Internet technologies and, in turn, it was philosophically underpinned by the dominant discourses of the time.

Meanwhile, in 1989, Peter Vergo suggested through the idea of 'new museology' that collections were increasingly to be viewed with 'a more recent sense of an obligation that museums should not merely display their treasures to the curious and make their collections accessible to those desirous of knowledge, but also actively engage in mass education' (Vergo 1989: 2).

This social communication agenda, while relatively new to the museum program at the time, is not dissimilar to that which drives social networking in museums. Online social networking, facilitated through the use of social media, provides opportunities for audiences to access, discuss and engage with cultural collections. In turn, this broader access enables new collaborations and conversations between audiences and institutions, thus providing an environment to achieve Vergo's new museology. In other words, social media extends the audience/institution relationship beyond 'the captions, the information panels, the accompanying catalogue, the press handout' (Vergo 1989: 3).

The media museum responds to these earlier reflections on the changing role of the audience. In technological terms, it is the product of two fundamental changes: digitization, which has enabled cultural institutions to make aspects of their collections available online; and the convergence of media technologies, which has fuelled the rise in social media networking applications such as Facebook, Ning and content-sharing sites.

The media museum responds to these parallel stimuli in two ways. At an institutional level, the media museum attempts to create new types of relationships between audience and institutions where content sharing is at the heart of new knowledge (see the National Library of Australia[3] and Library of Congress[4] Flickr initiatives). At a community level, the media museum develops 'trusted cultural networks' (Trant 2010 [1997]); for example, the National Museums Online Learning Project[5] in the UK (2006–2009). This was a three-year, multi-partner project focused on making cultural content from multiple organizations available through a single portal. It included the facility for audiences to create their own content and save their searches, thus developing an individually curated experience. Additionally, the project included educational materials in the form of WebQuests, which students could use as a resource when researching topics that could be illustrated by content from within designated museums.

The most significant difference between these audience/institution relationships and those developed prior to social media is in the ability for audiences to build and widely disseminate knowledge, content and conversations across multiple platforms within the museum sector. This remains a significant evolution in the relationship between audience and institutions described by Vergo with reference to mass-media communication (1989: 2).

Online cultural interactive experiences

Today, social media provides a real possibility to respond to social agendas by forming communities of interest and networks that recontextualize the nature of the museum space in relation to the cultural interactive experiences taking place online. Creating online cultural interactive experiences requires a change in the ways in which collection materials are considered for public distribution and interpretation purposes. Weil (2007) observed that museums had changed from being 'about something' to being 'for somebody'. To move beyond an emphasis on technology and reframe social media communication in terms of audience experience, the media museum should use methods that elicit engagement, participation and co-creation in a structured fashion (Russo and Watkins, 2004, 2005a). These methods would recognize the mission of the museum and develop audience experiences that are in keeping with its resources and remits, thus enabling museums to connect media to collections in an effective way. However, even when adopted, 'structured methods' that privilege audience experience in the development of museum communication can only go so far in shifting museum agendas.

The variety of experiences, from branded cultural experiences (i.e. blockbuster exhibitions) to virtual experiences (i.e. virtual heritage reconstructions) provide an increasingly complex environment in which to interpret collections and develop compelling narratives. In this environment it becomes increasingly important to structure the relationship between audience and institutions in ways that can meet audience expectations while remaining true to museum missions.

While we could continue to develop exhibitions and social media initiatives with the hope of capturing a target audience, in this chapter I propose to reframe audience experience as a relationship that is conducive to creating new instances of collective memory and community. When experience is contextualized in this way, the resultant communication builds on traditional museum practices and situates technology as a medium through which to create cultural experience rather than a tool to produce an experience that is engaging in its own right (Russo, 2004).

Supporting collective memory

Museums have played an authoritative role in the creation of memory. Enabling visitors to engage with their collections, albeit from a distance, has been fundamental to such a role. So how has the museum acted as a memory institution?

Halbwachs (1992: 78–84) suggests that memories are recalled by time periods, by recollecting places visited, and by situating ideas or images in patterns of thought that are specific to distinct social groups. Memory is essentially social; it can orient experience by linking an individual to family traditions, customs of class, religious beliefs or specific places. For Halbwachs, memory is based on *lived experience*; it is something that can be plucked from the past and seized by the individual in the manner of naive and immediate knowledge. If not linked to lived experience, memory is reduced to *history* and may become abstract reconstruction or faked recollection. In museums, memory makes the visitor aware of time and offers a perspective on the past. According to Halbwachs, memory always unfolds in places and it is based on spatial reconstruction. When these places cannot be located in the social space of a group, then remembrance would fail.

Similarly, Christine Boyer (1996:135) proposes that museums present a fundamental distinction between history and memory. If, as Halbwach asserts, history begins where tradition ends, then as long as memory stays alive within a group's collective experience, it is not necessary to write it down or to fix it as the official story of events. But as a gap opens up between the enactment of the past and the recall of the present, then history begins to be 'artificially' created. According to Boyer, history divides time into static periods and didactic stages, when in reality there are no such boundaries. History presents fragments and details as a whole, relocating these within new frameworks, outside the collective experience.

It is within such frameworks that the historian (and the curator) establish comparisons and contrasts, recomposing the variety of times and places into a uniform pattern. This newly formed structure becomes the basis of a vision of the past that in the traditional museum was often erected and credence maintained as an universal truth, not subject to change.

Today globalization, nomadic work practices, migration and a cult of individualism have severed the ties between people and the social and physical environments in which collective memory unfolds. If collective memory relates to the transmission of the values and traditions ascribed to the cultural spaces it creates, then it is possible that as Deleuze (1989) suggests, we are in the grip of a memory crisis. But Deleuze (1989: 251) also argued that this memory crisis is balanced out by our need to establish counter-memories, resisting the dominant coding of images and representations that are embedded in our way of being. He suggested that in doing so, we recover in our own right the differences in site, action, intention and experience that have been erased by globalization. If so, then the 'next wave' of museum practice will need to create new sites for exploration, to present new connections between spaces, places and people, and to give rise to new social and cultural imaginaries. These new sites will need to allow for individual experiences to be drawn together in the context of emerging communities and produce new instances of collective memory.

Fostering community

Museum-going is widely accepted as a social experience where visitors' knowledge, previous experiences and expectations influence the ways in which they experience cultural content (Hooper-Greenhill 2000; see also Wakkary et al., this volume). Wallace (1996: 109) even suggests that visitors enter museums with well-stocked film banks, carrying both raw footage and narrative sequences in their heads. This results in visitors with a malleable sense of past, present and future. Besides calling for new relationships with visitors and communities based on interpersonal methods of communication as advocated by Hooper-Greenhill, Wallace proposes that these mental 'film banks' offer museums an avenue through which to reconceptualize themselves. They offer an approach to present a particular set of interpretations that audiences can recognize as mediations rather than universal truths and that can be used to build new relationships.

Building community around memorable experiences can produce unexpected associations for the creation of new museum audiences. The contemporary museum continues to provide authoritative knowledge but is increasingly experimenting with a many-to-many communication model to engage its audiences. In this model, communities have an opportunity to develop around collections and disciplinary knowledge and are provided with an avenue through which to explore new relationships with the institution. This is usually achieved online by providing 'spaces' where communities of interest can connect with the institution while contributing their own knowledge to the debate (see for instance the Sydney Observatory blog[6] and the community of the Brooklyn Museum[7]). This shift in cultural practice, while initially seeming to undermine the primacy of collections and the authority of the museum, can provide significant interpretative knowledge (Russo and Watkins 2005b).

Simon (this volume) emphasizes the social implications associated with offering museum spaces, specifically online spaces, as productive places for assembling diverse groups of people to engage in 'an interactive practice of remembering', and argues that these online spaces constitute a new arena of participation in the formation of cultural memory.

Simon suggests that 'digitally mediated platforms' are a lived social practice that situates audiences in relation as they 'express and remake their connections to specific historical events and each other' (p. 91). He also argues: 'digital practices of remembering together constitute a collectivity that publically displays its own process of formation' (p. 91). Such a notion could be well illustrated through the Imperial War Museum's new initiative, Lives of the Great War. In 2014 the world commemorates the centenary of the beginning of World War I. This commemoration will occur without any 'living voices' contributing to the discourse. As a result of the worldwide interest and attention that will occur during the centenary years 2014–2018, Lives of the Great War will allow millions worldwide to collaborate and piece together the life stories of those who gave their lives in World War I. This will be constructed as an end-to-end media experience where audiences will be able to engage and participate across a variety of web platforms, social media services, mobile devices and television channels. Such an approach to a subject of global significance offers a unique case study for the formation of an interactive practice of remembering (Simon, this volume).

The first half of this chapter has attempted to contextualize the impetuses for creating active cultural experience through new relationships between audiences and institutions. I will now consider how social media can be integrated in such contemporary museum practices to create online cultural interactive experiences based on the interplay of new instances of engagement, participation and co-creation.

Creating new cultural interactive experiences through social media

The authority of cultural institutions by virtue of their control of interpretation to their collections is challenged when collections are digitized: once cultural content is converted to digital media and distributed on multiple platforms, it is part of the public domain and accessible through several channels. This shift is coupled with the individual ability to collect, archive and share across peer-to-peer distributed networks. People can build, control and distribute their own experiences on demand. Significant amount of museum content is now readily available via simple web search engines such as Google: people engage with the museum while creating and sharing knowledge and experiences of value to them.

Social media facilitate knowledge exchange by taking advantage of network effects (Dawson 2002), that is, the distribution of content across multiple organizations (see Culture Victoria by the Victorian Cultural Network[8]), the creation of new distributed cultural content (see the Powerhouse Museum[9]), and the development of new public forums for describing museum practices (see Ning Museum3[10]).

In the longer term, social media provide an exceptional platform from which to explore the convergence of disciplines related to museum communication with the goal to:

- position museums to take a primary role in debates on the implications of new social media practices;
- provide practical examples of ways in which public investment in museums can engage audiences with issues of social history;
- generate cross-disciplinary connections between museum communication processes, media design and digital content creation.

Cultural institutions, with their large technological infrastructures and well-developed education programs, could lead a new wave of cultural programming, particularly through increased production of creative and cultural content across a wide range of digital platforms. An extremely successful example of this new relationship between audience and institution across networks is the successful BBC series *Who Do You Think You Are?*

The series started as a television program focusing on genealogical information related to British identities, and has expanded to include a magazine, public forums, events and research development workshops. Importantly, the series has created strong partnerships with commercial entities, providing access to comprehensive ancestry databases and to the British Library. In this example, the 'networked effects' has resulted in audience interest expanding beyond the individual programs into the collection-based materials that make up social history documentation.

By partnering with the British Library, the BBC has improved access to cultural materials. The live forum demonstrates the veracity of online social networks that form around collection materials, and the workshops and events are excellent literacy initiatives by institutions with strong educational agendas. Yet the collection materials and the audience of 'amateur' family historians have existed for a long time. This initiative has achieved a new form of participation, because it was based on capturing the audience experience and linking it to 'authoritative' voices within the community.

While the reach and scope of the distributed BBC program is beyond most museums, the structure can be adapted to suit specific purposes if it is strategically developed with audience experience at its core. From this perspective, there are specific considerations that need to be addressed when social media is used to create online cultural interactive experiences. These considerations concern engagement, participation and co-creation. Each area provides an insight into how to plan for social media in museums to ensure that collections remain at the heart of the cultural experience.

Engagement

Social media are often being used to engage in discussion and share subject knowledge outside of the museum. Sites like Technorati[11] represent venues where audience comments are collated well beyond the walls of the museum. Such conversations provide valuable insights into the 'meanings' that audiences construct from their museum experiences. Museum professionals such as curators and educators should be aware of these conversations, particularly as to whether: the audience is seeking to speak with them; the museum is interested in engaging in conversations; or, the museum is ready to listen to the issues that are being raised. While audiences can gain agency through this use of social media, museums risk irrelevance if they ignore audiences' public reflections and conversations of their own experiences.

Another form of engagement is for audiences to personalize or 'tag' content by adding their own key search words for collection databases. 'Tagging' establishes independent taxonomies (also called 'folksonomies') that can be used by others to enable personalized online searching. In 2006 the Powerhouse Museum launched its OPAC 2.0 online collection database, allowing visitors to the site to tag their collection items, while the Museum's formal taxonomies and specialist knowledge were still available. These are just some of the ways in which social media can bring together collections, audiences and content creators in cultural knowledge exchange.

Participation and co-creation

A more active form of participation concerns content creation and sharing. People are encouraged to express opinions and views, engage in activities, and sometimes even contribute to the main displays (Salgado et al. 2009; Simon 2010). Social media is proving very effective in facilitating this, with major museums around the world (such as the Metropolitan Museum of Art, the Smithsonian Institution, the Liberty Science Center, among others) utilizing different ways for people to communicate, promote, enrich and sometimes create exhibits.

Content sharing is a relatively new initiative in the museum sector and demonstrates the ways in which instances of collective memory and community can be achieved through social networking and audience participation. For example, the National Library of Australia and Yahoo!/Flickr collaborated to develop Click and Flick, a site where individuals contribute their own images to the PictureAustralia[12] online image repository. Previously, PictureAustralia had only provided access to images within existing library, archive, museum and gallery collections. With Click and Flick the National Library of Australia not only acknowledges the value of community content, it privileges and thereby validates community content within its collection.

A step on from content sharing is content creation and 'crowdsourcing', that is, the ability for audiences to participate in the development of new content that responds or relates to existing museum collections. Here are a number of interesting examples. Art Mobs[13] are students who create podcasts of their visits to the Museum of Modern Art (MoMA) in New York and then upload them to an independent website where other potential visitors can access them. The Victoria and Albert Museum in London developed Every Object Tells a Story,[14] a project that enables visitors to the site to upload personal and family objects and create informal community records describing the history and use of these objects. In some instances, visitors also provided extra information to offer additional knowledge around these informal collections.

These projects provide novel online experiences that encourage public debate and social networking. In these projects, the museums play an important role in knowledge exchange by providing tools, infrastructure, digital literacy and access to their collections. Social media can extend the authenticity of collections by enabling museum professionals to establish and maintain a cultural dialogue with their audiences. At the same time, when social media initiatives are supported by the museum, they have the potential to expand collection knowledge and to create communities of interest that support and extend cultural participation. Museums can play an active role in encouraging such participation and reviving their authority by embedding themselves into the everyday life of the community and actively encouraging knowledge sharing, 'voice', education and acknowledgement.

Conclusion

Even with enormous cultural capital locked in their collections and public status achieved through their increasingly virtual presence, museums struggle to situate themselves in the contemporary, media-saturated environment.

As already suggested by the DigiCULT study (European Commission 2002), technologies alone should not be assumed to foster structural change within cultural and memory institutions (archives, libraries and museums). Rather, cultural institutions would need to 'reinvent' themselves if they were to implement technological initiatives that were of benefit to their missions. The report describes information and communication technologies as systemic technologies that would affect all practices and procedures of an institution, if properly integrated (European Commission 2002: 82–83). Therefore, the report emphasizes the limitations of applying technology without adapting institutional practices to cultural programs by means of structured processes and systems. The study also points to the need for strategic implementation of technology across multiple areas of the museum. These considerations are even more relevant today when discussing how social media can capture and engage new audiences.

Museums are the mirror through which institutionalized knowledge, spectacle and display are conceptualized in terms of a civic state and defined in global terms. Their appeal derives from their ability to engage with social, cultural and political agendas. The practices of the museum are interdisciplinary and make specific reference to evolving knowledge and changing technology. Until the early 1960s, museum practices were largely uncriticized, as the tensions between knowledge ownership and power, changes in cultural contexts, representation, and mediation of knowledge were played out in relatively local fields. The rise of social media has created a new dispersed landscape through which to discuss and critically analyze museum programs and practices.

If the museum is to provide a trusted, authoritative source through which to create new forms of cultural participation, then it must look to situating its traditional roles within the media environment. The media museum is here. But technologies of social media must be discussed and described in terms that engage all museum professionals, not only those dealing with technology. Because social media provides an exceptional opportunity for interdisciplinary solutions to the creation of meaningful cultural experiences, social media should be of interest to the entire organization.

Notes

1 See National Museum Australia, Annual Report 2002–2003. http://www.nma.gov. au/shared/libraries/attachments/annual_report/annual_report_20022003/nma_ annrep2003_part02/files/344/nma_annrep2003_part02.pdf (accessed 22 November 2011).
2 Australian Museums and Galleries Online (AMOL) Task Group: http://www.cmc. gov.au/working_groups/past_working_groups/collections/collections_-_australiam_ museums_and_galleries_online_amol_task_group (accessed 23 November 2011).
3 National Library of Australia, Picture Australia: http://www.pictureaustralia.org/; see also: http://www.flickr.com/groups/PictureAustralia_ppe/ (accessed 23 November 2011).
4 Library of Congress on Flickr: http://www.flickr.com/people/library_of_congress/ (accessed 23 November 2011).
5 Victoria and Albert Museum, National Museums Online Learning Project: http:// www.vam.ac.uk/about_va/online_learning/index.html (accessed 23 November 2011).
6 Sydney Observatory blog: http://www.sydneyobservatory.com.au/blog/ (accessed 23 November 2011).
7 Brooklyn Museum community: http://www.brooklynmuseum.org/community/ (accessed 23 November 2011).
8 Culture Victoria by Victorian Cultural Network: http://www.cv.vic.gov.au/ (accessed 23 November 2011).

9 Powerhouse Museum collection database: http://www.powerhousemuseum.com/collection/database/about.php (accessed 23 November 2011).
10 Museum3 powered by Ning: http://www.museum30.ning.com (accessed 23 November 2011).
11 Technorati provides real-time search for user-generated media (including weblogs) by tag or keyword: http://technorati.com/ (accessed 23 November 2011).
12 See note 2.
13 MoMA Art Mobs: http://mod.blogs.com/art_mobs/ (accessed 23 November 2011).
14 Victoria and Albert Museum, Every Object Tells A Story: http://www.vam.ac.uk/vastatic/microsites/1303_every_object/ (accessed 23 November 2011).

References

Abercrombie, N. and Longhurst, B. (1998) *Audiences: A Sociological Theory of Performance and Imagination*, London: Sage.

Boyer, C. (1996) *The City of Collective Memory: Its Historical Imagery and Architectural Entertainments*, Cambridge, MA: MIT Press.

Dawson, R. (2002) *Living Networks: Leading Your Company, Customers, and Partners in the Hyper-Connected Economy*, Upper Saddle River, NJ: Prentice Hall.

Deleuze, G. (1989) *Cinema 2: The Time-Image*, Minneapolis, MN: University of Minnesota Press.

European Commission (2002). *The DigiCULT Report. Technological landscapes for tomorrow's cultural economy: Unlocking the value of cultural heritage.* Luxembourg: European Commission. http://digicult.salzburgresearch.at/downloads/dc_fullreport_230602_screen.pdf (accessed 23 November 2011).

Halbwachs, M. (1992) *On Collective Memory*, Chicago, IL: The University of Chicago Press.

Hooper-Greenhill, E. (2000) *Museums and the Interpretation of Visual Culture*, London: Routledge.

Kenderdine, S. (1996) 'Diving into shipwrecks: Aquanauts in cyberspace', *Spectra* 24 (1): 32–42.

Miller, S. (1998) *A Theory of Shopping*, Cambridge: Polity.

Pearce, S. (1995) 'Collecting as medium and message', in E. Hooper-Greenhill (ed.) *Museum, Media, Message*, London: Routledge.

Russo, A. (2004) 'Media museum: Sites of virtual display. towards an ontology for museum exhibition development', PhD dissertation, University of South Australia.

Russo, A. and Watkins, J. (2004) 'Creative new media design: Achieving representative curatorial practice using a Cultural Interactive Experience Design method', in E. Edmonds and R. Gibson (eds) *Interaction: Systems, Practice and Theory*, Sydney: University of Technology, Creativity and Cognition Studios.

Russo, A. and Watkins, J. (2005a) 'Post-museum experiences: Structured methods for audience engagement', *Proceedings of the 11th International Conference on Virtual Systems and Multimedia (VSMM 2005)*, 173–182, Brussels: ENAME.

Russo, A. and Watkins, J. (2005b) 'Digital cultural communication: Tools and methods for community co-creation', *Proceedings of the International Conference on Engaging Communities*, Brisbane: Queensland Government. http://eprints.qut.edu.au/3983/ (access 23 November 2011).

Salgado, M. (2009) 'Designing for an open museum: an exploration of content creation and sharing through interactive pieces', PhD Dissertation, University of Art and Design Helsinki, Finland.

Silverstone, R. (1994) 'The medium is the museum: On objects and logics in times and spaces', in R. Miles and L. Zavala (eds) *Towards the Museum of the Future: New European Perspectives*, London: Routledge.

Simon, N. (2010) *The Participatory Museum,* Santa Cruz, CA: Museum 2.0.

Trant, J. (2010) 'When all you've got is "The Real Thing": museums and authenticity in the networked world', in R. Parry (ed.), *Museums in a Digital Age,* London: Routledge [originally published 1997]. Original paper online at http://www.archimuse.com/papers/jt.cidoc.97/trant-cidoc97.pdf

Vergo, P. (1989) (ed.) *The New Museology*, London: Reaktion Books.

Wallace, M. (1996) *Mickey Mouse History and Other Essays on American Memory,* Philadelphia, PA: Temple University Press.

Weil, S (2007) 'From the design of something to the design for somebody', in R. Sandell and R. Janes (eds) *Museum Management and Marketing*, London: Routledge.

PART III
Sense of place

PART III

Space and...

9

MOSAICS AND MULTIPLES

Online digital photography and the framing of heritage

Richard Coyne

Digital photographs do not just come in ones, twos and carefully assembled collections, but in vast numbers, arrayed in file stores and as outputs on web search engines, as well as social media and photo sharing sites. Digital images appear as thumbnails arranged on grids like collectibles in display cases or postage stamps in an album. A stamp makes little sense to the collector as a singular item. The digital collector similarly deals in multiples. Digital photographs are deposited in very large numbers from digital cameras, to be sorted, arranged, ordered, compared and shared (Treib 2011). Digital photographs present themselves in large numbers to both the individual photographer and to audiences and consumers.

Ernst Gombrich's influential book *Art and Illusion* and W. J. T. Mitchell's *Picture Theory* pay attention to individual images and classes of images (Gombrich 1960; Mitchell 1995, 2005) without overtly addressing images en masse. In this chapter we examine the implications for heritage matters of the dynamic flow of large volumes of imagery.

This strategy affords a critique of digital photography and an opportunity to examine the role and impact of emerging online practices on how people come to understand space, place and heritage. What does this hyper-accretion of images mean for heritage matters?

Digital archives

Those responsible for heritage matters have an obvious investment in presentation and display. Digital images serve as media for the presentation of heritage, for documentation, analysis, and as cultural resources in their own right. Neil Silberman provides a helpful definition in the context of digital media: 'Heritage is an ever-changing array of objects and symbols, a complex mosaic of artefacts, images, monuments, and customs that demand our attention and demand that we give some meaning to them' (Silberman 2008: 82).

Of course, the origins of heritage reside less in concepts of dynamic mosaics than in ideas about property, the preservation of a lineage, and traditions and artefacts passed from parents to their children over generations. The Convention of World Heritage (UNESCO 1972) defines heritage in terms of places (and we could add *artefacts*) that have 'universal value' and that are to 'be protected for future generations to appreciate and enjoy'. So heritage, at least in its inception, relates to conservation, the preservation of tradition and values, and by extension the conservation of professional judgement, expertise and authority.

Understood traditionally, heritage is an issue for institutions, who must be concerned with conservation in order to persist and to carry out their functions. Institutions such as universities, banks, hospitals and museums outlive their human functionaries, and need artefacts and records in order to endure across the generations. In the case of those institutions whose particular business is heritage, such as UNESCO, preservation societies, such as the National Trust in the UK, museums and galleries, heritage also implies the preservation of objects of value.

This is a *traditional* view of heritage. The changing relationships between expertise, amateur interest, the diversity of user communities and publics, and the multitude of perspectives each bring to the understanding of cultural resources and artefacts, pose challenges for those concerned with producing and managing heritage assets (Srinivasan *et al.* 2009). As indicated in the chapter in this volume by Silberman and Purser, the traditional view is under increasing challenge from heritage institutions themselves. Projects such as Europeana, and its attempt (among many) to deploy crowdsourcing as a way to create active user communities, exemplify this challenge. Digital photography is ubiquitous and operates ostensibly with little regard for the authority of professionals and experts, adding further challenges to the authority of institutions and heritage practices (Silberman 2008). But in spite of trends towards open-ended, community-oriented heritage as the nurturing of collective memories, it still falls to institutions to garner and manage heritage assets and to broker debates about heritage.

The instrument of the archive provides a useful way of thinking about heritage and institutions, and provides access to more radical understandings. The philosopher Jacques Derrida encourages us to regard the challenges faced by any institution as a problem about the archive (Derrida and Prenowitz 1995; Coyne 2011), including how the archive is created, conserved, protected and made public. Archives are not incidental to institutions but are central to their operations. Contemporary heritage practices wrestle with concepts of the institution, authority, expertise and the archive, all of which are challenged by the proliferation of technologies and practices that facilitate openness, the putative democratization of knowledge and expertise, and the proliferation and increasing exposure of archives and materials able to be archived. Sophia B. Liu addresses something of this complexity of the archive in her characterization of the curatorial role in her chapter in this volume.

So the concept of the institution (and its archives) provides a helpful link between digital photography and heritage. Archives are potentially vast. In a sense they are infinite (Bell 2004). There is no end to what we might think of storing away. Archives take up space, they grow over time, and the media and technologies of their preservation, analysis and interpretation change. They also cross-reference each other, and are cross-referenced through digital media (Churchill and Ubois 2008; Van House and Churchill 2008). The issue of the quantity and scale of the archive is a problem for digital photography. Put another way, the exponential growth in digital photographic resources exposes the problems of the archive, and of heritage.

Digital photographs in quantity

What are the features of digital photography that encourage the proliferation of images? Amateur digital photography is an art of permutations and cherished misjudgements, differing in many respects from analogue film-based photography in the plethora of imagery it encourages, and in emphasizing processes of collating, sorting, editing, archiving, embedding and sharing large numbers of images, abetted by functions integrated into image capture software.

Rather than languishing unsorted in envelopes, boxes and slide trays or lovingly folded into bulky and half completed photograph albums, digital snaps are immediately and automatically organized by date and location and displayed as thumbnail images to be tagged, shared, scanned visually, searched and embedded, i.e. brought into service in some way. The deployment of such images is commonplace in professional life, as images are embedded into electronic slide presentations, printed publications, reports, web pages and blogs. Digital snaps feature in communications among people working out in the field: i.e. surveyors, building inspectors, architects and conservators visiting communities, monuments, construction sites and archaeological digs. Digital snaps supplement formal modes of evidence gathering and are major instruments of professional working.

Innovations in camera technologies contribute to the plethora of imagery. Smartphones with cameras constitute a major source of innovation. Researchers into digital photography identify the special nature of mobile phone cameras (Foster 2009; Lee 2009). The phone is generally ready to hand. Unlike most single-function digital cameras, the smartphone does not need to be packed away in a protective case. Mobile phones are discrete and have multiple functions, so people in the vicinity of the camera need not even be aware they are witnessing or are part of a photographic event. The need for flash is diminishing in many cases, and even inexpensive cameras deliver high quality imagery under adverse lighting conditions. Digital photographers can readily target subjects close up, via zoom, and in wide-angle formats. Digital photography can improve on the naked eye in situ. The viewfinder of the camera displays pictures just taken to reveal details in the world not readily perceived. As well as providing records, digital cameras have secondary functions as telescope, microscope and periscope. As reliable, inexpensive, multifunctional devices, these factors conspire to deliver very large numbers of images from digital cameras.

One of the most radical features of photography on mobile phones and smartphones is that images can be shared instantly through phone or wi-fi networks to other phone users, and uploaded to specialised image sharing sites (e.g. Flickr), to blog sites, and virtually anywhere on the web. Images can also be tagged automatically with locational coordinates, face recognition, and of course with captions and accompanying commentary. They are also in the company of other media, with which they readily elide, including video and audio recording, synthetic images, digital animations, and real-time video, audio and text communication. At the same time, the user has access to a steady stream of media from external sources, some of which includes consumer-generated content: YouTube clips, podcasts, playlists, and much of this is shared with others. Digital photographs are also in the company of aerial photography (i.e. Panoramio on Google Maps and Google Earth) to which they can be attached. Google Maps' Streetview service for seeing what it is like to walk down the street of a town consists of views stitched together from photographs taken from cameras mounted atop a moving vehicle adapted for the purpose. Imagery streams steadily from ubiquitous surveillance cameras to disks, servers and the desks of security personnel, and some finds its way into public forums such as YouTube, news broadcasts and television programmes about policing.

In the words of media critic Friedrich Kittler writing in the 1980s, 'Modulation, transformation, synchronization; delay, memory, transposition; scrambling, scanning, mapping — a total connection of all media on a digital base erases the notion of the medium itself.' Echoing the insight of Marshall McLuhan he adds, 'the contents of one medium are always other media' (Kittler *et al.* 1987: 102). Mitchell also draws attention to the ability of images to reference themselves, and other images, coining the terms 'metapictures' and 'meta-metapictures' (Mitchell 1995). These are pictures of pictures and pictures about pictures. The artist Diego Rodríguez de Silva y Velázquez's famous painting *Las Meninas* provides an obvious example of the latter. Here the artist appears in his own painting, along with representations of other paintings, as well as conventionally posed human subjects. So many digital photographs at heritage sites inevitably include the presence of other photographers, and may include images of other images and displays. Mosaics of digital images are themselves pictures of pictures. The term 'metadata' already indicates data about data. Archives similarly cross-reference other archives, and as any electronic library catalogue will indicate, the contents lists of different archives are themselves archivable items. The medium references itself.

In keeping with this media maelstrom, digital photographers are immersed in images, professional and amateur, of their own making and by others. Most browsers and search engines support the delivery of page after page of ordered images in response to search terms. As well as broadcast media and advertising billboards, there are display screens, information screens, urban screens, and of course images are consumed on the screens of smartphones, laptops and ubiquitous tablet screens.

As the cost per image at source for amateur photography is negligible, and images can be deleted readily, the medium of digital photography can be deployed with a minimum of care. The digital photographer can take many pictures in large numbers, even of the same subject, reserving the process of selection for later, if at all. Digital photographs do not come singly and in small sets, but in vast numbers, and digital cameras and storage devices can hold thousands of images. Studies into digital photography by Van House reveal how people keep many such images to hand for display through smartphones and other mobile media, and deploy them in their storytelling, helping to construct one's self-image and that of a group (Van House and Churchill 2008; Van House 2009). The plethora of imagery is complicit in social formation.

Researchers into online photo sharing, Amparo Lasén and Edgar Gómez-Cruz, foreground the everyday nature of digital photography, which continues the trajectory of development from the earliest days of specialized and expensive equipment and expertise, to handheld cameras as consumer products, and ubiquitous consumer services for processing images (Lasén and Gómez-Cruz 2009). Cameras are ready to hand on various portable devices: laptops, tablet computers, mobile phones, smartphones and of course as stand-alone, single-function cameras. The latter are evolving into yet more sophisticated SLR (single lens reflex) cameras with interchangeable lenses, restoring to some extent the idea of the sophisticated, specialized and conspicuous apparatus of the tourist. This simply means that any individual may have more than one camera on their person at any time: smartphone, laptop camera, SLR camera and handy instant camera. Static photography also merges into video, as digital cameras and camera phones typically support both functions. Many cameras have functions for taking a rapid sequence (or burst) of photographs suitable for rapidly moving subjects.

In sum, the point I wish to emphasize here is the step change in the quantity of photographs engendered by digital photography, a change that affects the qualitative understanding of photography as it relates to heritage.

Digital photography and heritage

There are several obvious ways that digital photography impinges on heritage practices (Kalay *et al.* 2008). Digital photographs serve as a means of documentation, of keeping and sharing records, from the point of view of the heritage specialist as well as audiences and consumers. Digital photography features in the analysis of heritage artefacts and sites. Recording and reconstructing artefacts through scanning and photogrammetry are advanced forms of digital photography. Three-dimensional (3D) models of heritage sites and artefacts may deploy textures and surface materials collected from digital photographs. Photo sharing reveals what interests people most about heritage sites. It serves as a means of disseminating interest, education, publicity and raising awareness.

Digital photography is complicit in many innovations in the service of heritage. Amongst the most unusual are the experiments with very large numbers of images taken from sources such as Flickr in order to reconstruct 3D models of places and artefacts. Microsoft's Photosynth[1] is a program that takes any set of digital photographs with overlapping content (such as a random set of photographs along the Grand Canal in Venice) and stitches them together to make a composite, or at least provides a compellingly visual way of navigating through a series of overlapping images: registered, spatialized and hyperlinked. Increasingly we are seeing the use of old maps, available as overlays on services similar to Google Maps. As the tourist walks through a town they can see their location on their smartphone according to how the place was mapped 100 years ago (see Speed, this volume).

Digital photographers and their audiences can tag photographs and elements within photographs presented online, contributing to a kind of community-based metatagging or 'folksonomy' (Cattuto et al. 2007; Vander Wal 2007). Technologies exist for the collection and tagging of stories surrounding artefacts, as in the case of the so-called 'Internet of Things' (Barthel et al. 2010). Colleagues and I have also developed uses of mobile phone cameras to expose so-called 'hidden art' or graffiti, using automated image matching techniques as if the art is concealed on the walls of buildings (Coyne et al. 2009). Such techniques have gone mainstream with 'augmented reality' applications for smartphones such as Aurasma.[2] Digital photographs in very large numbers constitute data to be processed, analysed, navigated, mined and displayed.

The innovation that is digital photography, and its spinouts, in the realm of social media operate not only in the service of heritage, but are complicit in its definition. For example, the Mukurtu website[3] is designed for managing cultural resources (e.g. images) for which European and Western ownership-oriented rights do not necessarily apply. Whereas the liberal impulse is to value openness and free access for all, certain indigenous communities may feel that open access fits uncomfortably with local kinship and authority structures. For example, the Mukurtu protocol may restrict access to a photograph that shows the image of a recently deceased person. If it is tagged as such then members of that family may be spared seeing the image on searches. The site allows for the negotiation of access rights to people within and outside the community according to local custom and sensitivities. According to the developers, Mukurtu is: 'A free and open source community archive platform that provides international standards-based content management tools adaptable to the local cultural protocols and intellectual property systems of indigenous communities, libraries, archives, and museums' (Srinivasan et al. 2009). Heritage no longer, if it ever did, references a state of affairs that can be assumed, to be recorded, documented, interpreted and disseminated, but is in flux. As attested in this volume, as society changes so do issues of heritage, and in ways that are heterogeneous across diverse communities (Isaac 2011).

Digital images, as raw data, processed and versioned, also constitute new heritage items. The question arises as to what uses archivists, archaeologists, audiences and visitors of the future will make of the inordinately large collections of images stored on the world's growing numbers of hard drives and cloud servers, not to mention how these resources might intentionally be forgotten or disposed of (Mayer-Schonberger 2009).

In this highly industrialized and technologized age, the issue of quantity brings to mind mass markets and mass consumption. Archives deal in large quantities and carry risks. Quantity also pertains to crowds, which involve bodies in number whether assembled or dispersed, whether taking photographs or being photographed. One way to manage quantities is to classify and thereby think of the ways in which objects are the same, but then quantities also highlight differences. In what follows I will deploy theses themes as a schema for investigating photographic mosaics and multiples: massification, the archive, crowds and the unfamiliar.

Digital photographs and massification

It is tempting to think of the production of very large numbers of digital photographs as yet another step in the industrialization of image production to which critic Walter Benjamin refers, constituting a diminution in the value of the image (Benjamin 1992). It is worth unpicking the mass market aspect of this medium. Governments and economists identify heritage as part of the creative and cultural industries (Gray 2009), particularly as consumed through tourism. The adoption of a commodity for mass consumption is often referred to as 'massification', that also implies a process by which societies become 'mass societies' and deploy mass media.

Digital photography is a mass phenomenon, especially in so far as it is tied to photo sharing via social media. Rather than the lone consumer, social media technologies start with the premise of mass communication between thousands of people, so-called many–to–many communication, an unpredictable mass of expert and inexpert potential collaborators (Ofcom 2008). As with conventional broadcast media, the default condition is openness. Organizations or the state have to introduce controls if they want to restrict communication to smaller groups. On the one hand social media photo sharing promotes consumer-led creation, i.e. the power of the crowd through shared resources and innovations — 'crowdsourcing' (Rheingold 2002; Feld and Wilcox 2008; Hand 2010). On the other hand, photo sharing also implies access to mass markets, amplifying the modernist conflation of freedom of expression with free markets and competition.

Massification constructs a particular frame around the concept of the unique and the individual — it brings singularity into its mass discourse. The concept of the 'long tail' accounts for consumer demand that is modest and of small scale (Anderson 2006). The long tail is what you get when you rank individual products according to the volume of sales, and find that there are only a few products with large sales but many products with only small markets. Add up these niche markets, and you end up with the potential for high volumes of sales at the niche end overall. Economists present the Internet as a means of enabling large numbers of small-scale producers to establish their own niche markets. In other words, social media and photo sharing provide an environment for the assertion and satisfaction of minority interests, thus supporting the possibility of highlighting, supporting and circulating heritage materials appreciated by only a small number of people.

There are specific websites for the exercise of such specialist interest, notably the Landscape/Portrait site,[4] where individuals can record a self-portrait telling what they think about where and how they live in the UK. This site allows people to compare these self-portraits with the stereotypes that already exist for each UK postcode area. There will usually be someone out there with whom you can share your photographs and interests. Alternatively, any individual can exercise their own interest for future generations to pick up on. With online photo sharing, for any digital photographer there is potential satisfaction in the anticipation of a posthumous contribution to a heritage pool.

The Geographic British Isles project[5] attempts large-scale organized photo sharing with heritage objectives. It declares that it: 'aims to collect geographically representative photographs and information for every square kilometre of Great Britain and Ireland, and you can be part of it'. All images, and hence all subjects so represented are commoditized, are available on an even grid for mass consumption. On the other hand such compilations make a space for the otherwise unacknowledged and the marginal. I explore this tension further under the section on Defamiliarization. Attending to the margins borrows support from ideas about appropriation. Opportunities for tactical appropriation of the everyday release otherwise acquiescent consumers from subservience to capitalism. For arguments along these lines see Henry Jenkins (1992) and Michel de Certeau (1984).

Toxic archives

There are risks in holding large numbers of records, not least the archiving of digital photographs. As indicated already, heritage has an institutional aspect. It is concerned with the conservation of traditions, places and artefacts. No matter how liberal, open and inclusive, one of the main functions of any institution is simply to perpetuate itself, and to conserve its existence, functions and values. Institutions are after all those organizations usually charged with responsibility for preservation. Derrida links this institutional function to the conservation of information, suggesting though that the desire to *preserve* information is in some way a symptom of an inbuilt and unavoidable desire to *destroy* it (Derrida and Prenowitz 1995; Bell 2004). Drawing on Sigmund Freud's concepts of the pleasure principle and the death drive, Derrida argues that an information store (archive) on the one hand involves a desire to safeguard information for the internal consumption and edification of the people holding on to it, but it also entails the need to reveal information to the outside world and for the benefit of others. Letting information out in some way destroys it. At the very least exposure of the archive has the propensity to damage the institution's functioning.

Fragile paper-based photographs need eventually to be exposed to unpredictable climatic conditions and the touch of human hands in order to be scanned, digitized and studied. There are risks in so exposing the physical archive.

In order to conserve, there is a sense in which you have to risk destroying the thing you want to preserve by exposing it to the outside world. Then there is the risk that comes from putting your own images and information out to public view. Images can be copied and exploited by others — as documented in the case of employees brought to account for the content of images circulated on photo sharing sites regarded as no longer appropriate in professional life. But Derrida was referring not only to the fragility of old documents or risk to one's reputation or claim on intellectual property, in highlighting the destructive tendency inherent in the keeping of archives.

The supposed problems of the archive are well illustrated through the phenomenon of WikiLeaks[6] and similar 'whistle-blowing' websites. This very public revelation of secret government communications, including images, exposes a propensity within organizations and institutions to *keep* secrets (Žižek 2011). Institutions, as well as individuals, want and need to be secretive, to keep information hidden, as a way of preserving their authority and reputation. But government departments, private organizations and individuals also insist on *storing* those secrets, deliberately harbouring information they would rather not expose.

Institutions store records, memos, transcripts, emails, cable messages and images in drawers, file boxes and on servers. Taking a lead from Derrida, it seems that such incendiary documents are time bombs of an organization's own making, kept officially and ready to be stumbled upon or leaked. Even if their exposure fails to destroy the institutions that harbour these secrets, they at least require the expenditure of labour to restore order, effect cover-ups and reinstate the organization's authority. The secrets on which the organization depends entail risks and costs, but are after all essential for its operations.

It is worth reflecting here on the meaning of 'information'. As well as giving something a form, information has its origins in the concept of the secret. Think of 'to inform' as to disclose incriminating evidence, the first meaning outlined in the Oxford English Dictionary. The archive is a collection of secrets; some of them are essential, such as staff records, and some can be exposed for the organization's and its clients' benefit, as in the case of a database of e-books for purchase, or the Home Office's instructions on how to get a passport, and of course the image libraries of museums and galleries. But some collections can be lethally destructive of their hosts. Derrida is referring to this primary characteristic of information. At the core of the information concept is this tendency, if not the desire, to destroy, which is the opposite of educating, edifying and preserving.

The revelations from the WikiLeaks website raised many questions about the probity and trustworthiness we invest in leaders, organizations and records. Why must people say and do what they don't want *everyone* to hear and see? The same question hangs over the propensity to produce photographs, especially pictures that are personal and private, revealing and potentially salacious. Then there are the technologies and motivations at the disposal of those instigating leaks, those who would reveal what is obviously meant to be secret. The WikiLeaks revelations also raised questions about why those secrets are *stored* in the first place. Why are such records retained? The answer resides in the nature of organizations and institutions. We should not be so surprised when we reflect that no institution can survive without its secrets, and that concealment is at the heart of the information concept. This is a propensity that seems to spill over to individuals, though with more limited consequences.

According to Derrida, '[n]othing is less reliable, nothing is less clear today than the word "archive"', and this trouble is due to 'the trouble of secrets, of plots, of clandestineness, of half-private, half-public conjurations, always at the unstable limit between public and private, between the family, the society, and the State, between the family and an intimacy even more private than the family, between oneself and oneself' (Derrida and Prenowitz 1995: 57). Neither should we be surprised that one of the weapons deployed against the WikiLeaks figurehead Julian Assange was the exposure of his own apparent private indiscretions, though as yet unsupported by digital photography.

Individuals are also creatures of institutions, and have a vested interest in their preservation. Individuals also have an interest in maintaining their own reputations, especially in institutional and organizational contexts. Photo sharing, exercised willingly or maliciously by others, highlights the inevitable riskiness of both storing and circulating digital photographs. This risk in part is attributable again to the very large numbers of images involved. As is the case with WikiLeaks, the revealed archives and their contents exist in extremely large numbers. It is easy for institutions to lose track of any potentially salacious or toxic record. One thinks of the crate containing the supposedly lethal 'arc of the covenant' portrayed in the film *Raiders of the Lost Arc*, eventually secured and lost in a vast warehouse, ready to be stumbled upon by a future archivist or janitor. As improved forensic techniques are able to uncover crime scene evidence formerly concealed (e.g. DNA detection), so there are now technologies for transporting, searching and mining mega databases of textual records. The visual archive waits for such time as the tools exist for sifting through and analysing millions of images available online, to uncover secrets otherwise occluded in the noise of massive photographic production.

In this volume, Liu makes cogent reference to the Bhopal gas leak records, the availability of the material for future analysis, and the role of the online archive in keeping an issue alive, though dormant for the time being. Such materials include photographic images.

Bodies and crowds

Multiplication is in any case a device used by institutions to perpetuate power and control, as well as to unsettle it. Museum theorist Eilean Hooper-Greenhill develops an analysis of museums on the basis of social theorist Michel Foucault's understanding of the way institutions promote power (Foucault 1977; Hooper-Greenhill 1992). Museums and other custodians of heritage are not only storehouses of knowledge, but also instruments of power. Extending Hooper-Greenhill's analysis, they are complicit in various means of exercising power. This invariably involves bodies, a theme that provides further access to the potency of digital photography en masse.

There is an inevitable physicality to photography. Cameras have to be carried. Their operation requires physical movements, positioning to get the right shot, and human subjects freeze and comport themselves in stock poses in front of cameras. Early cameras were mounted on heavy tripods that had to be carried around, and subjects would have to stand very still. Personal and portable cameras have undergone various changes in relation to the body. Box cameras would be suspended at waist height via a cord looped around the neck of the photographer, who would peer down onto a translucent plate showing what was in front of the camera. The plate would be shielded from extraneous light by a series of collapsible shutters. Cameras also deployed eye-level viewfinders. Many cameras are still held to the eye of the photographer. With improved LCD displays, fewer cameras have an eye level viewfinder, the scene to be photographed appearing on a screen at the back of the camera. This is also the case with mobile phone cameras, encouraging the photographer's pose now of holding the camera at some distance from the eye, and even at arm's length. With the panoramic feature enabled, this posture is also translated to a steady sweeping motion of the body in a 180–360 degree turn. Photography involves procedures and practices that require bodily movement and comportment. These practices are changing and evolving as the technology changes. With fast electronic 'shutter speeds' a steady hand is no longer required, other than in exceptional lighting conditions, and manual or automatic corrections can be made after the image has been taken.

The body is complicit in behaviours and practices pertaining to places and environments, not least in influencing the character and definition of spaces designated as formal and informal, sacred and profane, public and private. The body is comported differently in different places, and certain locations tolerate or encourage the body of the photographer to varying degrees. Gatherings of people allow or encourage the photographic body as part of the background noise at public events, special occasions, the sites of monuments and in many heritage contexts. On the other hand, the photographic body presents as especially out of place when positioned in someone's private yard, among someone else's family, in the middle of a job interview or on a crowded bus.

The body is an issue for institutions. Foucault identifies the ways in which institutions manage the body (Foucault 1977). He focuses on schools, military establishments, hospitals and prisons. These institutions perpetuate orderliness by containing and confining the body. People are contained in classrooms, dormitories, hospital beds and prison cells, and these confinements are imposed on bodies. There is a physicality to this containment, sometimes even involving restraint, and other pressures to keep bodies in their allotted space. Another method at the disposal of institutions is to keep a watch on what people are doing, i.e. to keep an eye on their bodies. There are obvious technologies for implementing surveillance, including cameras, but space can also be arranged such that you are always under the watchful eye of someone or other, from balconies, towers, windows and other vantage points.

We are now at a stage where these points of prospect are also for people with cameras. Space can also be arranged such that there is the *possibility* that you are being watched or photographed, or that people may be watching or photographing each other. People tend to behave differently in places where they know that they might be seen than in places where they are invisible to the gaze of others. Not only might you be seen, but you might deliberately or inadvertently appear in someone's photograph.

Foucault also refers to the training of the body as a means of perpetuating order, i.e. the division of the body into parts, as when a piano player focuses on the wrists and fingers during an exercise. Foucault also refers to the strategy of stripping the body of any individual signifying dimension, by clothing it in a uniform that is the same as everyone else's, or requiring people to move in a uniform way, as in marching. Stripping the body is also a tactic for removing the usual means by which bodies signify. The other tactic is to require bodies to rise in the morning at set times, to follow standardized daily routines, in other words to partition time. A further mechanism to which Foucault refers involves posture, routines, orders and drills that require people to sit or stand, or assume a submissive, cowering, dignified or military bearing.

Digital photography cuts into each of these institutional mechanisms. Photography can restrict, partition and define movement. People behave differently in front of cameras, and are in a sense 'contained' in their movement by the lens, exemplified in the gathering of photographic evidence, acquired via mobile phones as a weapon by protestors, police and bystanders. Photography features as a medium for the exercise of power. Think of those infamous mobile phone photographs of naked prisoners in Abu Ghraib.

The body is present in the reception of heritage: bodies with eyes raised to cathedral ceilings or slumped in boredom, quietly and respectfully composed before a Rembrandt or in restless movement in the café or children's activity area, stooped over a box of old photographs or testing the weight of an ornament on the mantlepiece. Overlay with these comportments the body in reception of heritage, the photographing body, and the body as it appears in photographs, the body multiplied, and massified through digital photography.

A major innovation in computer graphics emerged with the easy simulation of crowds of people moving, walking and dancing with plausible variation and apparent individuality, famously demonstrated in the crowd scenes of James Cameron's 1997 film *Titanic*, an effect reproduced in many films since (e.g. *Lord of the Rings* and *Avatar*). The software commonly used for simulated battle scenes and crowds in demonstrations, stadiums and sports is appropriately entitled Massive.[7] Massive is emblematic of the way we think of bodies in digital photography, and in heritage. Think of the appetite for role play, pageants and the reconstruction of events such as historic battles. Bodies in number appear in digital photography, as backdrops and in the panoramic capture of crowd scenes. Bodies also appear in quantity in the mosaics and multiples of very large numbers of casual portraits online.

Defamiliarization

It is easy to assume that digital photography diminishes our engagement in place. A digital photograph, taken in haste during a fleeting visit might mean we spend even less time at the place. The digital image capture is sufficient to consummate the occasion of being there. Then we move on. Participation is transformed into the acquisition of yet more digital photographs. Such practices transform our involvement in, and definition of, space and spatial experience, and render us less inhabitants of places than transients in non-places (Augé 1995). Museum theorist Gwyneira Issac asserts that interactive digital displays in museums can 'enchant' the visitor, but with the technology rather than the artefact, creating new relationships that create distance rather than a sense of intimate engagement (Isaac 2011). Sandra Dudley calls for the need to attend to materiality in museums and heritage practice in *Museum Materialities* (Dudley 2009). Complaints about a loss of materiality are concomitant with the supposed diminution in a noble and elevating sense of craftsmanship (Sennett 2008). Place is no longer experienced and received as place; photography is no longer the careful exercise of a meaningful craft.

However, in the absence of hard evidence one may speculate just as readily that digital photography heightens the sense of place and materiality (Edwards 2009). Precisely because the plethora of images, for all its promise, fails to deliver the experience of the place, we value the actuality of being there all the more. No one would claim that viewing a street in Paris through a collection of photographs, in Streetview, Photosynth or 360 Panorama[8] would dampen our resolve to go there; it might possibly increase it. It might in any case make us want to explore back streets, unusual places, and seek out the unfamiliar, the less photographed. The argument here is similar to the defence that can be offered for the perpetuation of craft production. The concept of the local making of things, handcrafting, customized production, is a product of the industrial age. Machine production brings into relief the concept of craft, unrecognized before the introduction of large-scale mass production. One could argue, thanks to computers, that never before has there been such an emphasis on the tangible, the handmade and the possibilities in digital media to restore, appreciate or enhance a sense of craft (McCullough 1999).

As well as exposing concepts of the handmade, images displayed, sorted and arrayed also expose the abnormal and unusual. One of the themes developed in Eduard Tufte's compelling analysis of pictorial representations of data is the capability of images laid out on grids or mosaics to effect comparison, and thereby expose subtle differences that might otherwise go unnoticed (Tufte 1990). Two red squares may look identical when several metres apart, but differences in hue, saturation or lightness may only be revealed when they are immediately adjacent. As Liu describes in this volume, the curator invites similar subtle comparisons by the careful juxtaposition of images.

Digital photography revives the art of the multiple, as practised by Young British Artists (YBAs) in the 1990s. The organization of digital images, and their thumbnails, continues a fascination with, and necessity for, ordered arrays of graphical information. Printing processes encouraged the multiplication of images: wallpaper, fabric patterns and gift-wrapping paper, for example. The concept of the 'multiple' continues as an art form as illustrated in the artist Damien Hirst's colourful wallpaper designs consisting of repetitive arrays of pills and biblical quotations, or rows of pharmaceutical products on ordered shelves, as well as more recent work by the artist Julian Walker, involving the meticulous organization of small and ostensibly trivial found objects mounted and arrayed as if biological specimens behind glass.

It is well known that heritage consumers (i.e. museum visitors and cultural tourists) have a propensity to repeat and mimic what already exists in the cultural circuit (Urry 1990, 2007). As social creatures we tend to value what others value. Digital photography is one of these media of reproduction. It perpetuates the rapid reproduction of the standard view, the identification of what is valued. But by virtue of the sheer volume of low cost digital imagery in circulation, digital photography provides opportunities for some individuals to focus, deliberately or by accident, on the unusual, the marginal, the hidden and the peculiar perspective, if only others can then find the images so produced.

Heritage artefacts have a revealing function in any case, exposing current conditions and attitudes. The emerging practices of digital photography participate further in rendering the familiar strange, or to quote geographer David Lowenthal, render the past as 'a foreign country' (Lowenthal 1985). Emerging digital photographic practices also have this capability to reveal difference. The medium itself brings into sharp relief the nature of visuality. It reveals as much about the human understanding of environment as it transforms that understanding. Some commentators even claim of digital photography that it engenders a 'heightened visual sensitivity' (Lee 2009).

Photography in any case renders the familiar strange, by planting it on a two-dimensional surface, statically, from a particular angle. It also invites experimentation: the use of strange angles, fisheye lens, the panorama and 3D stereoscopic imaging. The various operations possible with digital photographs amplify the possibilities.

The introduction of the high dynamic range (HDR) feature into digital cameras arguably brings sky conditions and cloud formations into prominence, as HDR evens out exposure readings for the sky and the ground, by taking photographs with different exposure settings in rapid succession. I might see the sky differently after using HDR, even when the camera is back in my pocket. At the very least HDR revives issues of foreground and background.

Emerging digital photographic practices also reveal much about people's attitudes to time, heritage and place. There are now digital photographic practices that would have appeared unusual even ten years ago: visitors photographing paintings at an exhibition, diners sending photographs of plates of food to friends, individuals recording portraits of themselves every day for a year from a camera held at arm's length, and the celebrated case of painter David Hockney emailing a new artwork produced on his iPhone or iPad to his circuit of friends every day.[9] Digital imagery emphasizes the human propensity to collect and hoard, to order things in time, to date stamp and in a sense to arrest time. According to Kittler, early film (and the gramophone) promised the 'ability to store time' (Kittler *et al.* 1987), a trajectory continuing with digital photography.

Digital photography also amplifies the anticipatory aspect of human experience, in other words it amplifies the concept of a future. Heritage and the archive are not only about holding on to what we designate as belonging to the present or the past, but draws attention to futurity. What will the technologies enable, how will culture have purchase in a future? Bell and Derrida allude to this theme as it pertains to the archive (Derrida and Prenowitz 1995; Bell 2004).

The temporal aspect of the archive and digital photography brings to light the nature of interpretive experience as an excursion into the unknown, a process driven by the temporal phenomena of expectation and anticipation. Photography involves collecting, sifting and transporting objects and information back to home base. It is fieldwork of a kind. Most importantly, digital photography takes on the character of an excursion into another country. To move into the field, even when it is close to home, involves configuring circumstances so that the familiar presents as something new. In this respect the pilgrim is the typical fieldworker, undertaking a transformative rite of passage (Turner 1967). Studies in tourism amplify this process. For John Urry: 'Like the pilgrim the tourist moves from a familiar place to a far place and then returns to the familiar place' (Urry 1990: 11; Urry 2007). Part of this encounter involves the provision of a new backdrop to the ordinary aspects of the researcher–tourist's life, such as walking, shopping, eating and looking. The gaze of the tourist 'renders extraordinary activities that otherwise would be mundane and everyday' (Urry 1990: 13). There is pleasure in eating as we usually eat, even from the same menu, but at a café in a Prague rather than our own dining room or in front of the television; or to walk as we usually walk, but by a lake or in the streets of Macau. The new territory can be 'sensuously 'other' to everyday routines and places' (ibid.: 155).

The digital photographer in the field operates under similar processes of defamiliarization. Travellers often carry instruments that aid the recording process: notebooks, optical instruments, sound recorders, personalized electronic devices (smartphones, GPS, digital cameras, video), which not only allow them to capture information, but are complicit in the filtering and invention of the phenomenon under observation. Instruments amplify the strangeness of the encounter. Networked devices and social media invite experimentation that further renders the familiar strange, defamiliarizing the ordinary activities of moving about, talking and looking.

And what of the homecoming? Not only does the fieldworker, tourist or photographer bring something back to the laboratory, home or studio, but encounters the starting point again, renewed. The home is different. As for Alice returning from Looking Glass World the familiar sitting room takes on a different cast.

Theorists of interpretation (hermeneutics) present such mundane processes of excursion and return as key means by which we come to read, understand and interpret texts and images. The act of interpretation has been described as the transformation brought about by negotiation across a threshold, the excursion of the traveller, the alien encounter that in fact discloses something about the familiar context of the home. The movement is repetitive, and even obsessive, involving recurring excursion and return. Interpretation and fieldwork involve re–presentation and re–creation. Interpretation is an operation of repetition and multiplication. I develop these themes elsewhere in relation to the seminal writing of Hans–Georg Gadamer on hermeneutics (Gadamer 1975), Joel Weinsheimer on the excursion (Weinsheimer 1985), and insights from working with the defamiliarizing media of smartphones and other mobile instruments (see Coyne 2010).

Add to this interpretive practice of repetitive excursion and return the phenomenon of the multitude. The vastness of the record is itself a vehicle for defamiliarization. By what other means would we come to see so many images, some of which are familiar, but in such profusion, and thrown together in multiples and mosaics?

Conclusion

Multiplication relates to repetition, a theme close to the uncanny, as developed by Sigmund Freud, Giles Deleuze and many others (Caputo 1987; Deleuze 1994; Kierkegaard 2001). In this chapter I claimed access to the implications of digital photography for heritage studies via concepts of the archive, which is in turn a mainstay of institutions, including museums and other custodians of heritage matters. The sheer volume of easy and incessant digital image production represents a step change in our understanding of the image. Digital images are not only pristine targets for isolated theorizing and interpretation as suggested by much of Mitchell's 'picture theory' (Mitchell 1995), but are also to be understood as multiples, as mass phenomena, as vast archives in which may be buried risky and toxic materials, and on which might be printed crowds of bodies. Each aspect of the digital mosaic harbours the potential for revealing differences, and heightening as well as occluding aspects of heritage and place.

Notes

1 Microsoft Photosynth, software tool for creating immersive 3D experiences: http://photosynth.net/ (accessed 24 November 2011).
2 Aurasma, augmented reality application: http://www.aurasma.com (accessed 24 November 2011).
3 Mukurtu, open source community content management system: http://www.mukurtuarchive.org (accessed 24 November 2011).
4 The Landscape/Portrait project: http://www.landscape-portrait.com (accessed 24 November 2011).
5 The Geographic British Isles project: http://www.geograph.org.uk (accessed 24 November 2011).
6 WikiLeaks, whistle-blowing website: http://wikileaks.org/ (accessed 24 November 2011).
7 Massive, suite of simulation and visualization tools for autonomous agent driven animation: http://www.massivesoftware.com (accessed 24 November 2011).
8 360 Panorama by Occipital, software application for real time panorama creation: http://occipital.com/360/app (accessed 24 November 2011).
9 David Hockney website: http://www.hockneypictures.com (accessed 24 November 2011).

References

Anderson, C. (2006) *The Long Tail: Why the Future of Business is Selling Less of More*, New York: Hyperion.

Augé, M. (1995) *Non-places: Introduction to an Anthropology of Supermodernity*, trans. J. Howe, London: Verso.

Barthel, R., A. Hudson-Smith, M. de Jode and B. Blundell (2010) *Tales of Things: The Internet of 'Old' Things — Collecting Stories of Objects, Places and Spaces*, Working Paper, London: CASA, UCL.

Bell, D.F. (2004) 'Infinite archives', *Substance: A Review of Theory & Literary Criticism*, 33(3): 148–161.

Benjamin, W. (1992) 'The work of art in the age of mechanical reproduction', in H. Arendt (ed.) *Illuminations*, London: Fontana.

Caputo, J.D. (1987) *Radical Hermeneutics: Repetition, Deconstruction, and the Hermeneutical Project*, Bloomington, IN: Indiana University Press.

Cattuto, C., V. Loreto and L. Pietronero (2007) 'Semiotic dynamics and collaborative tagging', *PNAS (Proceedings of the National Academy of Sciences of the United States of America)*, 4(5): 1461–1464.

Churchill, E.F. and J. Ubois (2008) 'Designing for digital archives', *Interactions*, March 2008: 10–13.

Coyne, R. (2010) *The Tuning of Place: Sociable Spaces and Pervasive Digital Media*, Cambridge, MA: MIT Press.

Coyne, R. (2011) *Derrida for Architects*, London: Routledge.

Coyne, R., M. Wright, J. Stewart and H. Ekeus (2009) 'Virtual flagships and sociable media', in A. Kent and R. Brown (eds) *Flagship Marketing: Concepts and Places*, London: Routledge.

de Certeau, M. (1984) *The Practice of Everyday Life*, trans. S. Rendall, Berkeley, CA: University of California Press.

Deleuze, G. (1994) *Difference and Repetition*, trans. P. Patton, London: Athlone Press.

Derrida, J. and E. Prenowitz (1995) 'Archive fever: A Freudian impression', *Diacritics*, 25(2): 9–63.

Dudley, S. (2009) *Museum Materialities: Objects, Engagements, Interpretations*, London: Routledge.

Edwards, E. (2009) 'Photographs and history: Emotion and materiality', in S.H. Dudley (ed.) *Museum Materialities: Objects, Engagements, Interpretations*, London: Routledge.

Feld, L. and N. Wilcox (2008) *Netroots Rising: How a Citizen Army of Bloggers and Online Activists is Changing American Politics*, Santa Barbara, CA: Greenwood.

Foster, M.D. (2009) 'What time is this picture? Cameraphones, tourism, and the digital gaze in Japan', *Social Identities*, 15(3): 351–372.

Foucault, M. (1977) *Discipline and Punish: The Birth of the Prison*, London: Penguin.

Gadamer, H.-G. (1975) *Truth and Method*, trans. J. Weinsheimer, New York: Seabury Press.

Gombrich, E. (1960) *Art and Illusion*, London: Phaidon.

Gray, I. (2009) *Creative Industries: Technology Strategy 2009–2012*, Swindon: Technology Strategy Board.

Hand, E. (2010) 'People power: Networks of human minds are taking citizen science to a new level', *Nature*, 466: 685–687.

Hooper-Greenhill, E. (1992) *Museums and the Shaping of Knowledge*, London: Routledge.

Isaac, G. (2011) 'Digital enchantments: Identifying with electronic media at the National Museum of the American Indian', in H. Lidchi and H.J. Tsinhnahjinnie (eds) *Visual Currencies: Reflections on Native Photography*, Edinburgh: National Museums Scotland.

Jenkins, H. (1992) *Textual Poachers: Television Fans and Participatory Culture*, New York: Routledge.

Kalay, Y.E., T. Kvan and J. Affleck (2008) *New Heritage: New Media and Cultural Heritage*, London: Routledge.

Kierkegaard, S. (2001) 'Repetition: An essay in experimental psychology by Constantin Constantius', in J. Chamberlain and J. Rée (eds) *The Kierkegard Reader*, London: Blackwell.

Kittler, F., D. von Mücke and P.L. Similon (1987) 'Gramophone, film, typewriter', *October*, 41: 101–118.

Lasén, A. and E. Gómez-Cruz (2009) 'Digital photography and picture sharing: Redefining the public/private divide', *Knowledge, Technology and Policy*, 22: 205–215.

Lee, D.-H. (2009) 'Mobile snapshots and private/public boundaries', *Knowledge, Technology and Policy*, 22: 161–171.

Lowenthal, D. (1985) *The Past is a Foreign Country*, Cambridge: Cambridge University Press.

Mayer-Schonberger, V. (2009) *Delete: The Virtue of Forgetting in the Digital Age*, Princeton, NJ: Princeton University Press.

McCullough, M. (1999) *Abstracting Craft: The Practiced Digital Hand*, Cambridge, MA: MIT Press.

Mitchell, W.J.T. (1995) *Picture Theory: Essays on Verbal and Visual Representation*, Chicago, IL: University of Chicago Press.

Mitchell, W.J.T. (2005) 'There are no visual media', *Journal of Visual Culture*, 4(2): 257–266.

Ofcom (2008) *Report: Social Networking: A Quantitative and Qualitative Research Report into Attitudes, Behaviours and Use*, London: Ofcom (Office of Communications).

Rheingold, H. (2002) *Smart Mobs: The Next Social Revolution*, Cambridge, MA: Basic Books.

Sennett, R. (2008) *The Craftsman*, London: Penguin.

Silberman, N. (2008) 'Chasing the unicorn?: the quest for "essence" in digital heritage', in Y.E. Kalay, T. Kvan and J. Affleck (eds) *New Heritage: New Media and Cultural Heritage*, London: Routledge.

Srinivasan, R., R. Boast, J. Furner and K.M. Becvar (2009) 'Digital museums and diverse cultural knowledges: Moving past the traditional catalog', *The Information Society*, 25: 265–278.

Treib, M. (2011) 'The image: Print and pixel', *Architectural Research Quarterly*, 15(1): 16–23.

Tufte, E.R. (1990) *Envisioning Information*, Cheshire, CT: Graphics Press.

Turner, V. (1967) *The Forest of Symbols: Aspects of Ndembu Ritual*, Ithaca, NY: Cornell University Press.

UNESCO (1972) Convention Concerning the Protection of the World Cultural and Natural Heritage, Paris: UNESCO, 1972. http://whc.unesco.org/en/conventiontext (accessed 25 November 2011).

Urry, J. (1990) *The Tourist Gaze: Leisure and Travel in Contemporary Societies*, London: Sage.

Urry, J. (2007) *Mobilities*, Cambridge: Polity.

Van House, N.A. (2009) 'Collocated photo sharing, story-telling, and the performance of self', *International Journal of Human–Computer Studies*, 67: 1073–1086.

Van House, N. and E.F. Churchill (2008) 'Technologies of memory: Key issues and critical perspectives', *Memory Studies*, 1: 295–310.

Vander Wal, T. (2007) 'Folksonomy coinage and definition'. http://vanderwal.net/folksonomy.html (last accessed 2007).

Weinsheimer, J.C. (1985) *Gadamer's Hermeneutics: A Reading of Truth and Method*, New Haven, CT, and London: Yale University Press.

Žižek, S. (2011) 'Good manners in the age of WikiLeaks', *London Review of Books*, 33(2): 9–10.

10

MOBILE OUIJA BOARDS

Chris Speed

Introduction

Ten years ago, at the 'Habitus 2000: A Sense of Place' conference in Perth, Australia, the cultural geographer Steve Pile articulated the potential for cultural events within cities to bring back the dead and remind us of the past. During his talk, Pile described the occasion of an anti-capitalist march that had taken place on 1 May in London, and how a series of national monuments had been defaced. Pile drew the delegates' attention to some graffiti that had been spray painted on to a war memorial. He described how two doors had been painted on to the side of the memorial: one with a female symbol and the other with a male, denoting that they were toilet doors. Pile went on to describe how the editorials read in the newspapers that featured the images of the toilet doors. Whilst the damage to the familiar capitalist targets such as MacDonald's and Starbucks was taken as par for the course, the desecration of a war memorial was a step too far and the act had stirred the memories of the many thousands of people who had lost their lives during the Second World War. Pile described how the spray-painted doors had actually unlocked a passageway to the past; following their widespread publication in a national newspaper, the ghosts of thousands of soldiers could be understood to walk through them into the consciousness of the public.

This chapter reflects upon Pile's anecdote that was later explored in more detail through his article 'Spectral cities: Where the repressed returns and other short stories' published in 2004, and it places the phenomenon of 'haunting' into the context of mobile social media and locative tagging. The advent of affordable smartphones that come equipped with data free contracts and location services has meant that people are beginning to change the way that they interact with artefacts and architectures as well as the social connections that provide them with 'heritage'. Platforms such as the Apple iPhone and Google Android that contain GPS (global positioning systems) and camera technologies for reading quick response (QR) codes (two dimensional barcodes) are becoming powerful research platforms for exhuming narratives and representations of the past.

The cursive strokes written across public streets by the many people who 'walk the city' (de Certeau 1984) are now being written with the aid of mobile phones. iPhones, Androids and BlackBerries are all influencing the way in which people move across de Certeau's canvas of the city. For those who find themselves in an unfamiliar city, a smartphone is fast becoming a popular option with which to begin orientating themselves in a strange place. Using mobile versions of Google Maps, phone users are offered quick and direct instructions as 'way finding' solutions that solve the problem of asking local residents for help.

However, there are many types of visitors to a city: some require up-to-date directions to specific locations provided by maps that accurately represent the streets and traffic conditions; others are less concerned with the accuracy of the city 'now' and are prepared to negotiate a city through historical narratives or cultural themes. From ghost tours to walks associated with the famous, the geographical focus of a city shifts to a cultural perspective for the tourist, while the city is articulated as a representation of the past. A representation that the satellite navigation maps cannot support, as their satellite imagery of the present punctures the willing suspension of disbelief adopted by the tourist.

In the same way that the temporal emphasis of city maps differ for inhabitants and tourists, so too does the provenance of material artefacts that are purchased by different types of shoppers. Many people out in the high street on a Saturday are looking for new items to buy. Some shoppers expect items that are fresh, immaculate in condition and presented in such a way that obfuscates their point of social and personal origin, instead indicating a brand and a sell by date. Others are more interested in the history behind their objects; for them, antique dealers and second-hand shops offer a longer temporal perspective for artefacts, so that these may be identified as having a narrative that supports their integrity. Wearing the marks of previous ownership, these items, like the tourists' geography of the city are without barcodes and are valuable according to their fiction as much as their fact.

This chapter reflects on two software projects that explore the opportunities that mobile social media offers to reveal the historical characteristics of places and things. Whilst the production of much contemporary technology aspires toward closing the gap between the present and the future by presenting the most up-to-date information, the author (and colleagues) have enjoyed the chance to develop applications that point the arrow of time in the opposite direction – a creative approach that gives many of the ghosts of the past the chance to inhabit our present.

Out of the car and back on foot: the emergence of the smartphone into the city

Revisiting de Certeau's text 'Walking in the City' (Thrift 2004), Nigel Thrift asserted the role of the car as a socially sensitive technology through which we can experience the contemporary city. Through the development of automobile technology, its capacity to support the communication with others on the road, and our belief that we can affect its responsiveness to the road through our grip of the steering wheel and by shifting our weight as we sway around corners, Thrift describes a post-human condition in which the writing of the city is no longer restricted to our bodies. To complete the argument Thrift introduces the connections that the modern car has with GPS and network technologies that allow it to not only sense its immediate condition, but also the conditions of the road ahead and the environmental circumstances that the car will encounter. Written in 2004, the same network and satellite navigation technologies have now shrunk and have become integrated within the mobile phones in the pockets of pedestrians.

Smartphones such as Apple's iPhone, Google's Nexus series and BlackBerries all feature GPS technologies and a mapping application of one form or another that is able to stream a street or satellite map on to the screen and pinpoint the owner within it. Connected with data contracts that allow owners the ability to download huge amounts of data, smartphones are able to constantly update the base map and the owner's position as they move through the streets. Navigation services allow users to retrieve directions to addresses or well-known stores by simply entering a brand name or type, for example: 'Italian restaurant'. The software is also able to plot navigation routes between two points for walkers, by using public transport and by car, and even give an impression of the traffic conditions along the route.

With a smartphone in hand, de Certeau's 'Wandersmänner' (1984:102) remain constantly connected to the Internet, supporting a culture in which everyone is 'always-on' (Greenfield 2007) and always receiving information. Able to respond to SMS requests to meet people, to receive emails discussing work matters and to track the location of friends, the number of potential influences upon an individual's trajectory across the city has been extended tenfold. No longer is our navigation limited to specific destinations or innocent browsing, we have eyes that can see around corners, ears that can listen to the footsteps of friends that are streets away, noses that can smell the best coffee shops in town, and taste buds that can tell us what ingredients went in to a dish in our favourite restaurant. As the phones vibrate in our pockets indicating fresh incoming data, the city's meteorology has become superseded by a metrological climate: 'Once the whole social world is relocated inside its metrological chains, an immense new landscape jumps into view. If knowledge of the social is limited to the termite galleries in which we have been travelling, what do we know about what is outside? Not much' (Latour 2005: 242).

Nearly always-on

However, the 'always-on' culture compounds the urgency for information to be passed on at increasing speed. Failure to keep up to date with Facebook updates and Twitter feeds keeps us out of a social loop. Since Google Earth technology migrated to the phone, and satellite imagery can be seen to be streamed live under a person's feet in the street, it was inevitable to question how up to date or 'live' the maps really are. In a recent GPS mapping workshop in Dundee, Scotland, the author was asked: 'Wow, is that a live satellite image of where we are?' by a participant who had correlated the satellite imagery that was streaming on to the phone with her immediate surroundings, along with the blue dot that indicated her position in the landscape. The efficacy of maps being streamed onto a device that is also able to plot your position in real time was only going to lead to one conclusion: that if the data of my position is live, then the photographic image of the ground must also be live (Taylor 2009). The public uncertainty of the age of Google Earth imagery has its consequences though, and in order to retain its place in the market as providing accurate satellite data in the form of maps and photographs, Google are now compelled to develop ways of providing imagery that reflects new developments on the ground, for example: 'Google has been known to release much more recent imagery in GE [Google Earth] for unique events. For example, for the 2008 Beijing Olympics Google released 2-week old imagery for the Beijing area' (ibid.).

As maps get rewritten and updated at an ever-growing pace, the temporal integrity of the photographic satellite map we see on our smartphone begins to shift dramatically as some places are portrayed as they were five years ago, others months ago and some only weeks ago. This chequerboard of tiles complicates further our trust for the map to be considered as flat and consistent, revealing instead all sorts of irregularities and inconsistencies. However, whilst these temporal inconsistencies are unusual to the appearance of a base map, it is nothing new to how we expect to encounter a city. The city presents itself through the many ages of its architecture and built form, and as occupants we grow to expect dramatic differences between the age and style from one building to the next. In fact, the connections across particular buildings that are associated with certain histories represent the primary source of information for guided tours, travel guides and maps of a city. Visitors flock to cities around the world to re-envision what places would have looked like many years before, according to a particular subject or narrative. Armed with tourist guides, following signposts or listening to a drama student during their summer job, people spend enormous amounts of money and time transcending what they see as an actual place, in order to imagine where someone important once lived or something once happened. These tours evoke the architectural and social ghosts of the past and ensure that a city's history remains ever present across a landscape.

Exhuming spectral cities

However, the ghosts of the past are often hidden and harder for a tourist to elicit in a short visit to a place. In her chapter 'A landscape of memories', Kate Moles (2009) gave a rich account of Phoenix Park, Dublin, as a site in which the articulation of national identity is supported through an emphasis upon the recollection of the papal visit in 1979. Moles carefully describes how the darker side to the park's identity, the Phoenix Park murders, are obfuscated in favour for remembering the visit by the Pope: 'The construction of the park as a national space facilitates the formation of these shared memories and informs the personal ones, but it also excludes "other" alternative understandings and meanings that do not endorse the narrative necessary for ideas of nation and national identity' (Moles 2009:139).

During the *Habitus 2000* conference in Perth, Australia, the geographer Steve Pile rehearsed some ideas about cities and memories, in particular reflecting upon the anti-capitalist rally that had taken place on 1 May in London, earlier in 2000. As previously mentioned, Pile described how a series of national monuments had become damaged and defaced with graffiti during the rally. Amongst the most memorable monuments was a statue of Winston Churchill, defaced with a strip of turf placed over his head that gave him a Mohican haircut. Amongst the many other acts, Pile drew the delegates' attention to some graffiti that had been spray painted on to a war memorial (Figure 10.1).

Pile described also how the two doors that had been painted on to the side of the memorial had become portals to the past through which the memories of those who had suffered in conflict flooded back in to a public consciousness. Whilst the recovery of war-related memories is an important social process, it is something for which we use architectural installations such as memorials at specific times of the year. Exhumed in such an insensitive manner during the month of May and not November, when artificial poppies, public ceremonies and media channels prepare us to remember the dead, the graffiti released ghosts that on this occasion haunted the pages of the newspapers. Pile constructed a compelling argument for how the use of 'ghosts might reveal something about people's senses of place – about the way

FIGURE 10.1 The author's reconstruction of 'toilet door' graffiti on a London War Memorial. Photo © Karen Yee

affect is woven into the fabric of place; part and parcel of the processes that produce places as places' (Pile 2004: 241).

Edinburgh, Scotland, has two railway stations that serve the city, Waverley and Haymarket. The Haymarket station is to the west of the city and serves the many people coming in from Glasgow and the cities from the north. Outside the station a war memorial was erected and installed in 1922 to remember the footballers of the Heart of Midlothian football club who had fought in the First World War. In May 2009 the memorial was removed temporarily to allow work on a new tram scheme for the city, and commuters soon became used to the new landscape without the memorial. However, on 11 November later that year, a ghost of the memorial returned. Hanging from metal scaffolding, a collection of red poppy wreaths haunted the site of the memorial (Figure 10.2). Evocative because the architecture upon which the poppies hang is so crude, almost transparent, the wreaths hang in the air and remind passers-by of both the people who died in the war, but also the erasure of the memorial itself.

In the article later published in 2004, Pile uses the more complex scenario of a terrorist attack on the headquarters of the British Secret Intelligence Service in London. He uses the violent mortar attack by the Real IRA on the recently completed new building on the Thames that is home to MI6 as a model to describe how ghosts from the past haunt places through acts that don't have to kill anybody but are powerful enough to evoke dreadful memories of the past. The MI6 building was a strategic target for the IRA, not because it struck at the heart of anti-terrorist operations (if this was the case, the MI5 offices would have been the subject of the

FIGURE 10.2 The ghost of the Heart of Midlothian War Memorial, Haymarket, Edinburgh. Photo © Chris Speed

attack), but because the ghost could demonstrate their existence by firing upon a high profile building that is in close vicinity to the Houses of Parliament. Slipping away quickly, the ghost's attack upon the 'spooks' was scary enough to remind everybody of the death toll that the IRA's homeland bombing campaign had inflicted.

> The city haunts, then, because it gathers ghosts both in greater numbers of ghosts and in a wider variety than elsewhere. There is more to it. The city also commemorates those ghosts in more intense ways, in part by making the dead endure in its physical architecture, and in part by juxtaposing the dead and putting them into relation with one another. London, of course, has its fair share of actual memorials, but each new trauma creates a vernacular sacred architecture capable of calling forth the dead.
>
> (Pile 2004: 242)

Pile extends his use of ghosts through an analysis of M. Night Shyamalan's film *The Sixth Sense*. For Pile the film demonstrates the social and geographical tensions across time that become embodied within ghosts and that sustain trauma memories of the past. The film centres on a young boy (Cole) who builds a relationship with a child psychologist (Dr Crowe). Dr Crowe tries to understand Cole's claims of being able to see the dead. The suspense within the story increases as the identification of who is a ghost and why they should attach themselves to particular places becomes more complex. Children like Cole are used through cinema to tell stories, and often become the conduit through which we connect traumatic events of the past with a haunting in the present. As innocents, they represent a status in society in which time has yet to be formalized into the working day, and days centre around play (particularly through nursery and primary school).

Limited in their ability to read and write, young children have a temporal innocence similar to that which Thrift describes as distinctive of members of communities from the early middle ages, when 'natural rhythms dictate the pace of life and work and the content of language, and any expectation of a future centres on a short lifespan and the imminence of the Day of Judgment' (Thrift 1996: 180). Holding a position outside constructed history, children collapse time and space and offer networks through which communication with the dead becomes viable. Whilst Cole in *Sixth Sense* is able to sustain a position in the present, ghosts use him as a medium through which to relieve their attachment with a place, let them move to the 'other side' and become part of history. Understanding Cole as a medium, or an interface to the other times within places, also allows us to understand how delicately poised we all need to be when navigating places of great trauma.

Interfacing with ghosts

But the delicacy of straddling history in order to better understand trauma and perhaps overcome it is fraught with complexities. In Juan Antonio Bayona's 2007 film *El orfanato* (*The Orphanage*), a child fails to hold the position between the past and present and the house that is haunted by previous events 'takes him'. The mother, distraught at the apparent loss of her son, searches the contemporary 'space' of the orphanage in vain for the child. Upon understanding the history of the place, she begins to use memories and rituals of the old building to begin a fresh search across 'time'. Ultimately she finds that 'play' becomes the interface with which to get the attention of the ghosts of the children who occupy the place, and by engaging them in a game of hide and seek she is able to find her own child. However, in order to sustain the relationship with her son who is now part of history, she must remain with him and the other children who were 'lost' to the house many years ago, and become a ghost herself. Another classic tale of interfacing with ghosts is Spielberg's 1982 film *Poltergeist*, in which the young Carol Anne begins to communicate with ghosts through her parents' television. Eventually drawn into the 'other side' through the TV, like the children in *El orfanato*, it is Carol Anne's propensity to 'play' with an entertainment system that allows it to become the mechanism through which the connection is made.

Of course the contemporary form of television is not one in the corner of the room that is shackled to broadcast schedules, but laptops and smartphones that are part of a network culture of YouTube videos and allow us to watch television 'out of time' such as BBC's iPlayer or Channel 4's 4OD.[1] Connected and always-on, one of the many selling points used by manufacturers and service providers of smartphones is the ability to watch YouTube clips anywhere: 'You Phone, You Watch, YouTube' (bus stop poster for the television LG KU990 Viewty that allows uploads to YouTube). Having already established the mobile phone as a medium for play with the many games that come ready installed, or the thousands available for download at the press of the keypad, smartphones have become a 'playful' interface to transform our experiences as we wait for buses, sit on trains and use them to record events for sharing with others.

Using your iPhone to contact the dead

But just as television has broken away from the constraints of a universal broadcast model of time, and computer gaming has become mobile, maps are now open to many dynamic manipulations to change our experience of a place. The focal points of this chapter are three projects that received UK Research Council funding:

1   Walking Through Time: a software project that was funded through a Joint Information Systems Committee (JISC) rapid innovation grant and that concerned the development of a mobile phone application allowing users to overlay a Google map of Edinburgh with historical maps.
2   Tales of Things: a social media suite that allows the public to attach a personal story to any object. Using a new generation of printed barcodes called quick response codes or QR codes for short, Android and iPhone applications can use the camera functions of standard smartphones to read the codes and allow anyone to listen/watch the story through their phone.

3   Tales of a Changing Nation: an intervention into the National Museum of
Scotland, Edinburgh, which allowed visitors to attach personal memories to
particular items within an exhibition.

Walking Through Time

The application Walking Through Time[2] simply allows people to find themselves
in a Google map of the present, select from a long list of old maps and relocate
themselves in a nineteenth century map of the area (Figure 10.3). Retaining the
user's GPS marker, the moment that the map of the present becomes swapped
with a map from the past, the smartphone takes on the properties (albeit limited)
of Cole from the *Sixth Sense*, or the television that drew Carol Anne into the past.
The playful interface of the iPhone and our cognitive ability to identify with the
blue dot on the screen as ourselves, contests any truth in what we 'see' as the city
around us, and what is supplemented with the ghosts of buildings that have long
since disappeared. Holding a new user's hand, it is the 'supernatural' experience of
navigating two places simultaneously. People's mind's eye is using self–identification
with the dot on the screen as a proof of themselves, and yet it finds them located in
a place that has changed dramatically around them.

The ability to explore history whilst standing in a live location offers a host of
opportunities for user groups to 'walk' old streets, discover missing buildings and
extend their understanding of the past. Whilst an obvious target of the application
may be tourists, the author and developers of the application suggest that many
people will choose to navigate their city not in the technologically determined
'present' in which the map is as up to date and 'fresh' as possible, but may prefer to
use an old landscape that is occupied by ghosts. Walking through streets that aren't

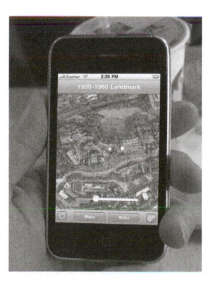

FIGURE 10.3   Walking Through Time, smartphone navigation software

'cleansed' of memories, or monitored by agents of institutions that want to guide our interpretation of the past in order to sustain our fear of particular ghosts, may help us 'see' the trauma that remains in a place and tread with understanding around its scars.

Tales of Things: The RememberMe Project

Developed in collaboration with the Oxfam charity shop in the student quarter of Manchester, the RememberMe project is a creative/technical intervention that explores how memories that are attached to objects can affect consumer habits. Oxfam is a charity that has 700 shops in towns and cities across the UK. The shops receive donations of clothes and artefacts from people, and sell them on to new owners as second-hand goods. A research associate of ours was working for one week in the local Oxfam shop in Manchester and asked people that dropped things off to tell a brief story about the object into a microphone (e.g. where they acquired it, what memories it brings back and any associated stories). These audio tracks were then uploaded to the Audioboo social media service (http://www.audioboo. com, accessed 23 January 2012) and linked to newly created stories on the Tales of Things[3] website. One week later, with the permission of people involved, audio tracks were linked to two-dimensional barcodes and RFID tags and were attached to the objects in the shop with a custom 'RememberMe' label. QR codes are a printed paper barcode that is able to contain an Internet address and, like RFID tags, can easily be associated with information or data files. Figure 10.4 illustrates a tag attached to an artefact in the Oxfam shop.

People browsed the shop using bespoke RFID readers and the Tales of Things iPhone and Android phone-based applications to scan the labels. Once triggered, speakers located in the shop played back the audio stories associated with the label.

Although the team anticipated an interest in the stories, we were surprised at how affective the very individual voices were upon visitors to the shop. The actual sound of somebody's voice associated with an object offered a supernatural extension to handling an artefact. People visiting the shop, browsing the objects and scanning the tagged donated items spoke of the 'personal connections' made as artefacts conjured an actual voice that gave the object additional meaning. The red silk toiletries bag that had no history or geography was transformed into an object loaded with place and personality as the story of its previous owner described a shopping trip in Bangkok that involved a near death experience in a tuk-tuk (Figure 10.5).

> Well my item is the little red silk make up toiletries bag, it's from a place called Narai in Bangkok, and it was one of the very first things that I bought when I went to visit my uncle and his wide Noi, who lived just outside Bangkok themselves, and I believe if this is the shopping trip that I'm thinking of ... I believe it's also one of the very first times that I got a tuk-tuk and nearly fell

FIGURE 10.4   RememberMe at FutureEverything 2010: tag attached to jewellery in Oxfam shop, Manchester. Photo © Jane Macdonald

out, on the middle of the motorway, on the way back … which I'm pretty certain it is actually so … yeah, that's my story, and I risked life and limb to get that toiletries bag.

(Red toiletries bag's anonymous donor)

The project's emphasis upon personal stories is an antithetical response to the quantitative data such as price, temperature or other logistical data that reside in supermarket databases and that are accessed through scanning the barcode on a product. The relationship between an object that is in someway labelled with a barcode or RFID tag, the database in which the tag is held as an entry, and the scanner that can connect the two has become of particular technical and social interest in recent years. Today software applications for smartphones have capitalized on the camera function and the constant connection to the Internet that contemporary mobile phones have. Using software applications that are able to read barcodes, users are able to scan products and draw down information from the Internet about the cost, price and whereabouts of a product. The sharing of data across the Internet and the use of artefacts as 'portals' to this data is one aspect of a cultural and technical phenomenon known as the 'Internet of Things'. The term Internet of Things, coined by Kevin

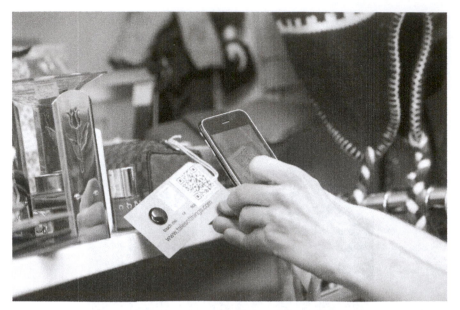

FIGURE 10.5 RememberMe at FutureEverything 2010: scanning the red silk toiletries bag. Photo © WeAreTAPE

Ashton at the Auto-ID research group at MIT in 1999 (Ashton 2009)) refers to the shift that is anticipated as society moves to a ubiquitous form of computing in which every device is on and connected in some way to the Internet.

The implications for the Internet of Things upon production and consumption are tremendous as this new paradigm has the potential to change the ways in which people shop, store and share products. The analogue barcode that has for so long been a dumb, encrypted reference to a shop's inventory system will be superseded by an open platform in which every object manufactured will be trackable from cradle to grave – from manufacturer to distributor, to potentially every single person who comes into contact with the object, following its purchase. RememberMe subverted the shopping experience in which people might expect to receive logistical data about an object and instead provided them with social information. The result of this supplementary information meant that every object (approximately fifty in total) was sold, even the types that are notoriously hard for a second-hand shop to sell, such as a sweater that had become frayed or a 7 inch vinyl record of a student band. The RememberMe project relied upon the web-based application Tales of Things (http://www.talesofthings.com, accessed 23 January 2012), which is able to associate different media types to a unique two-dimensional barcode. Members of the free-to-use system are able to submit an object to the database with a photograph and other information: name/title, keywords, location and most importantly a story that the object evokes for them. The interface also requests that other media be stored on services such as YouTube and AudioBoo and associated with the artefact: sound and video clips of the owner telling a story about the object. Once submitted, the

Tales of Things system creates a unique QR code for the artefact, which can be then printed out and attached to the object.

The Tales of Things social media suite also provides mobile applications for Android and iPhone platforms that allow anyone who comes across an object tagged with a Tales of Things code the opportunity to scan and retrieve stories, video and audio clips. The same phone applications also allow people to add additional stories to the artefact using text and video, thus contributing to the object's history. Tales of Things and RememberMe both offer a unique, social storytelling focus for the Internet of Things. This is in stark contrast to the current deployment of tagging technology that focuses upon providing consumers with logistical data about products and artefacts and offers no portal through which they can feedback. Judging from the affect on sales in the Oxfam shop (the charity recorded a 52 per cent increase in sales for this particular shop for the week of the exhibition, and 47 per cent for the subsequent two weeks) it may well indicate that consumers are interested in the provenance of an artefact, and not (as one might think) put off when they find out where it has been, who has worn it and what it meant to them.

Tales of a Changing Nation

The Tales of Things suite is facilitating a mechanism by which people are able to associate a personal memory to a physical artefact. The relationship between the 'thing' in material form and the memory that is held in a database in 'immaterial' form remains balanced so long as both forms of the 'thing' are in contact. However, there are occasions when this material/immaterial relationship becomes imbalanced and can lead to interesting opportunities and potentials for considering how memory and artefact become more complex.

The Tales of Things technology was used in the National Museum of Scotland through 2011 in an exhibition entitled 'Scotland: A Changing Nation'. The exhibition uses artefacts from the twentieth and the twenty-first centuries to tell the story of the nation's history, from a Hillman Imp motor car that was manufactured in Glasgow after the demise of the shipyards to a copy of J.K. Rowling's *Harry Potter* book. The exhibition was popular because it was filled with objects that could be said to have been from 'living memory' for many of the visitors. Tales of Things users were invited to tag eighty museum objects with QR codes that allowed visitors to do two things: access media footage such as video clips that were associated with each object, and add their own story to the object to extend the corpus of knowledge for a particular object.

The QR codes were located next to the objects and were accessible to anybody with a smartphone. Because of the presence of the codes close to the artefacts to promote the process, a number of items began to accrue a wide variety of social memories. The museum embraced the project, and particular artefacts were very successful at attracting multiple memories. The Singer sewing machine proved very popular, attracting ten personal stories in addition to the

1934 film by the Singer company that documented the making process. During its time in Glasgow, the European branch of the American company produced over 36 million sewing machines, making them one of the most accessible forms of domestic technology.[4]

The experiment to allow visitors to contribute to the historical knowledge of an artefact in the museum's collection offered some interesting outcomes for both the role of the museum as author of history, and also the role of a material artefact as instantiation of an immaterial memory. The potential for the public to add content to the collection meant that the museum no longer had complete control over an artefact's 'story'. Open and extendable, the artefacts became populated with personal stories that described intimate memories of using the object.

In order to trigger memories the research team ran a series of public workshops that used surrogate objects that would act as vessels upon which memories could be associated, but were not the actual thing. Unable to gain permission for workshop attendees to handle the 'real' dancing shoe (for example) the research team painted a similar object found in a second-hand shop white, as though it was a ghost of the 'real' thing (Figure 10.6). Even though the white dancing show had become detached from its owner and any sense of origin had been painted out, participants of the workshops who handled it in the museum were able to use it to trigger their own memories. The white ghost objects were interesting because they were able to bring back memories of things that had been lost and destroyed, and yet were able to recall a memory in the mind of a person. Able to recover an immaterial memory, the ghost objects became material 'vessels' for a selection of personal memories concerning things that no longer existed.

FIGURE 10.6   A ghost of dancing shoe, stickered with memories of the Scottish dancing hall culture. Photo © Chris Speed

Conclusion

As well as offering technical properties that are associated with networked computing, the contemporary mobile phone may have another unexpected capacity: that of being our spirit guide for navigating social and cultural geographies. Unlike Cole, whose connection with ghosts held him back from playing and consequently displaying the signs of a normal child, perhaps the phone can offer us an interface in which histories can be understood through the hacking of location services and the histories of artefacts. Traditionally seen as undialectical devices (Harvey 1996: 4), maps that are online and open to editing are beginning to afford an increasing number of contributions from web users. A project such as Open Street Map[5] is precisely intended to contest editorial control and rights for the ownership and production of maps. The project allows members to edit and define characteristics of a global map through an online interface and fill in the 'gaps' that mapping services such as Google Maps and Microsoft have to offer. Systems such as Tales of Things and the more commercial Sticky Bits[6] offer the same capability to 'write back' to an artefact and contest an object's value in the world.

The projects featured in this chapter open up a series of interesting properties for digital heritage to consider when dealing with the exhuming of ghosts through the use of smartphones. The Walking Through Time application offered a role in complementing maps that have a propensity to be seen as 'up to date' with cartographic material that is older, with the goal to reveal narratives that have been obscured due to a presiding representation of the present. Although trauma is not explicit as tourists use an application such as Walking Through Time, it is hoped that revealing the changes in the urban landscape of Edinburgh offers a sensitivity to change and perhaps loss. Standing on railways lines that no longer exist, such as those that used to run into the Princess Street Railway Station, Edinburgh, demolished in 1970, is an uncanny experience. In her exploration of Daniel Eisenburg and Rea Tajiri artworks, Wasserman (2007) examined the representational complexities of the past and memory in relation to the artist's family histories, each of which was formed by traumatic events relating to the Second World War. Both artists use photography as a medium with which to recover and explore the past or, as Wasserman describes it, 'events without experience' (Wasserman 2007: 166). Never as powerful as the subject matter of Eisenburg or Tajiti's artworks, the experience of walking over maps of long lost places is nevertheless done with a similar tenderness for the ground. Not exactly a postmemory, as Hirsch would have described it: 'The term "postmemory" is meant to convey its temporal and qualitative difference from survivor memory, its secondary, or second-generation memory quality, its basis in displacement, its vicariousness and belatedness' (Hirsch 2001: 9).

It is perhaps a fourth-generation postmemory: the distance from the subject of the image is too great to identify a traumatic event, but as the blue dot allows us to trespass across time, the viewer cannot help wondering whose spaces they are intruding upon.

Offering a cultural navigation, Walking Through Time draws the user across the city of Edinburgh to places that have seen dramatic change, a level of change that allows the user to walk vicariously across a historical landscape, imagining who's footsteps they walked in.

The Tales of Things platform, and the two projects that used it, RememberMe and Tales of a Changing Nation, offer a different connection with history, the ability to 'write' to an artefact, offer new histories, contest the veracity of any history that is presented to us, and offer alternative associations and pasts. Simon's exploration of Facebook and blogs that both afford a serial and dialogical reflection upon content on the Internet (Simon, this volume) emphasizes the role of social media in supporting a 'read/write' relationship between authors and audiences. Whilst for Simon this offers an emerging context in which groups may 'remember together', projects such as Tales of a Changing Nation also shows how tagged objects are beginning to offer the same properties. Able to extend a historical conversation upon reviewing an initial history offered by the National Museum of Scotland, or to contest such history, the ability to write back to an object has challenged how the Museum considers the management of its material artefacts. During similar workshops with community members of Wester Hailes, an area in the south-west of Edinburgh, images of the demolition of tower blocks were used to provoke questions about where the photograph was taken. Using tags to associate voice recordings to the images, participants discussed the exact whereabouts of particular flats and corrected the initial assumptions that were made by the local housing association.

The use of the white 'ghost' objects in the National Museum of Scotland also introduced mobility to memories, allowing them to be recovered from the past as a recollection, and then transferred to the ghost object via the use of paper tags. It has been suggested that people in general surround themselves with between 1,000 and 5,000 objects (Waldner 2007), many of which are discarded and replaced through consumption and subsistence. However, some objects are lost, stolen or mislaid forever and are irreplaceable because of the memories with which they are associated. In the context of an Internet of Things, this status of absolute loss is already a thing of the past, as an artefact's data is likely to remain.

As we move to a time when objects are individually tagged through their production, we can assume that they will accrue more and more forms of data. Unlike the old adage 'a rolling stone gathers no moss', artefacts within the Internet of Things *will* gather moss. As they move from one place to the next, they will gather locative data; as people interact with them, they will gather social data; and even as they sit idly on a shelf, they may well be gathering data about the objects that are around them. This data will exist in virtual form even when the actual object has been broken, lost or thrown away. Stored safely in the cloud and accessible for eternity, the object lives on as a ghost in the network, waiting for a chance to be exorcised.

Although lost in the actual world, the things that no longer exist in physical form do remain in the world in an immaterial form, as demonstrated by the return of the wreaths to the absent War Memorial outside Haymarket station in Edinburgh. Evidently, we find that things that are not actually in the world are still able to find a thing to which they can be associated and therefore be remembered. It is likely that memories will far outweigh the number of actual things in the world, simply because people throw so much away. If this is the case, then we are likely to see more and more circumstances in which physical objects will become associated with social data looking for a host. In this context, we may need to design blank objects that have no other function than to become the host for memories that have lost their connection with the original physical artefact. Other times, discarded and culturally lost objects may be used, because they retain some of the physical attributes that trigger associations with memories that have lost their original material partner. In an Internet of Things scenario, objects may end up on your mantelpiece with associated memories of completely different artefacts. The value of these 'vessels' and our attachment to them will likely depend on the social data stored in them, rather than on their physical form.

Both Walking Through Time and Tales of Things embody a temporal 'turn' in the use of digital technology. So often driven by a technological determinism that promises that the next operating system, phone or computer will be better than the last, networked systems have the potential to engage people in such a way that timelines are not attached to the furthering of a technology, but to the people that are using them. If we are able to place social networks at the core of digital heritage, then the focus may shift from a linear momentum that focuses upon a future to a point when we may reflect upon the many historical contingencies that define our present. The digital heritage systems, within which the Walking Through Time and Tales of Things software can be bracketed, offer opportunities to introduce a point of temporal reflection and the ability to interface with ghosts.

Notes

1. In the UK, television broadcasting companies have introduced online applications that allow people to watch and listen to television programmes for a limited time period after they have been broadcast. The BBC's iPlayer and Channel 4's 4OD are two examples of these systems.
2. Walking Through Time is a web application for mobile phones funded by a Joint Information Systems Committee (JISC) rapid innovation grant. The application is a working prototype for the city of Edinburgh and was developed collaboratively between Edinburgh College of Art and the University of Edinburgh. Conceptual and historical development: Ian Campbell, Chris Speed and Karlyn Sutherland, the Edinburgh School of Architecture and Landscape Architecture (ESALA), Edinburgh College of Art. Technical development: Dave Berry, Petra Leimlehner and Peter Pratt, Applications Division, University of Edinburgh. Mapping support: James Reid, Ben Butchart and Tim Urwin, Edina, University of Edinburgh. The project website is: http://www.walkingthroughtime.co.uk (accessed 23 January 2012) and access to the application maybe granted with permission; see website for details.
3. Tales of Things is a project supported by a Digital Economy, Research Councils UK grant, and made 'real' by our team: Ralph Barthel, Ben Blundell, Maria Burke, Martin De Jode, Andrew Hudson-Smith, Angelina Karpovich, Kerstin Leder, Clare Lee, Jane Macdonald, Arthi Manohar, Simone O'Callaghan, Michael Quigley, Jon Rogers, Duncan Shingleton and Chris Speed. The project website is: http://www.talesofthings.com (accessed 23 January 2012).

4. Personal stories that were attached to artefacts from the Scotland: Tales of a Changing Nation exhibition at the National Museum of Scotland can be accessed here: http://talesofthings.com/totem/group_view/44/ (accessed 23 January 2012).
5. Open Street Map is a web-based mapping service that is editable to members. It allows members to upload information about geographical features and makes the maps available for use free of charge: http://www.openstreetmap.org (accessed 23 January 2012).
6. Sticky Bits is a smartphone software application that allows members to scan traditional barcodes on consumer items and access messages, write reviews and pick up offers: http://www.stickybits.com (accessed 23 January 2012).

References

Ashton, K. (2009) 'That "Internet of Things" thing', *RFID Journal*, 22 June. http://www.rfidjournal.com/article/view/4986 (accessed 4 December 2011).

de Certeau, M. (1984) *The Practice of Everyday Life*, trans. Steven Rendall, Berkeley, CA: University of California Press.

Greenfield, A. (2007) *Everyware*, Berkeley, CA: New Riders.

Harvey, D. (1996) *Justice, Nature and the Geography of Difference*. Oxford: Blackwell.

Hirsch, M. (2001) 'Surviving images: Holocaust photographs and the work of postmemory', *The Yale Journal of Criticism*, 14 (1): 5–37.

Latour, B. (2005) *Reassembling the Social: An Introduction to Actor-Network Theory*, Oxford: Oxford University Press.

Moles, K. (2009) 'A landscape of memories: Layers of meaning in Dublin Park', in M. Anico and E. Peralta (eds) *Heritage and Identity: Engagement and Demission in the Contemporary World*, London: Routledge.

Pile, S. (2004) 'Spectral cities: Where the repressed returns and other short stories', in J. Hillier and E. Rooksby (eds) *Habitus: A Sense of Place*, Aldershot: Ashgate.

Taylor, F. (2009) 'About Google Earth Imagery', Google Earth Blog. http://www.gearthblog.com/blog/archives/2009/03/about_google_earth_imagery_1.html (accessed 24 November 2011).

Thrift, N. (1996) *Spatial Formations*, London: Sage.

Thrift, N. (2004) 'Driving in the city', *Theory, Culture & Society*, 21 (4–5): 41–59.

Waldner, J.B. (2007) *Inventer l'Ordinateur du XXIeme Siècle*, London: Hermes Science.

Wasserman, T. (2007) 'Constructing the Image of Postmemory', in F. Guerin and R. Hallas (eds) *The Image and the Witness: Trauma, Memory and Visual Culture,* London: Wallflower Press.

11

EXTENDING CONNECTIONS BETWEEN LAND AND PEOPLE DIGITALLY

Designing with rural Herero communities in Namibia

Nicola J. Bidwell and
Heike Winschiers-Theophilus

Introduction

There are many electronic archives that store information about aspects of specific rural or 'natural' places in efforts to curate heritage or describe the indigenous knowledge or territories of rural people (e.g. Tripathi and Bhattarya 2004; Gupta 2005; Tjieka 2007; Dyson *et al.* 2007; Greyling and Zulu 2010). However, dilemmas arise in designing digital systems that enable rural dwellers themselves to create, store and share digital content about their connections with their land because the design and use of technologies manifests the priorities and assumptions of particular knowledge systems.

Technologies, and expectations about their use, privilege particular ways of encountering, organizing and making sense of the world, and these can conflict with the heritage that is lived in the connections between land and human dwellers in different parts of the world. In this chapter we express concerns in designing digital systems to extend the living heritage of those who live in places that are sparsely populated by people and, currently, technology. To do so, we refer to our endeavours to enable rural people of the Herero tribe, in southern Africa, to extend their local knowledge practices digitally. Our design activities reveal how the connections that rural dwellers experience in interacting with land differ from official narratives about relationships with land as well as from the connections on which existing technologies and design methods tend to focus. To illustrate dilemmas in designing systems that enable rural dwellers to create, store and share digital content, we describe three specific interaction issues. First we discuss how technological constraints can obscure relationships between people and their surroundings and metaphysical qualities of experience, and the way these constraints transform heritage narratives. Second, we show that the abstractions embedded in conceptions about heritage, such as impersonal and temporally fixed geographies, may be incompatible with the ways people manage place in their own living heritage practices. Third, we show that critically reflecting on prototype systems can bridge communities with different concerns by reflecting rural dwellers' priorities to designers and designers' understandings back to rural dwellers.

Challenges in designing systems for user-generated content about heritage

The significance of places to heritage lies in the ways that people conduct their everyday lives and experience their everyday connections in relation to those places rather than in a place's physical fabric. Social practices create distinctive communities; some, such as performing arts, rituals and festive events, clearly differentiate communities, however, others differ more subtly, such as ways to speak in public, systems of knowing about nature and cosmology, and expertise and skills in medicine, cooking, navigating, craft-making, cultivating or harvesting plants and husbanding animals. Many social practices are very finely nuanced expressions of living heritage, for instance everyday habits, communication protocols and bodily movements in and between places. Attending to social actions (Byrne 2008) and the cultural work through which places gain meaning, prioritizes relationships between people, land and artifacts that often remain hidden when we focus on the tangible qualities of land and artifacts. For instance, a museum display of the dried roots of a plant cannot express the ways people tend, gather, prepare, apply and talk about the plant in traditional medicine; yet, such actions contribute to the heritage significance of places (Bidwell *et al.* 2011a).

Designing tangible systems for generating, storing and sharing digital content that extend the living heritage of rural people faces many challenges. Firstly, there is a general issue that mechanisms aiming to preserve living heritage can ignore the elements of life most critical to those who live that heritage. Hester (1996) attributes this failure to the indetectability of those aspects: 'not distant enough in time or separable enough from daily life to be consciously seen as special' (Hester 1996: 13). This yields a set of problems for methods that enable mundane aspects of living heritage to shape the design of systems that enable people to author, store and share content about their connections with land.

Tensions also arise in designing systems through which rural dwellers author content about their connections with land, because heritage politics tend to privilege *official* narratives about places. Places are not some objective geographic milieu; they are loci of selected meanings, produced by different people and groups. As Byrne (2008) explains, each person or group may 'narrate' a place differently: emphasizing particular features, events or characters, and arranging relationships between these in different temporal or causal orders. Often the meaning of a place is contested locally; consider, for example, conflicts between the meanings of places inhabited by pastoralists and indigenous groups in Australia. Grazing cattle on large stations constitutes farmers' living heritage but ritual actions and movements to maintain the land's pre-colonial biodiversity constitute the living heritage of the land's traditional custodians (Standley *et al.* 2009). Indeed, thinking about relationships between people and land reveals how decisions attributing places with either social or natural heritage significance is cultural work itself.

User-generated content (UGC) about places appears, on the surface, to promise a rebalancing of power relations that affect the ways places are ascribed heritage significance, because such content selects and interprets places diversely. Multiple and publically visible interactions, reinterpretations and representations can certainly validate the heritage significance of places in a more democratic way than institutionally sponsored curation (Silberman and Purser, this volume). However, power relations also affect the ability of groups to produce and use digital tools for generating content about places (truna and Bidwell 2007). Consider how it is design teams, in cities far away, that mediate an elaborate 3D geospatial representation intended for the land's traditional custodians to tell their stories about their connection to 'Country' (truna and Bidwell 2007). Silberman and Purser (ibid.) further explain the danger of such hyper-real expert exhibits in authorizing certain views on heritage, particularly when these tools are inaccessible to those whose heritage they depict. Even social media, which some claim to support 'unofficial' heritage practices, are affected by power relations between the sites in which such technologies are produced and used and sites in which they are not. Consider highly technological places, where the daily lives of inhabitants entwine with an increasing range of repositories of personal stories and geographical representations, from Facebook to Twitter to web-based GIS mapping. Such repositories record existing social practices in relation to places and, simultaneously, shape new forms of producing and re-producing heritage (Bidwell *et al.* 2011a; see also: Coyne, this volume). Consider then, perspectives on relationships between people and social media in South Africa. Many studies imply that 10 per cent of the population frequent social sites (TNS 2009), that people focus their Internet use on social networking and claim that a particular mobile chat service, MXit, which has nine million registered users in South Africa, is "mainstream" (Donner 2010). However, research about cellphone use rarely considers rural Africa; and we have found in South Africa's Eastern Cape that almost no one frequents social sites and less than two per cent of the population locally use MXit (Bidwell *et al.* 2011b).

Another set of challenges in designing systems for UGC, to enable groups to record and express heritage in relation to their 'lived' places, arises because of the politics embedded in paradigms of technology design and use, as well as in the narratives about places that a given technology supports. As Christie observes: 'The work of turning the artefacts of knowledge production into discrete digital packages, and of organising them into searchable collections, turns them into politically and historically invested technologies' (Christie 2005:5). Tensions between the ways different knowledge heritages produce, organize and share information means, first, that even though the significance of places to heritage lies in the 'lived world of people', recording systems can focus only on that which can be made tangible. This perpetuates particular ways to validate heritage, for instance history is inscribed in written rather than in an oral text, and heritage is reified as places or objects rather than expressed in movements in places or interactions with objects. Second, embedded in the strategies privileged by technology design are certain cultural logics and literacies, or ways to organize, make sense of and communicate about the world (Dourish and Bell, 2011). Consider, for example, how the prime meridian of latitude used today in GPS is the product of an infrastructure of global exploration and control based in a perspective of the world that came to the fore in the Enlightenment (truna *et al.* 2009). Such information structures and representations reproduce priorities and assumptions about certain kinds of relations and dependencies. They contribute to 'problematic disjunctions' (Christie 2005) between technologies and the lived world of people, and can suppress and distort knowledge practices (Green 2007) even if marginalized groups engage enthusiastically in the process.

In this chapter we adopt a critical design perspective (Dunne and Raby 2001) to illustrate some of the challenges and tensions in designing systems for UGC suited to the living heritage of rural people. Critical design heightens our sensitivity to the ways local communities make sense of their settings, and inherit and practice heritage. Here, we refer to our ongoing work with rural Herero in Namibia to illustrate how the political, social and cultural factors that influence interactions between people, actions, places and technology can undermine designing UCG systems to support and extend existing practices. We propose this chapter has value to heritage practitioners, interaction designers and technology developers; as Dourish and Bell (2011: 205) observe: 'the creation of cultural artifacts and the exploration of them as cultural artifacts are not independent programs'.

Extending the rural heritage of Herero

There is increasing regard, in Southern Africa, for the role of traditional knowledge systems in social, economic and environmental sustainability. With globalization, alien technologies, from writing systems to water pumps, have destabilized many of the practices that support the identity and wellness of Africa's rural communities and the land they inhabit. Recognizing the significance of indigenous practices, we established a research project to design technologies suited to rural ways of knowing, doing and saying of the Herero tribe, a group constituting nine per cent of Namibia's population.

We aim to develop systems that will enable the Herero to create, store and retrieve content about rural knowledge, enable rural communities to communicate digitally their wisdom and skills to rural-to-urban migrants, and bridge intergenerational gulfs. In this section, first, we outline reasons for designing systems for UGC that will enable rural Herero to communicate their heritage, and summarize the methods we use in designing for a rural Herero community. Then, we introduce some of the differences between connections that rural dwellers experience in interacting with land and official narratives about the Herero's relationships with land that our design activities have revealed.

Rural-to-urban migration

Some 40 per cent of Namibia's very low population (1.6 million) is concentrated in a handful of cities, where many aspects of life are similar to Europe. Rural-to-urban migration accounts for much of the increasing urban population: rural youth live with relatives to attend school and remain in town for employment (Rumble and Koul 2007). However, migrants maintain strong links with their rural origins (see De Bruijn *et al.* 2001; Kok and Collinson 2006) and these have reciprocal benefit. Migrants live in low-budget urban settlements, such as Katatura, and save money to improve conditions for origin households or to buy homes or livestock. Some 60 per cent of households in Katatura receive farmed and wild foods via rural contacts (Frayne 2005). Migrants return home as often as affordable, to participate in seasonally intensive farming and social events, including the marriages and funerals of rural- and urban-based people.

Despite continuities between urban and rural Hereros, the migration of young people disrupts the intergenerational information transfer that, previously, bonded communities, produced knowledge suited to local factors and sustained the environment. An increasing epistemological and technological gulf accompanies rural-to-urban migration. Rural and formal knowledge systems are geographically polarized (Van Harmelen 2004); formal systems of education, such as schools, are often unavailable in rural areas, and traditional skills and modes of communication are excluded from national curricula. As a result, youngsters that migrated to the city are ungrounded in the minutiae of everyday rural life and the ways information is conveyed orally, and increasingly favour 'scientific', print-based systems over traditional knowledge systems. Migrants return to rural areas with urban-generated knowledge, assets and conveniences: now, travelling in vehicles not on horseback; now, listening to a radio not a storyteller around the fire; now, keeping more livestock than before.

Migrants' connections with rural habitat are also shaped by globalization, post-apartheid movements to unite tribes and build African nations, and media. Namibia's unbuilt, semi-arid landscape influences national identities and concerns for sustainable habitat, from food production to nature tourism; while media that is accessible to urban dwellers reshapes bonds with rural origins. For instance, national TV in Namibia frequently depicts rural settings, but there is only one weekly TV programme in the Herero language, *Otjiherero*: the news. Further the bonds of urban migrants with rural origins evolve with their use of media, since 'unofficial' heritage practices change as people use mobile, embedded and ubiquitous technologies (Giaccardi 2011). For instance, the international Herero diaspora often upload photos of their rural origins to the Facebook group 'Global Herero's Unite'; however, as we noted earlier, these media are inaccessible to rural people.

Systems for UGC, locally

In designing systems for UGC to serve marginalized knowledge traditions we are not concerned with whether local knowledge remains superficially the same, but what values, logics and literacies may be lost in transformation. Technologies to 'preserve' heritage often failed in the past to recognize incompatibilities between different knowledge systems and the values implicit in producing technology. Van der Velden (2008) argues that combining a wide range of technologies can facilitate preserving local intangible heritage, providing that the classification work is situated in a community's own knowledge traditions. However, rural inhabitants, around the world, encounter disjunctures between technology and their lived experience simply because the locale of technology production, sited in research labs and design studios in cities and industrialized regions, produces selective interpretations of rural life (Bidwell and Browning 2010). Such interpretations emphasize landscape from a detached tourist gaze, as resource for harvest or discovery or as rustic exotica for curation, rather than home or workplace. Thus, to enable rural Herero to extend their living heritage digitally, our endeavours aim to integrate their living heritage within our design processes (Winschiers-Theophilus *et al.* 2011) and attend to important, and multiple, interconnections between people and places. Recent innovations that support social, ubiquitous, tangible and 'whole-body' interactions offer new opportunities for representing and communicating oral traditions. For instance, combining GPS, Bluetooth or RFID with platforms for UGC might offer ways for people to express the heritage practices that 'live' within their movements in places or interactions with objects.

A participatory approach to designing systems for UGC

We commenced our project to design systems for UGC that can extend the living heritage of rural Herero in early 2008. Since then we have applied a perspective on designing that accounts for the social situation of interactions with technology and the varied non-technological factors that affect technology design and use. Through this lens, often termed the 'situated-paradigm' (Harrison *et al.* 2007), we use various methods, all of which interpret action, interaction and knowledge as embodied in people's actions in context. These methods include: ethnographic strategies, such as observation and contextual interviews, both with and without technology, and exploring the responses of community members to different prototype systems for creating and managing media content. We frame these methods within action research by designing prototype systems and reflecting upon their use, in a series of cycles. In other words, we treat our prototypes as formative: each prototype reveals factors that situate use and possibilities for technology development (Winschiers-Theophilus *et al.* 2011). We consider the various methods to constitute an emerging ethnographic action research (ERA) (Taachi *et al.* 2003) because Herero people participate in defining problems and opportunities and shaping the aims, methods and analysis and design processes. Our project team consists of: Herero residents of two villages in the Omaheke region in Western Namibia; Herero rural-to-urban migrants, including an information technology researcher; and, computer science and human–computer interaction researchers based in Southern Africa and overseas. Participants in the villages include: elders, whose knowledge community members hold in high regard; healers, who practice traditional medicine professionally; and other adults and youths. We connected to the villages through the kin and trust relations of rural-to-urban migrants (Bidwell *et al.* 2011a).

Participants in the rural villages do not have access to grid electricity, and limited access to communication technology. In one village, people watch TV if they can understand English, Afrikaans or Otjivambo languages and have sufficient fuel for their generator, and occasionally access an intermittent cellphone network. In general, however, people's use of technology is limited to radio. During the first year, we gathered thirty hours of video during seven field trips to uncover factors in interactions between media and heritage practices (Bidwell *et al.* 2011a; Bidwell *et al.* 2011c). Rural participants had not depicted their knowledge by photography or video before, rarely use writing materials, and some cannot read (Koch Kapuire *et al.* 2010). We chose video as the primary medium for recording in response to participants' enthusiasm for it, and also because it records aural and visual aspects of speech, movements and settings. In some fifty video clips, recorded by local and academic participants, community members tell stories, describe scenarios, demonstrate local practices and engage in everyday activities. In other video, community members view and interpret previously recorded video or interact with prototype systems. We derived themes from our ethnography and our detailed analysis of participants' interactions with video, including scrutinizing semantic and syntactic qualities of their speech and extra-lingual oral and multi-modal interactions (such as gesture, body and camera movement). Over the first year our insights shaped, and were shaped by, subsequent activities, analysis and discussion between participants. At the same time recording and viewing video provoked participant's ideas. Participants proposed various ideas for new systems, from specific media to enable disseminating herb lore to unique functions for kin-based social networking; as one participant said: 'when you take this [video] to the neighbouring place and show them they will also come up with their own ideas'.

At the end of the first year, and in subsequent years, we explored different prototypes for creating sets of media, and organizing the media recorded by the community. In this chapter, we limit reflection to three prototypes for organizing UGC, all of which run on laptop computers. The first prototype that community members attempted to use and evaluate was counterintuitive as it concentrated on enabling users to retrieve video using text-based meta-data. The second prototype aimed to enable elders to disseminate their choice of videos to selected people using thumbnails and icons, and showed that community members appreciated the concept of sharing content based on relationships between people (Koch Kapuire *et al.* 2010, Bidwell *et al.* 2011c). A more recent prototype embeds members' videos in a 3D visualization of participants' villages in which models of people and animals depict scenarios of local practices (Rodil *et al.* 2011). Participants found this prototype more usable and engaging than earlier prototypes for organizing video, which, in part, reflects some of the transformations in their understanding of technological systems that occurred through ERA.

Rural Hereros' lived heritage places

We first describe some broad insights about the relationships between Herero people, places and heritage, which provide some grounding for more specific interaction issues that our design activities in the first years of the project revealed.

In both our everyday observations and specific design activities Herero participants from the villages noted the significance of some of the tangible fabric of their 'lived' heritage. They indicated items such as calabashes for souring milk, and particular physical infrastructures, such as the layout of corrals and fires, and the orientation of their homes in rural homesteads. Sometimes participants retained artifacts they related to their heritage as mementos, for instance one participant displayed, on her wall in Windhoek, the leather 'apron' warn by male youth until two decades ago. However, although participants identified particular objects and aspects of homesteads as signifying their heritage, they do not emphasize tangible relics as objects or features. Nor do they note particular attachment to the places that the wider Herero community of Namibia marks as ancestral land. Such differences, between local and institutionalized accounts of heritage, reflect politics.

Until 50 years ago, the Herero continuously relocated according to their customary nomadic practices of cattle herding and, later, due to colonial and apartheid strategies. The Herero tribe descends from migrants who entered northeast Namibia from central Africa in the sixteenth century to settle around the Kalahari. Although the tribe was highly mobile throughout the eighteenth and nineteenth centuries, the national Herero community refers to the vicinity of the Waterberg, in north-eastern central Namibia, as their original settlement because they established rights to access the water and graze their livestock there over other tribes who inhabited the area (Forster 2005). The Herero's reference to the Waterberg as their ancestral lands may be a response to their forced relocation by Germans and South Africans who converted the land to commercial cattle farms in the early twentieth century. Survivors of the 1904–1908 wars were forced to settle in minimal sections of their homelands or far away, such as in Omahake, where project participants have lived for over thirty years. Thus, like other displaced peoples, the national Herero community use the strategies of their colonizers with respect to land, in narratives that 're-claim' place (Harrison 2010).

In former times, Herero families appropriated areas of land during their nomadic movements by grazing cattle there (Grinker *et al*. 1997; Henrichsen 1999; Kavari 2002; Forster 2005). However, the concrete, fixed points, such as wells and settlements, that marked this appropriation were rarely permanent; they decayed or were abandoned as a result of seasonal or lasting migration. Thus, the Herero's heritage connections to places are primarily oral. For instance, verses (or 'praise songs') recall and describe almost all the places Herero society inhabited, permanently or temporarily, before the German conquest (Henrichsen 1999; Kavari 2002; Forster 2005; Bubenzer *et al*. 2009). Participants in our project explained that village names depict stories about their settlement, for instance how people came to a river so broad and deep that horses could not cross. The forms and properties of the Otjiherero language itself are also rich with environmental concepts that relate land to economics, ethnicity and other natural and social dimensions (Bubenzer *et al.* 2009). Interpretations of names and elaborate poems, which are used in various contemporary depictions of Herero history, often emphasize the idea of 'settling' when mapping people or events to land. However, such a perspective on relationships between people and places does not necessarily depict the connections that the Herero experience in interacting with land. African traditions have their own narrative forms and functions for vocal imagery (Bubenzer *et al.* 2009). However, when we interpret concepts, culturally and linguistically, we tend to selectively emphasize those that are similar to dominant models. For instance, elsewhere, authors (Dourish and Bell 2011) use anthropological accounts of relationships between Native American wisdom and place to theorize about ubiquitous computing, even though these original accounts are grounded in secular European phenomenology and existentialism rather than the spirituality of the inhabitants (Ball 2002).

Sometimes communities use the physical fabric of places to communicate about intangible concepts, such that locations and objects perform in a 'reificative connection' (Wenger 1998). The reificative connections that communities collectively make to express experiences by linking them to certain places and objects become absorbed into practices and rituals. For instance, rural-to-urban migrants in our research observe silence when we drive through the site of a battle on the road from Windhoek (which is, coincidentally, marked by garish papier mâché models advertising a nearby, unrelated, taxidermist). Some reificative connections are re-reproduced by 'official' narratives about places and relics; for instance, the national Herero community recognizes venues in Waterberg to commemorate their ancestors' genocide and assert their tribal identity. However, power relations affect the concepts that are reified so that reificative connections do not necessarily align with the everyday practices that sustain a community's own meanings about places and their sense of belonging to them. For example, Namibian Herero refer extensively to the Waterberg in speeches, recitations, contemporary music and songs sung at schools (Kavari 2002; Forster 2005), but rural participants in our research have made no such references. Further, ancestral graves are often cited as 'stable' physical markers of the Herero's habitation of the Waterberg, and attributed spiritual significance (Henrichsen, 1999; Forster 2005). However, in our research, participants' everyday actions seem to articulate that temporality is a more vital dimension than spatiality in relation to ancestors. For instance, consider their connections with patrilineal ancestors with respect to the sacred 'Holy Fire', which men use in ceremonial slaughtering, in healing with herbs and in addressing social tensions. Like other fires, such as the fire on which women cook and heat water and the fire on which men cook goats, the Holy Fire has a specific location in participants' homesteads. However, in contrast with other fires, men must keep the Holy Fire burning *continuously* to maintain favour with ancestors.

These days rural Herero are sited, rather than nomadic pastoralists; but their attachment to land still lives in connections with others, both living and past, and between people and cattle. Their occupancy of community-owned land is based on verbal agreements with chiefs, and their attachments persist in linguistic and extra-linguistic acts not in written certificates about genealogy or land. The Herero have an intricate kinship system. They practice a double-descent system (people remain of their male or female lines), encourage cross-cousin marriage (from a parent's opposite sexed sibling), permit polygamy, share childcare across generations, and have considerable inheritance responsibilities. Kinship is signified in practices relating to cattle, including matrilineal inheritance, tendering cattle to a bride's parents to legalize marriage and in loaning. Cattle contribute to the Herero's characterization of places (Grinker *et al.* 1997; Forster 2005) and are a medium for social exchange, with many concepts about livelihood, economics, status and spirituality embedded in acquiring, owning, breeding, exchanging, donating and ritually slaughtering cattle. However, as we explained earlier, the interconnections people have with places, such as through kin and cattle, may not necessarily align with the social, technical and literary devices they use to reclaim place. Consider cases in other sparsely populated regions of the world where indigenous people have harnessed technology to exercise their cultural responsibilities for land. In Australia, for example, indigenous clans use video to record and teach younger members traditional knowledge as well as use representations that make sense to the authorities that govern access to, and decisions about, their homelands (Standley *et al.* 2009). However, the geospatial maps, chronological timelines and species classifications involved in these acts of reclaiming place differ significantly from their customary representations of land, such as songs and stories; and do not necessarily support the nuances of their heritage practices, such as 'walking Country' (Bidwell *et al.* 2008).

The Herero in Namibia have greater political power nationally than indigenous groups in Australia; however, regardless of national politics, a core part of the problem in designing technologies suited to living heritage is that details of interactions between people, and between people and objects, are often indiscernible to those performing them. As we said at the beginning of this chapter, 'lived' heritage lies in the details of everyday practices; but many of these practices are unconscious, and others are so tacit that they are difficult to articulate. The meanings of places are embodied in actions, and people can 'read' these meanings of places through patterns of actions in such places (Bidwell and Browning 2010; Dourish and Bell 2011). Often these patterns become conscious only when breakdowns arise, for instance consider the movements of participants, in our research in Namibia, relative to other people and livestock. A familiarity with daily and seasonal rhythms enables people to move around locations in villages and between cattle camps distributed over large tracts of pasturage. It is often only when people are uncertain of direction that they become aware that they follow passages created by cows' paths, read the movement of cattle between rivers, villages and corrals, or recognize individual cows' footprints. Mundane, conscious or unconscious actions render meaning, even when people do not verbalize these meanings. Consider rural participants' everyday movements in their homesteads. In front of people's huts lie cattle corrals, and in between these corrals and their huts is a fire for making tea and cooking farmed animals and the

Holy Fire, separated by an enclosure of stones or a hedge. Behind the huts lie goat corrals and places to slaughter goats and cook game. These tangible aspects of the homestead shape people's movements. Further, people's movements are shaped by protocols about gender and kinship, as women and men use the different fires to tend, slaughter and cook different animals. In other words, the tangible (e.g. fires) and the intangible (e.g. protocols) entwine in rural Herero's movements and actions, and in the way people perform their identity in relation to cattle and kin.

Critical design reflections

Our situated action research involves continuously and critically evaluating the details of design activities and prototypes in the context of broader insights about relationships between Herero people, places and heritage, such as those we described above. In this last section, we describe three specific interaction issues revealed by design activities that shed light on important tensions and that, we recommend, we must account for when designing systems for UGC to enable people to extend their living heritage.

Technological constraints on what is recorded transforms narrative

During our research we observed that local participants' video recordings tend to focus on people, and their camera use tends to embody social relations between speakers and listeners. For most clips a listener, other than local cameramen, was present (whether in view or not), and social relations shaped the cameramen's camera use and interactions with others (Bidwell *et al.* 2011c). For instance, cameramen waited for their subjects to speak and people's vocal interactions prevailed over their camera use, particularly if youth recorded elders. Indeed, one healer failed to record because he was absorbed in discussions with his mentor. In all viewings, participants listened carefully, and consistently noticed speech and gesture above other visual information. They used oral cues to recognize and disambiguate herbs and to identify speakers. Participants emphasized the importance of recording villages' and people's names involved in the video in order to assess the integrity of information based on the speakers' backgrounds. Acute attention to oral and person-based visual information, more than other visual context, may reflect earlier customs of storytelling around the evening fire and the ways oral custom accentuates imagery of people's characters, personhood, societal position and genealogical bonds.

Although seemingly empowering, equipping rural dwellers with video cameras does not always adequately record aspects of face-to-face, co-present communication important to their knowledge practices. Participants' discussions about video, recorded by themselves or academic researchers, often indicated that the content of clips incompletely depicted the knowledge they sought to represent. First, video may not show all links between visceral qualities of knowledge, bodily memory and communicating. For instance, as he recorded video a healer extensively and explicitly gestured to plants, the surroundings and/or his body, and held or touched plants; however, his clips show only some gestures and often all that is visible of these interactions is that the camera jolted or a branch twitched as a result. These issues are not addressed simply by introducing a professional cameraman or training local people with equipment, as such acts perpetuate the power relations between the knowers, as we described earlier. Sometimes the ways movements and actions shape the nature of people's experience of places are recordable, for instance video depicts relationships between places and gender roles. In yards women butchered meat, prepared food on the fire and supervised children, whereas men worked in the corrals and bush around yards. However, video, as a technology, often encourages people to take a particular perspective, which obscures relationships between the body and the surroundings in their heritage practices. For instance, participants did not record their paths or the sites where they prepare or administer herbal treatments, even though these shaped their oral narratives. Second, many qualities of interactions cannot be recorded. It was impossible to record some collaborative interactions because of their speed and complexity; connections between people's bodily experience; or, metaphysical qualities of experiences. For instance, a healer said he always tests herbs on himself then diagnoses patients' ill health by 'catching their hand' and that spirits help him to know 'the colour of the underwear you are wearing … where you have a birth mark …'. Thus, video records verbal descriptions and some bodily actions but excludes much information carried within interactions between bodies, settings and artifacts by projecting the lived world onto a 2D plane.

Existing media may influence participants' selectivity in recording as well as in classifying the content of recording. For instance, books on medicinal and edible plants in Namibia emphasize visual morphology, and participants distinguished recording information about herbs from recording other daily activities. However, participants did not always find plants legible in video and often found it easier to identify features from spoken sequences, as a taxonomy that separates plants from daily activities poorly represents participants' routine use of plants or the medicinal use of non-plant based products. Information about heritage is sometimes considered more valid if it derives from objective analysis and is 'shown' using particular systems of inscription and communication modes. Consider the power of carbon dating in validating an artifact's age over oral accounts. That is, print-facilitated culture and the politics of modernity valorize ways of knowing and promote those that can be formalized and articulated in sets of principles over informal and contextualized know-how, even though both ways of knowing contribute to the processes of producing and communicating knowledge. Holding recorded knowledge in higher regard than spoken or enacted knowledge associates with the view that recording systems foster objectivity, detached analysis, abstraction, categorization or memorization (Scribner and Cole 1981). Certainly, particular literacies certainly shape abilities, but cognition and verbal practice are also effected by schooling (Hull and Scholtz 2001) and linguistic contexts; indeed, a body of work in southern Africa shows that the creation and transmission of oral literature is rich with complex and abstract structures (see Kaschula 2001; Finnegan 2007).

When technology is appropriated in new practices of 'lived' heritage, it changes the focus on the content. As summarized above, video recordings can neglect aural, kinaesthetic or spiritual qualities residing in the performance, structure and form of oral communication and relationships between speakers and audience. Representations and accounts of knowledge entwine with the knowledge itself in an ongoing dynamic. Consider how participants ordered information differently when they watched clips rather than speaking without watching video (Bidwell *et al.* 2011a). When participants described a herb in situ or added stories about herbs unmentioned in clips, they tended to say symptoms or causes of ill health first. But when they discussed herbs concurrently with or just after seeing a clip, they identified the herb first, then described preparation and parts to use and, finally, symptoms and causes. Watching video prompts sequences starting with herbs rather than health; and participants associate recognizing herbs in clips with subsequent actions rather than, say, reasons for gathering.

The act of recording transforms knowledge, perhaps because video facilitates noticing different things in different moments, and this may have profound consequences in the way in which people experience places and objects and, in turn, derive knowledge. Heritage practices absorb intangible concepts about places and objects and, as we described earlier, the rural Hereros' movements and actions interconnect with tangible objects and intangible concepts. The entwining of the tangible and intangible, through movements and actions, not only shapes the way a Herero performs their identity but also shapes their experience of life in places. Consider how a woman's experience of her homestead and the surrounding desert land is affected by her garments which most aged over thirty wear. Her long, many layered dress restricts moving swiftly and she engages with her domestic and social tasks at a measured pace (Bidwell *et al.* 2011c). Her speed in encountering information in her habitat is part of the system through which she knows places, and through which she practices heritage, and, since video may not depict the tempo of her experience it obscures important aspects of her knowledge (for other examples see Ingold and Vergunst 2008).

Heritage abstractions disrupt temporal relations

Our own ways of thinking about location and time obscured relationships between places and movements within Herero activities. When we first interpreted interactions with video, we tended to abstract locations discretely, and tended to focus on their relationships to specific features and activities by noticing the ways participants' practices were situated topographically, or within 'discrete' places (Bidwell *et al.* 2011c). This distracted us from qualities that are 'topo-kinetic', or relate to bodily movement in and between places (Green 2007; Ingold and Vergunst 2008). Various activities showed that participants have good recall of chronology, and further analysis revealed that their movements influenced their use of spatio-temporal references in narratives, for instance they recalled how they learnt about herbs within activities sequenced across locations. Thus, it appears that rural Herero participants conceptualize time and location each as a continuum, and their narratives use frames of reference internal to the world not as abstractions that relate to imaginary fixed meridians, such as north. Participants related locations to people and activities, and the Otjiherero language expresses the land as a continuum in which vegetation increases with distance from the speaker. Viewing locations relative to people was particularly clear in participants' difficulty in creating a geospatially accurate, aerial view of familiar locations to which they had walked, directly, just a few moments before. Further, we frequently noticed that participants construct time relative to others, or polychronically, rather than in terms of discrete and quantifiable elements. They had difficulty in calculating durations (such as the years between events), and scheduled daily activities 'when we are ready' rather than according to impersonal units of hours or weeks.

Conceptualizing location and time as continual, not discrete dimensions shows that participants' lived reality differs from assumptions in accounts of places and heritage perpetuated by technology. Representing places by separating geographical locations from temporality is a worldview that is not held by all people. For instance, 3D visualizations of time-less locations inadequately depict Arawakan people's accounts of places in Brazil (Green 2007) and placeless events are nonsensical to Native Americans stories (see Dourish and Bell 2011). The significance of places to heritage resides in the ways people respond to those places whether or not we recognize those places as agents in social actions because they have some inherent spiritual power (Byrne 2008). Similarly, constructing time as past, present and future is also a social action. These relations about time are implied in the meaning of 'heritage' itself and also embedded within the operations of technologies, but they do not match the lived realities of the Herero, whose ancestors routinely communicate with them and are agents in current events. Further, abstractions that conceptualize places as spatial or temporal points along axes that are extrinsic to the world are incompatible with the ways Herero manage places in face-to-face oral interactions. Participants do not construct places with impersonal and temporally fixed geographies; rather their spatial references often relate locations to movements, and their narratives shape relationships between locations, people, livestock and events within journeys. When villagers meet and move together, within villages or to cattle camps, they experience links between their bodies, activities and the settings in which these meetings and movements occur (Bidwell et al. 2011c). But video encourages a particular spatio-temporal perspective on locations, and this may explain why participants had difficulty recognizing video clips by static thumbnail images even when they were distinctive to us. The same constraints are embedded in the perspectives on location and time in other technologies, such as applications in social media that aim to support meeting or recording events on particular dates.

Prototyping in envelopment

Our initial data gathering revealed how local people may use media to achieve various goals in preserving their heritage. For instance, participants mentioned that media might raise the government's awareness, so they 'see that we are living this way and help by giving [us] food ...'. Christie and Verran (2007) use the term 'envelopment' to describe the way that traditional owners in Australia harness media projects to continue their customs, exercise their ritual responsibility for country and ensure that clan lands and intellectual property (IP) stay in the right hands and in the right relations with other clans. However, to design for these types of considerations, all parties must sufficiently understand the politics framing their differing agendas. Misunderstandings can lead local participants to omit important information. For instance, consider how Herero participants in our studies explained to us that they did not reveal the numbers of cows they owned to previous data collectors, because they did not know how that information might be used. The government calculates local water needs based on estimates of cattle numbers and inaccurate information meant they installed insufficient solar panels to drive the pumps at the village borehole.

Our ethnography shows various aspects of causality and etiology in ill health that people were, at first, reluctant to discuss in English on camera. For instance, in-situ translations of the healer, as he recorded clips, did not mention spirits, ancestors or dreams, as he did in our healing experiences, while other participants rarely or never mentioned bewitching, possession, curses and bad luck. Indeed, an elder asked, 'must I tell you that?' before translating an explanation in a video about using a herb to purge malevolent spirits: 'someone killed people and those things... how can I say? Those things [that] are following him. Now he will maybe come and just touch you and these things will go to you.' Such omissions may reflect how, historically, Christianity and apartheid separated herbalism from spirituality or how Lutheran colonists were suspicious about tangibly representing divine forms (Bidwell *et al.* 2011a). However, unlike religious practitioners' opposition to filming rituals elsewhere in Africa (De Witte 2007) participants were not opposed to video recording in their syncrestic church, although we refrained, and, with time, participants became more comfortable in translating spiritual practices. For instance, in reviewing video a participant mentioned treating curse that went unmentioned earlier: 'You take a warm coal from the fire and you let the person bleed on this. It's the moving diplomat. ... The one who cursed you this one will take. It will go back to the person and that person will start bleeding. Things are happening in reality ...'.

Participants' explanations often seem to suggest they sought to make information comprehensible to those beyond their community. Thus, the ways they depict their knowledge is not only shaped by media but also by relations between those recording and/or viewing. Participants adapted the structure and content of their recordings according to those present. For instance, consider qualities of situated narratives about herb lore: early in our research we recorded a healer moving in the bush near his home while he, concurrently, self-recorded herbs as he spoke about them. The healer recorded separate clips of different herbs and we recorded constantly to include interactions when he was not recording, translations by his wife and interactions with researchers. Five months later we recorded the healer and his apprentice, to whom we gave a camera, together in the bush further from the healer's homestead. The healer intended his first tour to demonstrate how he might record and the second tour to inform his apprentice, who was so absorbed in listening to the healer he failed to record. Such insights show that participants realized that media take on local roles, context-specific meanings and can function to bridge different communities of practice. Media artifacts, such as videos on herbs, convey information between communities but also have interpretive flexibility since people draw on their existing knowledge to understand information that was embedded in the artifact when people created it, such as who was speaking and where a herb is. Participants attempted to assist researchers in making interconnections by referring to knowledge they assumed researchers might have, such as biblical metaphors to explain herbs: 'in the boat of Noah, they were male and female, so these plants are like that'.

Prototypes can also function to bridge different communities of practice by representing a designer's understanding to a community. The success of a prototype in bridging depends upon how identifiable the prototype is in community contexts. Community members responded more actively to our most recent prototype for organizing their video content within a 3D visualization than to previous ones, which used text, icons or images. The most recent prototype inserts video clips in a visualization of the village in which animated models of people and animals depict scenarios about local practices and follow some of the paths they routinely trace through the village (Rodil *et al.* 2011). In interacting with the prototype participants suggested scenarios, requested specific changes, and gave other critique and feedback. Like other visualization endeavours with indigenous groups, this prototype allows users to explore the setting without forcing a linear narrative between scenarios; and we remain wary that this compromises the information contained in the sequences of movement that contextualize knowledge (Bidwell *et al.* 2011c). Indeed, over the course of our research participants have become increasingly aware that technology cannot adequately represent the tacit knowledge of their face-to-face communication. For instance, based on his experience with video recording and prototyping, a healer expressed reservations about his earlier suggestion to record his knowledge in an interactive book.

Interestingly, the healer raised his reservations about the affordances of media for disseminating herb lore shortly after his city-based son had requested legally verified, written contracts to govern our collaboration with his father. Throughout our earlier discussions all participants said that they sought to share their knowledge for the benefit of 'nature and people' to all those who are interested. While we were comfortable with how this showed their recognition and pride in their cultural practices, we were also concerned that it suggested a lack of recognizing its economic worth. Thus, we devoted considerable time to provoking discussions about participants' rights in dissemination, confidentiality and IP. However, soon after discussions about legal contracts, the healer and his wife apologized for their son's interference and said that he did not understand the principles of trust established in our collaboration. That is, rural participants seem to conceive that written agreements are needed in the absence of trust and conflict with their heritage practices. The healer's son referred to the regulatory frameworks that attribute economic significance to knowledge practices, while rural Hereros draw upon local sanctioning that relates knowledge to principles of community sharing. Negotiating between the frameworks of IP versus the common good presents huge difficulties in design. The Namibian government, like others in southern Africa, strives to develop an appropriate indigenous knowledge policy to prevent further exploitation by external parties. However, at the coalface of designing a system to support community-authored content, we cannot differentiate between frameworks, tools and content and, as yet, have not achieved a model satisfying both systems. For instance, how do we ensure that participants' knowledge is valued within systems of IP without, simultaneously, devaluing their community values in relation to heritage? And how do we know who constitutes the 'common' given the concerns of rural community members about rural-to-urban migrants' reinterpretations of knowledge?

Conclusion

While rural Herero communities preserve connections with their rural homes within everyday practices and share these connections orally, rural-to-urban migration interrupts intergenerational transfer of local knowledge practices. To respond to this problem, we continue to explore ways to enable rural communities to appropriate new technologies to extend their own cultural heritage practices. By maintaining a critical design perspective as we develop digital tools, we started to recognize implicit and explicit assumptions about people's connections with each other, with places and with history, which may not match rural Herero people's lived reality. Social media and interactive technologies for UGC, more generally, and interaction techniques offer promising opportunities to extend rural indigenous practices, but, we must realize that technology also reframes reality and interacts with lived heritage to refocus practice. While community participation in generating content shifts recording to 'unofficial' heritage curation, practices in designing systems for UGC remain situated within political systems, so both the media and the recorder unavoidably constrain what is preserved.

Thinking about living heritage is helpful in generating insights about what is valuable in the past and present, and determining what is important for the future, but it also assumes certain concepts of time that do not reconcile well with some cultural practices. Thus, the conceptualization of heritage in the information age is problematic in itself, unless we leverage the ways media use can reveal assumptions within different communities of practice, and enable all involved to continually review their assumptions.

References

Ball, M.W. (2002) 'People Speaking Silently to Themselves: An Examination of Keith Basso's Philosophical Speculations on "Sense of Place" in Apache Cultures', *American Indian Quarterly*, 26(3): 460–478.

Bidwell, N.J. and Browning, D. (2010) 'Pursuing Genius Loci: Interaction Design and Natural Places', *Personal and Ubiquitous Computing,* 14: 15–30. First published online 17 March 2009.

Bidwell, N.J., Standley, P.-M., George, T. and Steffensen, V. (2008) 'The Landscape's Apprentice: Lessons for Place-Centred Design from Grounding Documentary', *Proceedings of the 7th ACM Conference on Designing Information Systems (DIS 2008).* New York: ACM Press: 88–98.

Bidwell, N.J., Winschiers-Theophilus, H., Koch-Kapuire, G. and Chivuno-Kuria, S. (2011a) 'Situated Interactions Between Audiovisual Media and African Herbal Lore', *Personal and Ubiquitous Computing,* 15: 609–627. First published online 31 December 2010.

Bidwell, N.J., Lalmas M., Marsden, G, Dlutu, B., Ntlangano, S., Manjingolo, A., Tucker, W.D., Jones, M., Robinson, R., Vartiainen, E. and Klampanos, I. (2011b) 'Please call ME.N.U.4EVER: Designing for "Callback" in Rural Africa', *Proceedings of The 10th International Workshop on Internalisation of Products and Systems (IWIPS 2011),* Kuching, Malaysia, July: 117–138.

Bidwell, N.J., Winschiers-Theophilus, H., Koch Kapuire, G. and Rehm, M. (2011c) 'Pushing Personhood into Place: Situating Media in the Transfer of Rural Knowledge in Africa', *International Journal of Human-Computer Studies. Special Issue on Locative Media:* 618–631

Bubenzer, O., Bollig, M., Kavari, J. and Bleckmann, L. (2009) 'Otjiherero Praises of Places: Collective Memory Embedded in Landscape and the Aesthetic Sense of a Pastoral People', *Studies in Human Ecology and Adaptation,* 4: 473–500.

Byrne, D. (2008) 'Heritage as Social Action', in G. Fairclough, R. Harrison, J.H. Jameson and J. Schofield, (eds.) *The Heritage Reader,* London & New York: Routledge: 149–173.

Christie, M. (2005) 'Computer Databases and Aboriginal Knowledge', *International Journal of Learning in Social Contexts,* 1: 4–12.

Christie, M and Verran, H. (2007) 'Using Technologies in Doing Digital Places', *Human Technology: An Interdisciplinary Journal on Humans in ICT Environments,* 3(2): 214–227.

De Bruijn, M., Van Dijk, R. and Foeken, D. (2001) *Mobile Africa: Changing Patterns of Movement in Africa and Beyond,* Leiden, Boston and Tokyo: Brill.

De Witte, M. (2007) 'Insight, Secrecy, Beasts, and Beauty: Struggles over the Making of a Ghanaian Documentary on "African Traditional Religion"', *The Journal of Sacred Texts and Contemporary Worlds,* Postscripts 1.2/1.3: 277–300.

Donner, J. (2010) 'Framing M4D: The Utility of Continuity and the Dual Heritage of "Mobiles and Development"', *The Electronic Journal of Information Systems,* 44(3): 1–16

Dourish, P. and Bell, G. (2011) *Divining a Digital Future: Mess and Mythology in Ubiquitous Computing,* Cambridge, MA: MIT Press.

Dunne, A. and Raby, F. (2001) *Design Noir: The Secret Life of Electronic Objects,* London: August/Birkhauser.

Dyson, L.E., Hendriks, M.A.N. and Grant, S. (2007) *Information Technology and Indigenous People,* Singapore: Idea Group Inc. (IGI).

Finnegan, R. (2007) *The Oral and Beyond: Doing Things with Words in Africa.* Oxford and Chicago, IL: James Curry/University of Chicago Press.

Forster, L. (2005) 'Land and Landscapes in Herero Oral Culture: An Analysis of Cultural and Social Aspects of the Land Question in Namibia', The Namibian Institute for Democracy: Analysis and Views. www.nid.org.na/Publications.htm (accessed 5 December 2011).

Frayne, B. (2005) 'Survival of the Poorest: Migration and Food Security in Namibia', in L.A. Mougeot (ed.) *Agropolis: The Social, Political, and Environmental Dimensions of Urban Agriculture,* Ottawa: IDRC.

Giaccardi, E. (2011) 'Things We Value', *Interactions,* 18(1): 17–21.

Green, L.J.F. (2007) 'Cultural Heritage, Archives and Citizenship: Reflections on Using Virtual Reality for Presenting Knowledge Diversity in the Public Sphere', *Critical Arts* 21(2): 308–320.

Greyling, E. and Zulu, S. (2010) 'Content Development in an Indigenous Digital Library: A Case Study in Community Participation', *Journal of the International Federation of Library Associations and Institutions*, 36(1): 30–39

Grinker, R.R., Lubkemann, S.C. and Steiner C.B. (1997) *Perspectives on Africa: A Reader in Culture, History and Representation (Global Perspectives)*, Chichester: Wiley-Blackwell.

Gupta, V. (2005) 'Traditional Knowledge Digital Library', paper presented at the Sub-Regional Experts Meeting in Asia on Intangible Cultural Heritage, Bangkok, Thailand, 13–16 December.

Harrison, R. (2010) 'Heritage as Social Action', in S. West (ed.) *Understanding Heritage in Practice*, Manchester and Milton Keynes: Manchester University Press in association with the Open University.

Harrison, S., Tatar, D. and Sengers, P. (2007) 'The three paradigms of HCI', *Alt.chi forum at 25th International Conference on Human factors in Computing Systems. CHI 2007*. http://www.viktoria.se/altchi/submissions/submission_steveharrison_0.pdf (accessed 1 August 2010).

Henrichsen, D. (1999) *Claiming Space and Power in Pre-colonial Central Namibia: The Relevance of Herero Praise Songs,* BAB Working Papers 1, Basel: Basler Afrika Bibliographien.

Hester, R. (1996) 'Economic Progress', *Prostor*, 4 (1/11): 7–26.

Hull, G. and Schultz, K. (2001) 'Literacy and Learning Out of School: A Review of Theory and Research', *Review of Educational Research* 71: 575–611.

Ingold, T. and Vergunst, J.L. (2008) *Ways of Walking: Ethnography and Practice on Foot,* Aldershot: Ashgate Publishing Limited.

Kaschula, R. (2001) *The Bones of the Ancestors are Shaking: Xhosa Oral Poetry in Context*, Cape Town: Juta and Co.

Kavari, J.U. (2002) *The Form and Meaning of Otjiherero Praises*, Cologne: Rüdiger Köppe.

Koch Kapuire, G., Winschiers-Theophilus, H., ChivunoKuria, S., Bidwell, N.J., Blake, B. (2010) ' A Revolution in ICT, the Last Hope for African Rural Communities' Technology Appropriation', in *Proceedings of the 4th International Development Informatics Association (IDIA) Conference 2010*, Cape Town, 3-5 November 2010.

Kok, P. and Collinson, M.A. (2006) *Migration and Urbanisation in South Africa*, Report 0304-02, Pretoria: Statistics South Africa.

Rodil, K., Winschiers-Theophilus, H., Bidwell, N.J., Eskildsen, S., Rehm, M. and Koch Kapuire, G. (2011) 'A New Visualization Approach to Re-contextualize Indigenous Knowledge in Rural Africa', *Proceedings of INTERACT 2011* (*Lecture Notes in Computer Science), 297–314*. Berlin: Springer.

Rumble G., and Koul, B.N. (2007) *Open Schooling for Secondary and Higher Secondary Education: Costs and Effectiveness in India and Namibia,* Vancouver: COL.

Scribner, S. and Cole, M. (1981) *The Psychology of Literacy*, Cambridge, MA: Harvard University Press.

Standley, P., Bidwell N.J., George, T. and Steffensen, V. (2009) 'Connecting Communities and the Environment through Media: Doing, Saying and Seeing Along Traditional Indigenous Knowledge Revival Pathways', *3C Media Journal of Community, Citizen's and Third Sector Media and Communication* 5: 9–27.

Taachi, J., Slater, D. and Hearn, G. (2003) *Ethnographic Action Research*, New Delhi: UNESCO.

Tjieka, L.T. (Aditya Nugraha) (2007) 'Desa Informasi: The Role of Digital Libraries in the Preservation and Dissemination of Indigenous Knowledge', *Bulletin of the American Society for Information Science and Technology*, 33(5): 37–42.

TNS (2009) *MWEB Friendship 2.0.* http://www.mweb.co.za/services/friendship/ (accessed 27 November 2011).

Tripathi, N. and Bhattarya, S. (2004) 'Integrating Indigenous Knowledge and GIS for Participatory Natural Resource Management: State of the Practice', *The Electronic Journal of Information Systems in Developing Countries*, 17(3): 1–13.

truna (aka turner, j.) and Bidwell, N.J. (2007) 'Through the Looking Glass on Gameworlds', *Proceedings of International Conference of Interactive Entertainment*, New York: ACM Press.

truna (aka turner, j.), Browning, D. and Bidwell, N.J. (2009) 'Wanderer Beyond Gameworlds', *Leonardo Electronic Almanac* 16(2–3). http://www.leoalmanac.org/journal/Vol_16/lea_v16_n02-03/JTurner.html (accessed 27 November 2011).

Van der Velden, M. (2008) 'Organising Development Knowledge: Towards Situated Classification Work on the Web', *Webology*, 5(3). http://www.webology.org/2008/v5n3/a60.html (accessed 27 November 2011).

Van Harmelen, U. (2004) 'Through the Eyes of Namibian Teenagers', in M. Roberson and M. Williams (eds) *Young People, Leisure and Place: Cross Cultural Perspectives*, New York: Nova Scientific.

Wenger, E. (1998) *Communities of Practice, Learning, Meaning, and Identity*, Cambridge: Cambridge University Press.

Winschiers-Theophilus, H., Bidwell, N.J., Blake, E., Koch Kapuire, G. and Chivuno-Kuria, S. (2011) 'Community Consensus: Design Beyond Participation', *Design Issues*, MIT Press. In press.

12

SITUATING THE SOCIABILITY OF INTERACTIVE MUSEUM GUIDES

Ron Wakkary, Audrey Desjardins, Kevin Muise, Karen Tanenbaum and Marek Hatala

Introduction

Interactive technology for museums and cultural heritage sites has been an active area of research for more than fifteen years, blending together work in ubiquitous computing, information retrieval and delivery, tangible computing and social media. Early prototypes such as Bederson (1995) provided evidence that it was possible to support visitor-driven interaction through wireless communication, thus allowing visitors to explore the museum environment at their own pace and according to their own interests and knowledge level. More recent prototypes and fully functional systems have even greater complexity, supporting a variety of media types, adaptive models and interaction modalities. Bell notes in her article on museums as cultural ecologies that 'the challenge here is to design information technologies that help make new connections for museum visitors' (Bell 2002: 15). Bell further argues for the importance of *sociality* in museums where visits are as equally social and entertaining as they are educational. While much work has been done on connecting museum visitors to *information* via museum guides, comparatively little work has been done on making *social* connections within the museum space. Addressing the social qualities of a museum visit remains a clear challenge when designing museum guide technologies, one that is accelerated by the increasing pervasiveness of social media and their impact on the notion of museum space itself.

In this chapter, we analyze emerging research approaches for interactive museum guides to describe the move from information delivery to sociability. As a result, we discuss the need to refine what we mean by sociability with respect to technologies in museums, and what impact the trajectory toward museum guides as social technology tools has on the notion of the interactive museum guide. We have selected research and experimental interactive museum guides based on their explorations of current boundaries, and in order to illustrate efforts in exploring social qualities across different types of systems and approaches. Our definition for an interactive museum guide is a device that uses information technology for the purpose of interpreting the artifacts, themes and concepts of the whole or main part of an exhibition.

This chapter is motivated by our previous research in interactive museum guides in which the main focus was on exploring interactivity and its influence on visitors' experience of the museum space as well as their learning process within the museum. In particular, our research has examined the opportunities of tangible computing for museum guides as a design and technology approach, and the role of adaptive systems relying on artificial intelligence and user models. An earlier publication of ours (Wakkary *et al.* 2008) examined these three aspects in a wide analysis of museum guide research. Since that paper there has been significantly more research in the area of tangible interaction and museums, and there has been an overwhelming rise in social media tools aimed at museums, with content created either by visitors themselves or by museum organizations. Hence this chapter revisits and deepens our earlier landscape analysis. We also decided to focus more explicitly on the idea of sociability in interactive museum guides. As a result, we analyze three categories: tangibility, interactive content and social media, and consider sociability as a concern across the three areas.

In this chapter, we use a 2 × 2 matrix for our analysis in each category of tangibility, interactive content and social media to help define and describe each category. The matrices also illustrate the relationship between the projects discussed in the chapter and situate their approaches with respect to sociability.

Situating tangibility in museums

In 1992, Durrell Bishop's Marble Answering Machine (Crampton-Smith 1995) was an early embodiment of the immediate and playful qualities of tangible interaction. The prototype used marbles to represent messages on an answering machine. A person replayed the message by picking up the marble and placing it in an indentation in the machine.

Tangible interactions or tangible user interfaces (TUIs) like the Marble Answering Machine imbue physical artifacts with computational capabilities. Ishii and Ullmer's foundational work on tangible interaction described the concept with the salient phrase 'coupling of bits and atoms' (Ishii and Ullmer 1997).

More recently, Hornecker and Buur (2006) offered a broader description of tangibility that relates well to our analysis. Their understanding includes physical manipulation of data, as well as the expressive and sensory interaction with objects and space. In our experience, a tangible approach to computation helps bridge between the virtuality of the museum guide system and the physical/social surroundings of the exhibition by leveraging our rich experiences in the physical world and our kinesthetic abilities.

With this in mind, one factor of the 2 × 2 matrix for tangibility that we use to describe tangible museum guides is the kind and quality of interaction (Figure 12.1).

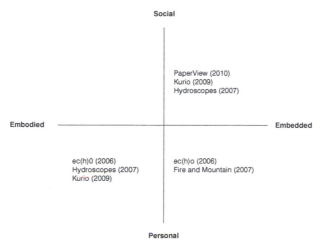

FIGURE 12.1   Matrix showing different types of interactive museum guides based on types of tangibility and degrees of sociability

We describe this factor as ranging from the *embodied* to the *embedded*. An embodied interaction relies on the whole body movements of visitors, i.e. their movements and paths within the exhibition. An embedded interaction relies on the local or smaller movements of wrist, hands and touch, e.g. the rotation and placement of an object by a museum visitor.

In addition to physicality and interaction, it is important to note that our social interactions are in large part mediated by objects and environments as much as by direct contact with others (Kaptelinin and Nardi 2006). Hornecker and Buur (2006) argue that social interaction may be the most critical feature of tangible interaction. In their own museum interactive work they comment on how interactive and hands-on installations attract groups that interact together in parallel or cooperative fashion. A second factor in analyzing tangible museum guides is the degree of sociability. This factor ranges from *personal* interaction to *social* interaction involving formal and informal groups of visitors.

Embedded and personal

We begin our analysis of the tangibility category with Rizzo and Garzotto's Fire and Mountain (Rizzo and Garzotto 2007). Fire and Mountain was presented as a temporary exhibit at the Civic Museum in Como, Italy, with the goal of supporting young visitors in their learning of the cultural heritage of the Como Lake region. The exhibition was composed of four digital installations with which visitors could interact tangibly and or by touch. The design of Fire and Mountain was based on four main objectives: creating emotional involvement in the young visitors by creating the sense of a 'magical' environment; developing interactions that were multi-modal to engage multiple senses; approaching learning as discovery-based so that content was uncovered by interacting with the displays; and making learning social to allow collaborative and cooperative interaction.

The four installations contained in the exhibition included: the Virtual Book, the Talking Dictionary, the Research Tables and the augmented reality representation of a cave. Fire and Mountain is a hybrid approach; it uses different technologies and components, but each installation allows for embedded interaction through either gesture, manipulation or the use of a tangible object. Even though all of the components of the exhibition allowed for groups of visitors, they relied on embedded interactions that were predominantly personal.

Our own museum project ec(h)o (Wakkary and Hatala 2007) was installed at the Canadian Nature Museum in Ottawa, Canada, in 2004 in an exhibition about the practice and history of collecting natural history artifacts and data. In ec(h)o, our approach included a tangible user interface designed to be playful and simple, a spatial audio display that relied on multiple voices and dynamic soundscapes and an integrated user modeling technique combined with semantic technologies that supported information exploration.

Visitors wearing headphones heard a binaural soundscape that changed as they moved through the exhibit. The sounds were related to habitat sounds of the animal artifacts in the exhibition and the dynamics of the sound were based on the visitor's proximity to parts of the collections. In certain areas or 'hotspots' in front of exhibit displays, the soundscape would fade and visitors were given three riddles related to the artifacts in front of them. Visitors selected which riddle they wanted 'answered' by rotating a wooden cube with colored sides (Figure 12.2).

ec(h)o is a hybrid approach in terms of interaction modalities. Visitors can interact in an *embedded* interaction mode since gestures with the cube are hand and arm movements. Yet visitors can also interact in an embodied modality in which their movements and their location in the exhibition influence the audio

FIGURE 12.2   ec(h)o: tangible user interface. Photo: used with permission by Ron Wakkary, Simon Fraser University, Canada

display. With respect to sociability, ec(h)o is based on personal interactions, with little social interaction.

Embedded and social

The PaperView system (Grammenos *et al.* 2011) is an experimental system that was installed at the Archaeological Museum of Thessalonki in Greece. Visitors gathered around either a table with a two-dimensional map or a glass case with a three-dimensional map. In either case, visitors could move sheets of paper across the map and satellite views of the map's location underneath the paper would appear projected on the surface of the paper. The paper acted like a magic lens that revealed virtual information based on the location of the paper. Visitors could navigate back and forth through the slide show by selecting virtual buttons projected on the paper or tilting the paper left or right to browse the content. PaperView utilized what is known as augmented reality techniques, i.e. combining virtual reality with physical environments, but also had a strong tangible component through the use of paper as the main interface component (Figure 12.3).

PaperView relies on embedded interaction. While the technology is not embedded in the paper, the paper reacts to sensing and it displays what is in near proximity to it, similar to ec(h)o. The interactions are local gestures, i.e. hand and arm movements as opposed to whole body movement. The system allows for multiple visitors to use the system at once by gathering around the table or glass display, each with their own piece of paper for interacting with the system. The social interaction is parallel rather than explicitly cooperative or collaborative.

Hydroscopes, a project presented at the Kattegat Marine Center in Denmark (Dindler *et al.* 2007), offered the visitors a creative way to summarize and finish their visit. In a room, visitors could create a fish by choosing parts with different characteristics (long tail, small fins, etc.) and assembling them together (Figure 12.4). All the parts contained RFID tags that allowed the system to give feedback on the strengths and weaknesses of the fish. Once this was done, visitors could release their fish in the virtual sea where fishes created by other visitors 'lived'.

FIGURE 12.3   PaperView: users interacting with the table (left); users lifting the paper (right). Photo: used with permission by Dimitris Grammenos, FORTH-ICS, Greece

FIGURE 12.4   Hydroscopes: the hydroscope (left); fishes with RFID tags (right). Photo: used with permission by Christian Dindler, Aarhus University, Denmark

This project relies on tangibles for two things. First, the fishes are tangible, with technology (RFID) embedded in them. Secondly, the hydroscopes are the way through which visitors can explore the virtual sea. They are constructed with a large tire tube that supports a screen and an acrylic dome (which protects the screen). To explore the sea, visitors have to move the hydroscope on the floor. The size, the shape and the required movement all encouraged social interactions between visitors (whether they knew each other or not). This fosters a closer contact and thus a more engaged experience. Hydroscopes is social and both embedded (creating the fish) and embodied (moving the Hydroscope on the floor of the exhibition room).

A recent project of ours, Kurio, is a museum guide system supporting families and friends visiting the museum (Wakkary *et al.* 2009). In Kurio a family imagines themselves as time travelers that are lost in the present because their time map is broken. In order to repair the time map, family members have to complete 'assignments' and collect information from the museum. The overall 'mission' is collaborative; the assignments are individually assigned, but they explicitly invite help from family members and friends. The main feature of Kurio is a set of custom designed tangibles, including Pointer, Finder, Listener and Reader (Figure 12.5).

The Pointer is in a shape reminiscent of a flashlight and was used to point at and select information in the museum. The tip of the pointer glows blue when a selection is made. The Finder is used to find different locations in the exhibition space and is shaped like a branching stick or water diviner. This tangible glows and vibrates as a visitor moves closer to a part of the exhibition they need to find. The Listener is used to hear audio information in different locations within the exhibition space. This tangible is in the form of a walkie-talkie and the tip of the antenna glows when a visitor is in a location where they can hear audio. Lastly,

FIGURE 12.5 Kurio: Kurio's tangibles from left to right: Pointer, Finder, Listener and Reader (left); mother and son reviewing information obtained with the Reader on the personal digital assistant (right). Photo: used with permission by Ron Wakkary, Simon Fraser University, Canada

the Reader is a large magnifying glass that collects text from didactic displays. Similar to other tangibles, the Reader allows visitors to select text from the various didactics in the exhibition to help complete assignments. Kurio also includes an interactive table for gathering around and a personal digital assistant (PDA) while on the move, which are used to manage the overall mission, the assignments and the selections from the tangibles. Kurio, like Hydroscopes, is primarily embedded and social, however, aspects of the system like the Listener and Finder are embodied and personal.

Embodied and personal

ec(h)o, Hydroscopes and Kurio can additionally be categorized as embodied and personal. We have described each of these systems above, including their embodied aspects. In summary: one mode of interaction in ec(h)o is a dynamic soundscape that responds to body movements and location in the exhibition; Hydroscopes encourages visitors to view the virtual aquarium by moving through the space while looking through the hydroscope; and aspects of Kurio like the Listener and Finder are location-based and rely on visitors moving through the exhibition.

Summary

Tangible interaction in museum guides can add to the critical social dimensions of museum visits, without precluding personal experiences. By means of our examples it is clear that tangible museum guides can lead to (at minimum) a passive sociability through shared or parallel interaction.

As shown in our matrix (Figure 12.1), the area of *embodied* and *social* interaction is relatively unexplored. This can be explained in relation to the fact that in many instances the fine motor skills required for selection by tangible museum guides limit the social aspects of interaction. For example, in ec(h)o the soundscape is personalized to a particular visitor and would be an incoherent garble if all soundscapes were played publicly instead of via headphones. In Kurio we used displays that visitors could share because they were either handheld through PDAs or located on an interactive table. This allowed for social and embedded interaction. Yet the table clearly limited mobility and anyone who has bumped into things or people while walking and texting on a phone understands the inherent challenges of embodied interaction with handheld displays.

Situating interactive content in museums

Our next category examines approaches to how we interact with content through museum guides. In particular, we focused on individual or group experiences in museum visits and strategies for content delivery. In our 2 × 2 matrix analysis (Figure 12.6) of interactive content approaches one factor we propose describes visitor interaction as ranging from *information delivery* to *game-interaction*. Information delivery refers to the approach of using an information repository to present the visitor with relevant content either adaptively (i.e. by recommendation of the system) or by user selection. Game-interaction refers to providing the visitor with the ability to interact with the exhibit content in a playful and less guided manner. Often the game-interaction approach will use games as a way of learning, as opposed to solely providing information about artifacts and exhibits. A second factor, similar to that used for the matrix of tangibility, analyzes the sociable quality of the systems ranging from *personal* to *social*. Here we use personal to refer to systems that target interaction with single individuals, whereas social refers to interaction aimed at groups of individuals.

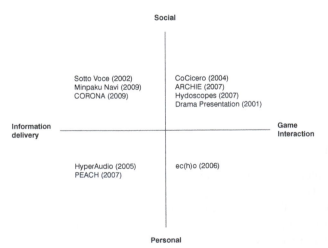

FIGURE 12.6 Matrix showing different types of interactive museum guides based on interactive content and degrees of sociability

Information delivery and personal

Many of the systems we reviewed were information delivery in style, while also falling under the personal category. Typically they involved a PDA and an audiovisual interface. Among the first of such guides was HyperAudio (Petrelli and Not 2005). In the HyperAudio system, individual visitors were encouraged to walk around the exhibition with the handheld device and headphones, stopping at various exhibits to learn more about specific artifacts in their surroundings. As the authors, Petrelli and Not note, 'the presentation (audio message and hypermedia page) would be adapted to each individual user, taking into account not only their interaction with the system, but also the broad interaction context, including the physical space, the visit so far, the interaction history and the presented narration' (Petrelli and Not 2005:307). The presentation thus displayed also provided a link on which the participant could click with a palmtop pen to gather further information. By doing so, the visitor was provided with a map of the museum; on this map, the location of a new artifact of interest was displayed in order to allow visitors to see the artifact in person if desired. The authors also describe their interest in keeping the graphical user interface to a minimum so as not to distract the visitor. It is for this reason that audio was chosen as the main channel of information delivery.

The PEACH (Personal Experience with Active Cultural Heritage) guide (Stock *et al.* 2007) provided the visitor with a digital character on their PDA that supplied information on various artifacts within the exhibition. Showcased at the Hecht Museum of the University of Haifa, this system also contained rich media in the form of video close-ups of frescoes and detailed descriptions of paintings of the museum exhibition. Unique to this system is the availability of a printout, which provided the visitor with an overview of the exhibits encountered while at the museum.

Information delivery and social

The Sotto Voce system (Aoki *et al.* 2002) provided the first instance of a museum guide where researchers focused on group activity. The system contained an audio sharing application called 'eavesdropping' that allowed paired visitors to share audio information with each other while on an information delivery tour. The application was designed with three main factors in mind: the information source, the visitor's companion and the museum space. The authors remarked that they found that the visitors used the system in creative ways and with social purpose, when presented with the opportunity for interacting with each other through the system.

Following Sotto Voce, CORONA (Heller *et al.* 2009) was another project focusing on group activities and exchanges that was deployed in the historic town hall of Aachen in Germany known as the Coronation Hall (Figure 12.7). The system was an audio guide that immersed the visitor in an audioscape, while also allowing conversations to be possible as a result of very light earphones. Visitors that were close to each other could experience and share the same audio space;

FIGURE 12.7 CORONA: a map of the system (left); the Coronation Hall (right). Photo: used with permission by Florian Heller, RWTH Aachen University, Germany

at the same time, the audio was less intense and softer in order to encourage conversation between visitors. Other social interactions supported by the system included following someone and eavesdropping. This is an example that challenges the idea that audio guides with headphones prevent visitors from having interactive and social exchanges.

Hope *et al.* (2009) proposed a project named Minpaku Navi that aimed to engage Japanese families in interactive information delivery systems in the Japanese National Museum of Ethnology. The device provided the visitor with quizzes about the artifacts and information about where other visitors were in the museum. Initially, the project was meant to be a single-user device in order to allow for free exploration of the museum. However, because the system was developed with enough flexibility to support group interactions, the authors observed a significant amount of interaction and collaboration between family members concerning the quizzes.

Game-interaction and social

In recent years, research has continued in the area of group-based museum tours, although the orientation has shifted from information delivery tours to game-interaction activities. This is evident in the CoCicero project implemented in the Marble Museum in Carrera, Italy (Laurillau and Paternò 2004). The CoCicero prototype focused on four types of group activities: (1) 'shared listening' – similar to the Sotto Voce system, (2) 'independent use' – to allow individuals to choose not to engage in group-based tours, (3) 'following' – to allow an individual to lead other members of a group and (4) 'checking in' – to allow members in a group to know how others are doing through voice communication while not being physically present. The guide functioned by offering museum groups a series of games, such as puzzles and multiple choice questions, which required the visitors to gather clues through viewing the exhibits within the museum.

Similarly, the ARCHIE project (Loon *et al.* 2007) developed a learning game for school children that allowed visitors to trade museum-specific information to gain points in order to win a game. Because each player played a different role, the visitor had to understand various levels of information gained from exploring the museum in order to trade them and improve his score. Initial findings of the ARCHIE project showed that game-interaction does foster user interest in museum content.

Callaway *et al.* (2011) designed a Drama Presentation System to specifically engage members of small groups of visitors in discussions about the artifacts in the museum. The emphasis on narratives and drama created a playful way to foster conversation in a natural and unobtrusive way and we therefore consider this to be a game-interaction approach. In this system, each visitor used a mobile device (i.e. a smartphone). Depending on where the visitors were located in the exhibit and in relation to each other, they all received different parts of the narrative. The parts could be complementary or contrasting, but either way they were meant to foster conversation between the visitors. This project was clearly a group museum guide, since each visitor needed the other visitors to understand the meaning of his part of the story.

Game-interaction and personal

Our system ec(h)o (Wakkary and Hatala 2007) is exclusively a personal system yet it uses a *game-interaction* approach. Its interface aimed for an interaction based on open-ended game qualities or what we referred to as play. The play took on two forms: (1) 'content play' in the delivery of information – in the form of puns and riddles and (2) 'physical play' – consisting of holding, touching and moving through a space; in other words, simple playful action along the lines of toying with a wooden cube.

Summary

In summary, we can see an increasing desire to create systems that are more social, whether informed by an information delivery approach or a game-interaction approach. If there is a discernible trend, it is that recent explorations have shifted toward social and game-interaction factors.

Situating social media and user-generated content in museums

In this section, we look at how museums use social media and user-generated content technologies to enhance visitors' social engagement and experience. Our goal is to rethink the museum guide through the lens of social media and its growth in recent years. We investigate how social media can transform museums from a visitor–artifact connection to a visitor–visitor connection that supports interpretations of the exhibition. We also explore the shift from an expert curator's single interpretation of the artifacts to multiple visitors' interpretations of the exhibits. Social media is defined by Kaplan and Haenlein (2010) as a 'group of Internet-based applications that build on the ideological and technological foundations of Web 2.0 and that allow the creation and exchange of User Generated Content' (Kaplan and Haenlein 2010:61). By Web 2.0, they suggest that the content and applications on the web are created, published and modified by users. User-generated content is defined as the sum of all the ways people make use of social media. Such content has to be published on a publicly accessible website or a networking website, it has to show a certain amount of creativity and it has to be created outside professional practices. Kaplan and Haenlein include a range of social media types from blogs to virtual social worlds despite the differences in the medium's richness or degree of social presence. Related to social media, Boyd and Ellison (2007) define social networking technologies as having three characteristics: (1) users can create a public or semi-public profile, (2) they can articulate a list of other users to share their profile with and (3) they can view and traverse lists of connections. To ground our work, we took these three definitions and expanded them to the museum space. For this part of our study, we considered both 'in-museum' guides using social media to allow visitors to interact and online systems that invite visitors to contribute to cultural heritage collections. Second, we only considered content that has a component of user-generated content, even if it is combined with expert-generated content. Finally, we considered the scalability of the network and the participatory channels used.

The 2 × 2 matrix for this section (Figure 12.8) classifies projects around two axes: the type of content shown (*user content* or *user and expert content*) and the situation in which the content was presented (*in museum* or *online*). We define user and expert content as content that combines expert comments with visitors' opinions. Projects that were online and that helped visitors make sense of the exhibit in general were also considered to be museum guides, following our definition of museum guides stated at the outset of this chapter.

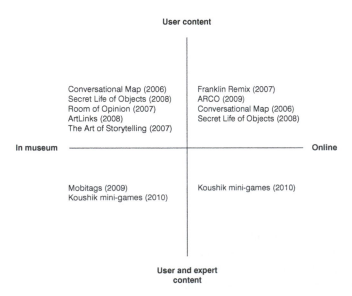

FIGURE 12.8   Matrix showing different types of social media guides based on degrees of user-generated content and user location

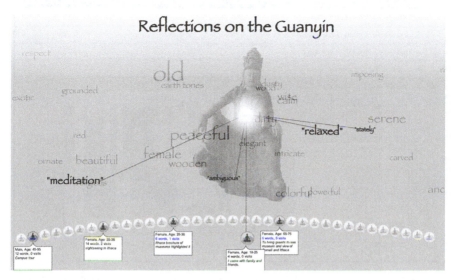

FIGURE 12.9   ArtLinks: user interface. Photo: used with permission by Dan Cosley, Cornell University, USA

In-museum and user-generated content

First we investigate a group of projects characterized by user-generated content and in-museum situations. We describe four projects: ArtLinks (Cosley *et al.* 2008), the installation Room of Opinion (Ferris *et al.* 2004), The Art of Storytelling (Fisher and Twiss-Garrity 2007) and two digital boards developed by Mariana Salgado (2009).

ArtLinks was a visualization tool that helped visitors explore other visitors' opinions about the exhibit (Figure 12.9). The visualization was shown on a pedestal, close to one of the art pieces of the exhibit. Visitors could log in, create their profile (with basic demographic information), write comments about the exhibit and record a sound representing their thoughts about what they discovered throughout their visit. They could also view other visitors' profiles based on the words from the written comments, the recorded sounds by other visitors and demographic information.

The Room of Opinion was part of Re-Tracing the Past, an exhibition held at the Hunt Museum in Limerick, Ireland. A number of objects in the museum were misclassified in the past, or never had a clear explanation of what they were used for. In the Room of Opinion, the 'Interactive Radio' invited visitors to record their theories and opinions about these mysterious artifacts in exhibition. Visitors were very curious to listen to possible interpretations of the objects and the system supported reflection and collaborative discovery in order to help visitors construct their own understanding of the exhibit.

The Art of Storytelling was similar, but instead of 'tuning' others' opinions with the dial of an interactive radio, visitors created podcasts for other visitors to carry with them in the exhibit (Figure 12.10). The authors suggested that by inviting

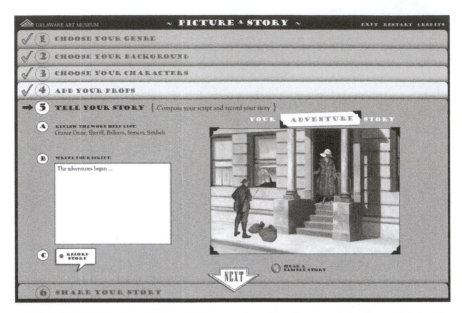

FIGURE 12.10   The Art of Storytelling: user interface. Photo: used with permission by Michelle Ghadfa, Night Kitchen Interactive, Philadelphia, USA

visitors to construct their own narrative about the exhibit, the activity supported and promoted knowledge construction skills.

Conversational Map (Salgado 2009) was a participatory digital board that was designed to collect visitors' comments in the form of text and external links. These comments concerned an art exhibition that was presented both in the museum Kunsthalle in Helsinki and on the museum's website. This project allowed visitors to exchange their comments with previous and future visitors of the same exhibit. The Secret Life of Objects (Salgado 2009) was also a participatory digital board that invited comments and reflection about the exhibit in the Design Museum in Helsinki. This project particularly encouraged creative artistic comments such as poems, pieces of music and videos. Salgado's two projects contain both user-generated content and they take place in the museum, but can also be viewed and accessed online.

In-museum and user and expert content

Mobitags (Cosley *et al.* 2009) is a project that combined both expert and user content in the Johnson Museum of Art at Cornell University. This mobile system offered guidance in three navigation aspects of the exhibit: (1) social – the users can create tags for objects that will be accessible to other visitors, (2) spatial – the system provides an interactive map of the space and artifact and (3) semantic – the system offers information about the artifacts (Figure 12.11). The system allowed visitors to tag objects, but also to look at how others tagged the same objects within the physical space of the museum. Visitors could use the tags as recommendations for

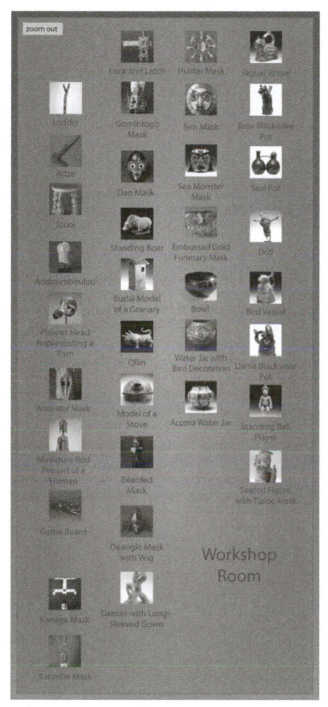

FIGURE 12.11 MobiTags: user interface. Photo: used with permission by Dan Cosley, Cornell University, USA

the next artifacts to observe and they could also read the expert interpretation of the objects 'on the move' with a web application on an iPod touch.

Some projects also combined in-museum and online experiences, user- and expert-generated content. For example, Koushik *et al.* (2010) and Hope *et al.* (2009) describe games that were produced by experts and played by visitors. These games included an online component that also allowed for user-generated content.

Koushik *et al.* (2010) proposed five mini-games on iPads in order to enhance collaboration during the visit of the California Academy of Sciences. The game began by asking the visitor to create a profile and an avatar on an online website. Once this was done, the visitors played a number of collaborative mini-games based on the items of the exhibition and accumulated points. After the visit, they could revisit the website, see their friends' scores and even buy new outfits for the avatars.

Online and user-generated content

We encountered several projects that were taken out of the museum's physical location into online space. Franklin Remix (Fisher and Twiss-Garrity 2007) and ARCO (Zhang *et al.* 2009) are all examples of this phenomenon. The Franklin Remix combined two physical exhibitions in Philadelphia (at the Benjamin Franklin Tercentenary and the Rosenback Museum) and asked students to choose artifacts from both exhibits to create their own online exhibition about Benjamin Franklin (Figure 12.12). The authors defined the concept of remix as 'the process of understanding a body of knowledge by using technology to rearrange and recontextualize its elements in order to construct an original narrative' (ibid.).

In ARCO, users could create their own exhibitions online, while keeping them clearly separated from the expert curator's view. The objective was to empower users to discuss and communicate their shared heritage. Even though this project did not happen in the museum, we believe it served some of the same purposes as museum guides: it helped visitors make sense of what they saw, reflect on the exhibit and gain a better understanding of what the museum was trying to communicate.

Summary

Sociability is an important part of the learning and cultural experience of going to the museum, as well as of making sense of heritage in general. User-generated content is currently gaining a lot of interest in museum settings. While still providing expert content, cultural heritage institutions are promoting ways for visitors to share their interpretations and opinions. Increasingly, there also seems to be a common effort in creating museum guides that engage visitors in collaborative activities. However, there are also drawbacks. Most of the projects based on user-generated content that we reviewed entailed legal issues. As warned by the creators of these projects, problems regarding copyrights and similar intellectual property issues have to be addressed carefully. Sometimes, curators and museum staff are also

FIGURE 12.12   Franklin Remix: example of a personal online 'remix'. Photo: used with permission by Michelle Ghadfa, Night Kitchen Interactive, Philadelphia, USA

afraid that people will confuse user-generated content with expert interpretations of the artifacts in the museum, causing confusion or the spread of inaccurate information.

Discussion

We have presented sociability as a dimension and a growing concern of interactive museum guides, which extends current notions of interactive content and tangible interaction. Social media tools and social networking are creating new approaches to interpreting museum collections that include the social and entertaining aspects of a typical museum visit. We believe that in order to have a meaningful experience in an exhibit, it should be possible for visitors to not only interact with people that are there, at the same place and at the same time, but to also connect with previous and future visitors. Social media can broaden the shared social experiences that visitors have.

We have looked at how sociability is supported by the inclusion of embodied/embedded interaction and game-interaction approaches and it is integral to the use of social media and user-generated content. Yet questions remain as to what exactly is the nature of sociability within museums. In addition, it is important to consider how the move to sociable interactive museum guides alters or impacts the notion of the interactive museum guide.

Sociability

In past and current research there is a clear effort to address sociability with respect to interactive museum guides. From our analysis, we can see that engaging visitors (socially) in the interpretation of the museum experience is a dominant trend, with many directions being actively explored. Our analysis so far has painted social activity with a broad brush, so now we turn to a more detailed discussion of the quality and kind of sociability within the systems we analyzed.

Adhering to our matrix analyses of this chapter, we look at sociability across two factors. The first concerns itself with the kind of social interaction that ranges from *independent* at one end to *cooperative* at the other end. By independent social interaction we refer to a group activity in which actions are side by side or simultaneous but essentially do not rely on each other. Cooperative refers to social interaction that consciously shares a goal through the interaction: visitors can work together on the same activity or collaborate by helping and sharing. The second factor is the kind of people who share the activity with respect to familiarity. At one end of the spectrum people are *familiar* with each other and at the other they are *anonymous* (Figure 12.13).

Social media tools have increased the degree to which social interactions (either anonymous or familiar) can become part of the museum experience and aid in interpreting and learning from that experience. For example, a project like ARCO enables activities among visitors within a common social network that are parallel

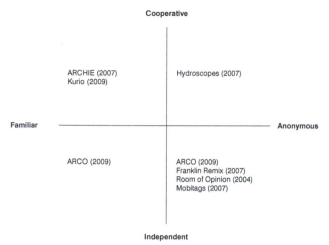

FIGURE 12.13 Matrix showing different kinds of social interaction and degrees of familiarity

in nature. ARCO is an example of a guide that connects people from the same social network (i.e. knowing each other) through their own personal exhibitions online, thus it occupies our quadrant of familiar and independent interactions. However, as is expected with social networking, interactions can move from people who are familiar to us to those who are anonymous as social networks expand and mix. ARCO is for this reason also in our quadrant of anonymous and independent interactions.

Anonymous and independent interactions appear most commonly in our review. For example, the Franklin Remix project aims to solidify what children learned in two previous exhibits by asking them to create their own exhibition. The result is a collection of different student projects that are not considered as a whole. Mobitags is also an anonymous exchange of information, comments and recommendations for future visitors. This type of user-generated content looks at the role of the interactive museum guide as a common forum for individual contributions or expressions to be shared with people they do not know. In the Room of Opinion, visitors record and share opinions, comments and interpretations on the interactive radio for future visitors to listen. Visitors try to make sense of the artifacts in the Hunt Museum and to construct meaning for themselves, knowingly sharing their understanding with others who are anonymous. We view this as independent; although in a general sense there is a collective intent, we see this as different from conscious cooperation or a shared pursuit of goals or experiences.

For example, in projects like Kurio and ARCHIE, visitors consciously know they are working toward a collective experience. Typically this experience is cooperative, as in the case of Kurio, but it can also be competitive, as in the case of ARCHIE. In each case, the guides are clearly structured as games that involve roles and activities such as trading or collaborating. In this case the game-interaction is used as a means to support familiar and cooperative interactions.

Game interaction or playfulness is evident in Hydroscopes, where we find cooperative and anonymous interaction. Hydroscopes engage visitors to interact with both people they know and people they don't know. Small groups often collaborate by exchanging ideas and thoughts about the creation of fishes, before releasing them in the virtual ocean.

Impact on the interactive museum guide

As we mentioned in the introduction, the interactive museum guide has been developing as a concept for many years. In our analysis it has become evident that the concept is shifting as multiple directions for sociability are being explored. For example, game-interaction aims to strike a balance between an engaging experience and allowing for reflection within museum exhibitions.

In tangible interaction, we find that technology aims to integrate with the exhibit through the distribution and embedding of technology into the architecture, the displays and even the artifacts, or become the artifacts of interest themselves as in Hydroscopes. The notion of an interactive museum guide as a handheld device with a graphic interface is quickly ceding territory to hybrid systems like Kurio.

Perhaps the biggest shift through the inclusion of social media and user-generated content tools within interactive museum guides is that these tools tend to be 'audience-focused'. By this we mean that the systems orient around the visitor and aim to connect visitor to visitors' content (their own or others) or to other visitors. In many respects this challenges the traditional confines of the museum guide orientation, traditionally centered on the exhibition. This idea refers to the issues of engagement and participation that Russo addresses in this volume. As a result, many systems move past the boundaries of any given exhibition or museum and typically ground in a visitor's collection of experiences, contents and connections that make up the visitor experience. For example ARCO is an example of 'virtual' collections given coherency through the visitor and their social connections (which, of course, raises the questions of whether 'visitor' is even the appropriate term). These collections serve as a public forum to interpret and reflect, often across the boundaries of more than one exhibit or museum. Arguably, this represents the largest challenge and opportunity in future research of sociability and interactive museum guides.

Conclusion

As shown in this chapter, there are currently several approaches for situating sociability within interactive museum guides. Through a review and analysis of current contributions in the three key areas of tangibility, interactivity and social media we have constructed a comprehensive outline that provides a theoretical grounding for future research in the design of museum guides that support sociality. Our analysis led to a discussion of the quality and kind of social interactions arising out of different strategies and projects. It also highlights the influence that sociability and social media have in the changing notions and definitions of an interactive museum guide as well as the meaning of the museum space and the museum visit.

References

Aoki, P.M., Grinter, R.E., Hurst, A., Szymanski, M.H., Thornton, J.D. and Woodruff, A. (2002) 'Sotto Voce: Exploring the Interplay of Conversation and Mobile Audio Spaces', *Proceedings of the ACM Conference on Human Factors in Computing Systems (CHI '02)*, New York: ACM Press, 431–438.

Bederson, B. (1995) 'Audio Augmented Reality: A Prototype Automated Tour Guide', *Conference Companion of the ACM Conference on Human Factors in Computing Systems (CHI '95)*, New York: ACM Press, 210–211.

Bell, G. (2002) *Making Sense of Museums: The Museum as 'Cultural Ecology'*, Pittsburgh: Intel Labs..

Boyd, D.M. and Ellison, N.B. (2007) Social Network Sites: Definition, History and Scholarship, *Journal of Computer-Mediated Communication*, 13(1), 210–230.

Callaway, C., Stock, O., Dekoven, E., Noy, K., Citron, Y. and Dobrin, Y. (2011) 'Mobile Drama in an Instrumented Museum: Inducing Group Conversation via Coordinated Narratives', *Proceedings of the 15th International Conference on Intelligent User Interfaces*, New York: ACM Press, 73–82.

Cosley, D., Lewenstein, J., Herman, A., Holloway, J., Baxter, J., Nomua, S., Boehner, K. and Gay, G. (2008) 'ArtLinks: Fostering Social Awareness and Reflection in Museums', *Proceeding of the 26th Annual SIGCHI Conference on Human Factors in Computing Systems (CHI '08)*, New York: ACM Press, 403–412.

Cosley, D., Baxter, J., Lee, S., Alson, B., Nomura, S., Adams, P., Sarabu, C. and Gay, G. (2009) 'A Tag in the Hand: Supporting Semantic, Social and Spatial Navigation in Museums', *Proceedings of the ACM Conference on Human Factors in Computing Systems (CHI '09)*, New York: ACM Press, 1953–1962.

Crampton-Smith, G. (1995) 'The Hand That Rocks the Cradle,' *ID Magazine*, May/June, 60–65.

Dindler, C., Krogh, P.G., Beck, S., Stenfelt, L., Nielsen, K.R. and Grønæk, K. (2007) 'Peephole Experiences: Field Experiments with Mixed Reality Hydroscopes in a Marine Center', *Proceedings of the 2007 Conference on Designing for User eXperiences (DUX '07)*, New York: ACM Press.

Ferris, K., Bannon, L., Ciolfi, L., Gallagher, P., Hall, T. and Lennon, M. (2004) 'Shaping Experiences in the Hunt Museum: A Design Case Study', *Proceedings of the ACM Conference on Designing Interactive Systems: Processes, Practices, Methods and Techniques (DIS '04)*, New York: ACM Press, 205–214.

Fisher, M. and Twiss-Garrity, B.A. (2007) 'Remixing Exhibits: Constructing Participatory Narratives with On-Line Tools to Augment Museum Experiences', in J. Trant and D. Bearman (eds) *Proceedings of Museums and the Web 2007*, Toronto: Archives & Museum Informatics. http://www.archimuse.com/mw2007/papers/fisher/fisher.html (accessed 9 March 2011).

Grammenos, D., Michel, D., Zabulis, X. and Argyros, A.A. (2011) 'PaperView: Augmenting Physical Surfaces with Location-Aware Digital Information', *Proceedings of the ACM Conference on Tangible, Embedded and Embodied Interaction (TEI '11)*, New York: ACM Press, 57–60.

Heller, F., Knott, T., Weiss, M. and Borchers, J. (2009) 'Multi-User Interaction in Virtual Audio Spaces', *Proceedings of the ACM Conference Extended Abstracts on Human Factors in Computing Systems (CHI '09)*, New York: ACM Press, 4489–4494.

Hope,T., Nakamura,Y.,Takahashi,T., Nobayashi,A., Fukuoka, S., Hamasaki, M. and Nishimura, T. (2009) 'Familial Collaborations in a Museum', *Proceedings of the ACM Conference on Human Factors in Computing Systems (CHI '09)*, New York: ACM Press, 1963–1972.

Hornecker, E. and Buur, J. (2006) 'Getting a Grip on Tangible Interaction: A Framework on Physical Space and Social Interaction', *Proceedings of the SIGCHI Conference on Human Factors in Computing Systems (SIGCHI '06)*, New York: ACM Press, 437–446.

Ishii, H. and B. Ullmer (1997) 'Tangible Bits: Towards Seamless Interfaces Between People, Bits and Atoms', *Proceedings of the ACM Conference on Human Factors in Computing Systems (CHI '97)*, New York: ACM Press, 234–241.

Kaplan, A.M. and Haenlein, M. (2010) 'Users of the World, Unite! The Challenges and Opportunities of Social Media', *Business Horizons*, 53(1), 59–68.

Kaptelinin, V. and Nardi, B.A. (2006) *Acting with Technology: Activity Theory and Interaction Design*, Cambridge, MA: MIT Press.

Koushik, M., Lee, E.J., Pieroni, L., Sun, E. and Yeh, C.W. (2010) 'Re-Envisioning the Museum Experience: Combining New Technology with Social-Networking', *Proceedings of the 9th International Conference on Entertainment Computing (ICEC '10)*, New York: Springer LNCS, 248–253.

Laurillau, Y. and F. Paternò (2004) 'CoCicero: Un Système Interactif pour la Visite Collaborative de Musée sur Support Mobile', *Proceedings of the 16th Conference of the Association Francophone d'Interaction Homme-Machine*, New York: ACM Press, 101–108.

Loon, H.V., Gabriëls, K., Teunkens, D., Robert, K., Luyten, K. and Coninx, K. (2007) 'Supporting Social Interaction: A Collaborative Trading Game on PDA', *Proceedings of Museums and the Web 2007*, Toronto: Archives & Museum Informatics, 40–62.

Petrelli, D. and Not, E. (2005) 'User-Centered Design of Flexible Hypermedia for a Mobile Guide: Reflections on the HyperAudio Experience', *User Modeling and User-Adapted Interaction* 15, 303–338.

Rizzo, F. and Garzotto, F. (2007) 'The Fire and The Mountain: Tangible and Social Interaction in a Museum Exhibition for Children', *Proceedings of the AMC Conference on Interaction Design and Children (IDC '07)*, New York: ACM Press, 105–108.

Salgado, M. (2009) 'Designing for an Open Museum: An Exploration of Content Creation and Sharing Through Interactive Pieces', PhD dissertation, University of Art and Design Helsinki, Finland.

Stock, O., Zancanaro, M., Busetta, P., Callaway, C., Krüger, A., Kruppa, M., Kuflik, T., Not, E. and Rocchi, C. (2007) 'Adaptive, Intelligent Presentation of Information for the Museum Visitor in PEACH', *User Modeling and User-Adapted Interaction*, 17(3), 257–304.

Wakkary, R. and Hatala, M. (2007) 'Situated Play in a Tangible Interface and Adaptive Audio Museum Guide', *Journal of Personal and Ubiquitous Computing*, 11(3), 171–191.

Wakkary, R., Muise, K., Tanenbaum, K., Hatala, M. and Kornfeld, L. (2008) 'Situating Approaches to Interactive Museum Guides', *Museum Management and Curatorship*, 23(4), 367–383.

Wakkary, R., Hatala, M., Muise, K., Tanenbaum, K., Corness, G., Mohabbati, B. and Budd, J. (2009) 'Kurio: A Museum Guide for Families', *Proceedings of the ACM Conference on Tangible and Embedded Interaction (TEI '09)*, New York: ACM Press, 215–222.

Zhang, W., Patoli, M.Z., Gkion, M., Al-Barakati, A., Newbury, P. and White, M. (2009) 'Reanimating Cultural Heritage through Service Orientation, Workflows, Social Networking and Mashups', *Proceedings of the 2009 International Conference on CyberWorlds*, Washington, DC: IEEE Computer Society, 177–184.

AFTERWORD

Dialogue in the space between ethnography and heritage

Peter Wright

When I was invited to write a short afterword for *Heritage and Social Media*, I was already in the thick of researching and writing another book with John McCarthy on the experience of participation. As part of that, I'd tasked myself to find some good examples of social media in action. I was looking for examples that provided a basis for a discussion of liveness, dialogue and diversity in participation. It was 11 September 2011. I launched YouTube and the top hit was a clip of Paul Simon singing 'Sound of Silence' at Ground Zero, New York, as part of the 9/11 ten-year memorial service. I'm a bit of a sucker for Paul Simon and for memorialization. My wife and I grew up and courted to Simon and Garfunkel, they were the soundtrack to our teenage years. As I watched Paul Simon at Ground Zero, I remembered back to earlier in the year when, with my wife and teenage daughters, I visited the graves and battle sites of World War I in Belgium, and how powerful that experience had been for all of us. I remembered, too, where I was when the Twin Towers came down. I was in Siena with John McCarthy working on our previous book *Technology as Experience*. Together, John and I watched the towers fall on live TV in an office in Antonio Rizzo's Media Lab. It was the dying weeks of an idyllic study leave amidst the Tuscan hills. It seemed to me then that the world would never be the same again, and it wasn't. As I watched the video of Paul Simon performing, I also saw how he had aged, I remember him as so young, and I wondered how old I must look now, and realized how long ago these remembered things must have been.

If living heritage is about an encounter in which personal memory and cultural memory come together in an aesthetic moment of reflection, then I guess my story (at least as much as I have recounted so far) must be a pretty good example. So, as I planned my afterword it seemed to make perfect sense to repurpose my ethnographic notes on the Paul Simon video and frame them not as an experience of participation, but as an experience of living heritage. It has all the ingredients of an iconic, historical moment (Paul Simon performing at Ground Zero on the tenth anniversary), a remediation though participatory media (the YouTube video) and a 'visitor' encounter (well, my story anyway).

But now I have embarked on this journey, I seem to be inexorably drawn to two questions that I can neither avoid nor answer with any certainty. The first question is: when does people 'just doing stuff' become 'heritage'? When does doing an 'ethnography' of YouTube, become 'heritage studies'? In trying to answer this question, two words keep popping up, *intention* and *framing*.

I guess there is a sense that we are all co-creating heritage all of the time. My wife sold a camera second-hand yesterday and forgot to take the memory card out, worse still we forgot to even reformat it, so there will be about two hundred pictures of our family life as bonus footage to the next owner. More interestingly, perhaps the memory card will be stored away somewhere and in 200 years time discovered by some cyber-anthropologist, who will be able somehow to recover the images and make all sorts of claims about family life back in 2011. But the point is, in just living my life, taking idle photographs, accidentally selling my personal photographs (worse still, actually – it was my daughter's camera, but we haven't told her), by just doing stuff, am I laying down heritage? Certainly I didn't intend those 200 photos to be our family legacy to the cyber-anthropologists. Certainly the photos weren't framed as heritage during their production.

In the case of Paul Simon and YouTube, clearly Simon is *intentionally* laying down heritage, his performance is *framed* as a performance of memorialization. Furthermore, it is understood as such by the audience, and it is even communicated as such by the person who uploaded the video. But is the actual *act* of uploading it onto YouTube a deliberate performance of memorialization, an act of preservation and curation for future generations? Is it an act of constructing heritage? Or is it just sharing stuff, or as YouTube would have it, 'broadcasting' one's self? Following Simon in this volume (Roger that is, not Paul), it seems that maybe there has to be some kind of dialogical orientation, a deliberate laying down of memory in conversation, an intentional curation of social syntax, for it to be an act of heritage construction rather than people just doing stuff.

In order to progress onto my second question, I need to tell some more of the story of my encounter with the Paul Simon video. Remember I was interested in examples of liveness and dialogue in social media? There is certainly a real liveness about YouTube, I didn't access the Paul Simon clip until a couple of days after the memorial service but videos of the service were appearing very soon after the performance. As more people watched, so the videos moved up the most viewed list and thus more people watched them and more people voted 'like' or 'dislike'. Such is the stuff of social media. But more importantly for my story, comment threads began to develop in response to the videos, and a dialogue emerged in real time. Some of the comments aligned with my emotional response recounted above: 'I was down at Ground Zero when he played this. It was incredibly moving. I had been holding back tears during the reading of the names, but when he played this song I broke down and started bawling.'

Others talked more lightheartedly about Paul Simon and the difficulties he had in composing the song, which added a kind of jokey facticity to the experience: 'Paul Simon took six months to write the lyrics, which are about man's lack of communication with his fellow man. He averaged one line a day.'

But other comments were contributed that revealed more than just a consensual construction of remembering, grieving and celebration. Rather they expressed a range of quite hostile and certainly dissenting voices including opinions about the legitimacy of the memorial service itself, objections to the US-centric viewpoint projected in both the event and the comment threads, questions about the USA's decision to go to war, and judgmental accusations about American society. I won't go into too much detail for fear of causing offence, but to give just three (slightly censored) examples:

> R.I.P the 2976 Americans who lost there lives, but does anyone spare a thought for the 48644 innocent Afghans and 1690903 innocent Iraqis who have paid the price for this?

> 911 was the pretext for the war on terror hoax, aimed at the american peoples bill of rights. wake up people. sheeple. when is paul simon gonna play that song for the over 1 Million dead innocent Iraqis' from the unconstitutional US occupation.

> America is godless, feeling-less society where right wing hate is spewed through church mouthpieces. god is striking your country down and will continue to do so ...

The risk of giving offense was a real issue as the following comment from the owner of the channel makes clear:

> A word about our comments. Requests are coming in to disable all comments as some are personally hurtful. I would hate to do this so please, vote down or Spam Label anything unkind and I will delete the most painful over the next few days. Also due to the large volume of objectionable videos, you now need to have your video approved before it will be displayed on the channel. Thanks very much.

Although it doesn't come over in this somewhat arbitrary selection of non-contiguous contributions, there was a strong dialogicality in the comment thread (again, see Simon this volume), definitely an exchange of opinions and definitely some voices of dissent.

Back to my story. As I read these comments at the time, my aesthetic moment began to dissolve before my eyes. Who were these people? What kind of people were they? I aligned with many of the sentiments but not the manner nor place in which it found expression. I could no longer see myself in this act of collective remembering if that is what it was.

So how do the comments figure in making sense of this particular experience of living heritage? With my liberal democratic hat on, I could now go on to talk about participatory media and freedom of speech, digital publics and social media as a force for democratization. Equally, I could use these examples to further explore my first question, namely, were the people contributing these comments *intending* to help frame a living legacy, giving expression to multi-voiced dialogue capturing the vox pop of our times? Or were they just saying stuff, just responding, just being angry and sad? What would our cyber-anthropologist make of these inscriptions were he to virtually excavate them in 200 years? The volume provides a framework to critically address these issues and also offers some suggestions, but those are not the substance of my second question. My second question is much simpler: what is the role of dissent and curation in the participatory heritage experience?

Let us imagine for a moment that the YouTube video of Paul Simon had been curated as an enactment of living heritage for future audiences. Then should the dissenting and potentially offensive comments be left in the frame as part of the heritage experience? If included, should they perhaps be curated in such a way as to cleverly make them a positive part of the aesthetic experience? But in being so rendered, would the dissent be neutralized? Does it matter if people are offended, or that an institution is associated with such voices of dissent? Perhaps should they be selectively curated (i.e. edited out), or should they be omitted but noted 'backstage' as 'visitor feedback'? In which case might we consider such strong reactions as a positive evaluation? These of course are the kinds of practical dilemma one gets into when content provider, curator and audience get intermingled through participation.

But while such participatory dilemmas are a relatively new problem for digital interaction designers (and perhaps for museum curators, too), within contemporary art such things are a matter of ongoing debate (Kester 2004; Bishop, 2006; Beech 2008). Beech suggests that, often enough, institutional approaches to participation instead of seeking to give voice to difference seek to neutralize dissent. They do this by enforcing the artists', curators' or institution's pre-given agenda onto the act of participation. But my question is whether this always a bad thing?

There are tensions here. Tensions between the practice of heritage as the capture of living dialogue (in the ethnographic sense of capturing the diversity of voices and practices of a culture) and the construction of a curated viewpoint on what is to be valued, and tensions also between heritage as the archiving of lived experience, and the designing of an aesthetic experience. This volume provides interactions designers and museum curators with a framework and vocabulary to explore how these tensions can play out in relationship.

Peter Wright
Culture Lab
Newcastle University, UK

References

Beech, D. (2008) Include me out! *Art Monthly* 4.08 pp.1–4

Bishop, C. (2006) (ed.) *Participation*, Cambridge, MA: MIT Press.

Kester, G. (2004) *Conversation Pieces: Community and Communication in Modern Art*, Berkeley, CA: University of California Press.

INDEX

188811

9 780415 616676